An Incredible Journey

An Incredible Journey

FROM A BARCELONA GRADE EIGHT
DROPOUT TO AN AMERICAN
UNIVERSITY PRESIDENCY

▲ ▲ ▲

By

Manuel A. Esteban, Ph.D.

Emeritus President, California State University, Chico

ISBN: 9798512173398 (paperback)

Table of Contents

▲ ▲ ▲

C.S.U. CHICO

Foreword

▲▲▲

An Incredible Life indeed. And an incredible recounting of that life. My friend, Manuel, has written an engaging, at times gripping, recounting of his multi-state journey starting from a modest family in Barcelona, where he was hardly a scholar at age 13, then to a small town, Souvigny, France, where he learned how to adapt to change and unfamiliar challenges. This move included not only his family but the family of Gloria, his eventual wife. Both fathers were professional glassblowers.

After a few years, both families again uprooted to re-settle in Alberta, Canada. There Manuel learned the glassblowing craft which could have been his life-long vocation had it not been for his younger brother, Julio, who encouraged, inspired, and guided Manuel to finally get his high school-equivalency degree and then go on to college. With Bachelor's and master's degrees in hand, he moved on to his third immigration, this time to the USA where his studies, career, and retirement took him to Michigan, California, and Arizona.

Manuel's early years were not always easy as he repeatedly confronted new circumstances and challenges. From these experiences, he gradually developed assets that were foundational to his professional successes and quality of life, so aptly described in his telling: family and friendships, adaptability, versatility, optimism, trust in his own skills and judgments, good humor, boundless curiosity, doing something well rather than so-so, joining with others to make good things happen.

Most of Manuel's memoir focuses on his academic career. We share his journey as a teacher-scholar, then into higher education administration, culminating as an acclaimed university president. Who could have imagined? This progression was built on a unique set of qualities already mentioned. Others include his abiding self-confidence, ability to make others comfortable and cooperative, having clear visions for doing good beyond himself, confronting others when needed, building community.

Manuel's story is more than personal. It illustrates millions of stories of immigrants succeeding and making our country a better place.

I was privileged to see all this up close during our near-daily noontime runs during the decade of his presidency at California State University, Chico. I listened and offered support as he worked through troubling and good times. Included, as you will read, were dealing with two years of unfounded and sometimes hateful attacks on campus and in the community as he assumed the presidency. As he said at one point during a run, "I am confident that if I stay true to myself, these attacks will diminish, and my presidency will succeed." He was correct on both counts.

Our friendship during that decade was the most treasured of my life and has transcended those challenging and rewarding times. Teresa and I are honored to have Manuel and Gloria as good friends to this day. Manuel, thanks for sharing with me and others this *Incredible Journey*.

Walter Schafer,
Emeritus Professor, Sociology
California State University, Chico

CHAPTER I

Barcelona 1940–1955

▲▲▲

WHEN I RETIRED AFTER TEN years as president of California State University, Chico, I was interviewed by Chico Statements, a CSU, Chico publication. It was published under the title *An Incredible Journey*. A good number of people who read the article and family members and friends encouraged me to write my autobiography. I thought it would be a good idea and seriously thought about doing it. This was eighteen years ago. The fact that I have not written anything until now does not mean that I have not been thinking about this project. In fact, and the last few years, hardly a day has gone by without reliving in my mind some of the experiences and events that have made me the person that I became and am.

I was born in Barcelona, in the Catalan region of Spain, 20 June 1940. My brother was born 14 October 1944. My parents called me *nen*, which means boy in Catalan. My brother called me *tete*, which was often the manner in which younger brothers called their older brother. He called me *tete* until he decided, without consulting with me, that he was too old to use this childish term. It should not have bothered me, but I was hurt. I loved to hear him address me in that manner. Everyone else in the family called me Manelet, or little Manel, the Catalan version for Manuel. Perhaps I should clarify that there are four official languages in Spain, Castilian, Catalan, Galician, and Basque, that correspond to four different regions. My parents must not have racked their brains for long to come up with my brother's and my name. My dad was called Manuel, so was I.

I guess they expected to have a girl after me. She would have been called like my mother, Julia. But, since they had another boy, he became Julio. Creative.

I have had an internal debate about what has been more influential in forming me, my parents and the familial context or the twists and turns that life has dealt me. I never had a large family. In fact, I know practically nothing about my father's own family. My father, Manuel Esteban Fandos, was born in 1911 in Burriana, to a Valencian family. He told me that he was the seventh child. His mother was by then relatively old and could not breastfeed him. As was customary in those days, he was passed on to a wet nurse. His *mare dida* lived in Onda, a nearby town, where she had lost her own child. In many ways, my father considered her his mother and her family his own. I met this family, but never his blood one.

I never knew my paternal grandfather, or the Esteban side of the family. Much of the same can be said for the Fandos side of the family. For those who may not be aware, in Spain and much of the Hispanic world, everyone has two surnames, that of the father and that of the mother. So, I am Manuel Esteban (my father's first surname) Beltrán (my mother's first surname). Supposedly, my grandmother lived with us in Barcelona, but she died when I was four or five. I have no memories of her. What was clear to me is that my father had no love at all for his blood family nor did he want to have any contact with whoever remained behind in Burriana. When I asked why this was so, he revealed that, when he was a child, the family sent him begging. He never forgave them this humiliation or repudiation.

My maternal family is a totally different story. My mother, Julia Beltrán Valdés, was born in Barcelona, in 1919. Her father died when she was only two. He was a soldier in Morocco during the 1920-1927 War of Melilla or Rif War. My grandmother remarried several years later. Three children were born of this union. I ended up with two aunts, one eight years older than me and the other one only six. But the only name that united my mother to them was the Valdés, since my step grandfather was a González. As far as my mother was concerned, he was her father and she adored him. But he, too, disappeared from her life. At the end of the

Spanish Civil War, when my mother was barely twenty, he took off for France with a nurse. He was never seen again.

My father had a very difficult childhood, probably not too dissimilar to that of many children his age, but it clearly affected him tremendously. In addition to having to beg, he was forced to work at a very early age. Consequently, he never went to school. He was illiterate. He only learned to read and write at a very basic level when he was already in his late twenties. When he was sent to fight in the Spanish Civil War, he had recently married my mother. If he wanted to write to her, he needed to find a soldier capable of doing it for him. He found this unacceptable and demeaning. So, he convinced this soldier to teach him to write. The language he learned, however, was Castilian, not Catalan, the language he and my mother spoke. He never really mastered the written language but managed to communicate well enough. This was an unusual situation as he not only spoke Castilian with a marked Catalan accent but had a limited vocabulary. Once, for instance, when my father started courting my mother, my grandmother asked him, in Castilian Spanish, if he wanted a *melocotón*, (a peach) he said he did not like them. My mother asked him in Catalan, don't you like *pressecs*? He replied, *pressecs si*. My mother laughed and told him that *melocotones* and *pressecs* were the same fruit. Much later in life, after his retirement, he became the translator in court cases for a lot of the Chilean refugees who left Chile to escape the Pinochet regime. He then improved both his Castilian and his English simultaneously.

He was equally handicapped when it came to basic arithmetic. Somehow, he invented his own way of adding, subtracting, multiplying, and dividing. As a teenager I asked him if he wanted me to teach him the correct way to do arithmetic. He said that his system met his needs. That was the end of our discussion.

Unlike my father, my mother had gone to school possibly past the age of fourteen, something not that common among working class families. Her family was normal in every way. The only unusual thing to me, anyway, was that even though we all spoke Catalan at home and with aunts, uncles, and cousins, everyone spoke Castilian when we were with my grandmother and grand aunt. They were both born in Madrid, came to Barcelona at age twelve and fourteen respectively, neither one of them however ever learned to speak Catalan although both understood it perfectly. But such were many families at that time, and one ended up thinking that this was quite natural and to be expected.

Many times, both my brother and I have wondered who had the greatest influence on us, our father or our mother. We both agree that my mother was more loving, more devoted to the family, very stable, and a moderating force at home. She loved us uncritically and unconditionally. Our father, on the other hand, was more critical, and demanding. He wanted for the two of us what had been denied to him by life. Our dad was mercurial, in need of affection, admiration, and attention. He was also a bit of a hypochondriac. All things considered, though, he was also far more fascinating. My brother was closer to my mother. I was drawn a lot more to my father. For whatever reason, I ended up sharing a lot of his interests. He enjoyed recounting his war time experiences as well as the six months he spent in France's concentration camp, Argelès-sur-Mer, where he and thousands of other Spanish Republican refugees lived in the most horrendous conditions. I loved listening to him. Years later, as I studied the period preceding, during and after the Spanish Civil War, and read, in particular, *Homage to Catalonia*, by George Orwell, I was amazed at how well an uneducated man, a simple foot soldier, was able to discern the complicated political situation and the chaos and rivalries that resulted from the myriad political parties and organizations that eventually led to the war, and, in a way, doomed the legitimate government and paved the way for General Franco's win.

Although our parents often argued about money, we were one of the few families in our neighborhood to own a radio. I recall many nights joining my father by the radio, searching for the short-wave connection to listen to news, which I realized later in life, came from Moscow. No one in Spain could believe anything that was reported either in the Spanish press nor on the radio. It was all Francoist propaganda. Very little was done by the Spanish government that did not mean to indoctrinate. Consequently, those who did not agree with the ruling party tried to have access to news from outside of Spain. I don't believe, though, that my father was totally conscious that whatever news we were able to hear from Russia, despite the Spanish attempt to disrupt any foreign transmission, was also communist propaganda. Listening to these transmissions at night was dangerous. We were all very afraid to be betrayed by our neighbors. No one trusted anyone. But this danger created in my mind a sense of valued complicity with my father.

My father had an unschooled but beautiful tenor voice. He loved singing and performing. He joined a local men's choir, where he was the soloist, and he took me with him. He also played the drum in a marching band, as I did eventually. He played the drum in the two bullfight rings in Barcelona and, when there were *corridas* (bullfights) in both, I played in one and he in the other.

I don't know how my parents managed financially, given how strapped for money we were, but they rented a piano so I could learn to play. This decision was not an unselfish act. My father had an ulterior motive. He wanted to have an accompanist. This explains the piano and the piano lessons, something that none of my friends in the neighborhood could even have dreamed of having. This made me a very special person and at times a source of derision among some of my friends. Nonetheless, I learned to play, specifically, the music to accompany him as he sang operatic and Spanish zarzuela arias and popular songs that my father wanted to perform. This linked me even further to my father.

My relationship with him, however, was not always the most endearing. Probably because of the very tough living conditions under which most working families lived and because he often had three different jobs in order to make enough money for us to survive, my dad was at times irascible and unpredictable. He was not very generous with my brother and me, unlike our mother who often tried to give us little pleasures to the extent that her meager resources allowed. He was also very demanding, particularly of me. When I was in my early teens, he would often ask me what I wanted to achieve in life. I had no idea and said so. His response, which hurt me deeply, was to repeat often that I would never amount to much in life with the attitude I displayed. To the degree that I could comprehend things then, I found this insistence on his part somewhat bewildering. The

A budding pian...

education I was receiving in school was incredibly lacking. I could not see any other option open than, at best, to work in some office that required little of me or, at worst, to work in some factory, something my father would never tolerate. Under no circumstances did he want me to be a glassblower like him. Future events, as I will detail, rendered his judgement ironic.

I do not recall with any degree of exactitude what my life was the fifteen and a half years we lived in Barcelona. My memory of those years is not linear at all. Instead, it is a series of occurrences, events and experiences, some of them good and others less pleasant, that may or may not have had a great deal of import for the person I have become.

The years that followed the end of the Spanish Civil War, particularly, the 1940s and the early 1950s were known as *los años de hambre, the* "hunger years." And indeed, they were. Rationing had been introduced in 1939 as soon as the Spanish Civil War was over, and it did not end until April of 1952. I was almost twelve years old by then. What was provided through the rationing system, however, was totally inadequate as it lacked the minimum level of nutrition for subsistence. Much of the scarcity was the result of the fields having been neglected during the war as well as a country without national resources to deal with a desperately poor populace. But, to a large degree, the government did little to ameliorate the condition under which the working classes had to live. To be sure, it suited Franco to have a population crippled by hunger and disease, particularly in Catalonia, one of the last regions to capitulate to him. Whatever was provided by the ration cards was far short of what a family needed to survive. A black market soon began to flourish for those who could afford to buy from *estraperlistas*, or black marketeers. To afford even the most essential parts of a basic diet, my mother had to purchase a few staple foods from such people. But she often lacked the resources for such purchases. I remember accompanying her to my grand aunt's apartment to borrow money. When my father was paid at the end of the work week, we went back to my grand aunt's home to pay back the borrowed money. This happened often. It became a vicious circle. My great aunt never complained about my mother's frequent requests for loans, but after each such visit I could clearly read the humiliation written all over my mother's face.

Humiliation was something many Catalans, particularly those who fought on the legal government's side against the forces of Franco, often experienced. I recalled going with my father to a government office. As we always did, since it was our language, we spoke Catalan to each other. When one of the clerks heard us, he ordered us to *hablad Cristiano, perros catalanes*, speak Christian, Catalan dogs. Under Franco's orders, Catalan was not to be taught at schools, heard on radio, theaters, and movie theaters, nor in any official government building. Even though our teachers were almost all Catalan and even spoke Castilian with a heavy Catalan accent, we were required to speak the "national" language. Our language and our culture were not only denigrated but every effort was made to obliterate them. And there were many other ways the Franco regime humiliated and cancelled more than the language and culture. My father and mother got married in 1938, during one of the times my dad was able to leave the front and come to Barcelona. When Franco took over, all the marriages that had taken place under the Republic were annulled, as if they had never existed. So, suddenly, my parents were not married under the new approved laws. For a while, they did not care. In their eyes and soul, they were married. Unfortunately, things got dicer when, in times of severe need, they were not able to get any of the family allocations benefitting the children of legally married couples. So, in December of 1944, when I was already four years old and my brother two months old, my parents had no choice but to get married again. This time the wedding was legally recognized but, as far as legal documents pertaining to my brother and me are concerned, we were born to an unwed mother. How could my parents ever forgive and forget such a mortification and indignity? But there was no official organ to which they could complain. Such irreverence would have been further cause for punishment.

Fear surrounded all of us constantly, as has been exhaustively detailed by Juan Eslava Galán in his recent publication *Los años del miedo*. Police were omnipresent. Snitches were everywhere. We did not consider ourselves free and safe even at home. We were always conscious that someone might be listening outside our door. The national atmosphere was oppressive. Franco's image was everywhere. Going to view movies was an escape from this oppression but also a constant reminder that we did not live in normal times. Before every movie we had to watch a clip that was called *No-Do*, which stood for *noticias/documentales*. These clips were almost exclusively about all the great things that Franco was doing to make Spain a better, greater nation. He was the leading character in all of these clips. As soon as the movie was over the Spanish anthem was played and everyone had to stand up, right arm up à la Hitler. Many tried to leave before the movie was over. No one had the courage to do it as soon as No-Do's leading character appeared on screen.

As I said, everyone lived in constant fear. My dad worked in a big glass blowing factory. Since the pay was greatly insufficient, the owners allowed some of the master glassblowers, of whom my father was one, to access the factory before working hours started and make some creative pieces that they could then sell and make some extra money. Working hours in the factory began at six in the morning. In order for my father to walk to the factory and have sufficient time to create a few pieces before six, he had to leave the house around four in the morning. One day, police stopped him and asked him where he was going. They asked him to produce his documentation. He got nervous and frightened and could not find it. He feared that he had left it at home. Despite the early hours, they forced him to go back with them. We were all terrified when we were awakened and saw my father with two men who were clearly police officers. There was absolutely no reason to treat a worker in this manner other than to elicit fear and humiliation. We felt that our home had been violated.

Although I was actually born in the neighborhood of Barcelona called Gracia, not too far from Gaudi's Sagrada Familia, my parents soon moved to new living quarters. We lived on the fifth floor of an old building in a street that was not paved. My street, Melchor de Palau, was not far from what is now the main Sants train station in Barcelona. The apartment was small and squarish. As soon as you opened the front door, you could see most of it. There was a relatively small space that functioned as a kitchen, dining room, and living room, from which you could see each bedroom.

On one side of the wall was a kind of counter that contained a sink, a sort of grill under which were the coals used for cooking, and space under the counter to store the coal, cooking utensils, potatoes, and whatever else could be kept there. It was all hidden from view by a sort of cloth apron. We also had a small cupboard and little else. We had no fridge. Consequently, like everyone else, shopping had to be done daily as most food did not survive for long without a fridge.

There were three small bedrooms. A small one, with a bed and little else, was shared by my brother and me. A somewhat larger one, was what we might call nowadays the master bedroom. It contained a bed, an armoire, and a night table. It also had a tiny balcony, with a view of the street below and the building across the street that seemed almost within reach with a long pole. The third bedroom became the home of the rented piano and a Singer sewing machine that my mother used to sew many of our clothes and do alterations for some neighborhood ladies. It also had a series of uncomfortable chairs. We had no internal rest room. Instead, to go to the bathroom, we had to go outdoors. We had what was then called a *galeria*, a kind of open-air balcony at the back of the building. It had a wash basin, where my mother did the laundry. It also had a small, enclosed area which contained a toilet. During the night, we did not go out to this cold toilet. Instead, like almost everyone else, we used chamber pots. And, obviously, we neither had a bathtub nor a shower. In fact, we would have to wait until we got to Canada before we had a fridge, a tub and a shower. But I am jumping ahead.

Barcelona, like the rest of Spain, was lacking in the most basic things. Long before recycling became popular, many, many decades later, we recycled everything. Almost everything we had was used and reused until it almost disintegrated into nothingness. We had appropriate containers and bags for almost everything we bought in small quantities. For milk, we had our own metal container which we took to the dairy store. We bought wine kept in huge barrels and filled our own bottles. Stores provided practically no wrappings. Even fish wasn't wrapped and if it was, it was wrapped in newspaper. Newspapers were used far more as wrapping and toilet paper than as providers of news. In fact, before we ever used whatever newspaper my parents could lay their hands on, my father wore it between his shirt and overcoat to protect himself against the cold, humidity, and windy days of winter. My dad even recycled whatever piece of tire he could find to re-sole our shoes. My shoes ended up being rather heavy and somewhat ugly, but I got great mileage out of them.

As I mentioned, we had very few toys. In fact, on January 6, when the Three Wise Men brought presents to children (in Spain, presents are delivered not by Santa Claus but by the three Wise Men), we used to get pencils, crayons, notebooks, for school, but also socks, underwear. Things that we needed at any time of the year but miraculously appeared as presents delivered by the Three Wise Men. Most of the time we played in the street, in front of our apartment building. There was hardly any traffic at all, other than, now and then, a horse drawn cart. Since it was dirt, we made holes on the ground and played marbles. The game consisted in driving the opponent's marble into the hole. We also played a sort of obstacle course jumping over a sequence of bent-down boys. There was also a more dangerous game called in Catalan *cavall fort*, or strong horse. It consisted of an increasing number of boys, the first of whom leaned against a railing or a wall, bent down, linked by grabbing the legs of those in front forming a longer and longer line. The idea was to run and jump as close as possible to the front and force the "horse" to collapse. Of course, we also played soccer in the street although instead of a normal ball, we used one made of scraps of clothing.

There were two things we were able to do for fun that did not cost any money. Summer Sundays, when we did not get together with family and my father did not have to play the drum at the bullfights, we went to the beach, either in the Barceloneta, which was much closer to home but less well maintained, or Castelldefels, a much nicer beach but one that required us to travel much farther. We did not have suntan lotion. So, regardless of the beach we decided to go to, Julio and I ended up the first time of each summer with severe sun burns. When we got home our mother prepared some concoction that included olive oil and some other ingredients. It relieved the pain somewhat, but we ended up smelling as if we had been immersed in salad dressing.

The second thing that gave us a lot of pleasure was the summer months during which each neighborhood had its *Fiesta Mayor*. The streets that had the greatest number of store fronts and some of the nicer buildings, and thus people with more means, dressed up the streets by constructing elaborate entrances celebrating a major theme, ran streamers and lights across the street in a manner such that when seen from one end of the street one could have sworn that the street was covered by colorful ceilings. Neighborhood stores and neighbors also built wood terraces on the sidewalks in front of their buildings from which they could, at night, listen to live music and watch all the activities perched higher than all the other participants. Everyone danced and everybody knew how to dance. Mothers taught little boys how to dance and fathers or mothers also taught little girls. These were fun and free events that allowed whole families to enjoy each other in the company of neighbors and friends. Boys in particular also enjoyed during the day the ability to jump from terrace to terrace. These were great summer days that filled us with joy and made our parents forget, however briefly, the difficult life they had to live.

Street life was not all the simple fun and games we played. Once we were old enough to be left alone in our apartment after school, my mother went to work. My brother and I spent a lot of time alone. In the absence of toys, we had to create our own games. My brother was always afraid of what our parents would say or do to us if we misbehaved. I was less concerned about consequences and thus got into trouble more often. I recall two incidents which cost me a serious spanking from my father. My parents had a nice armoire which had a full-length mirror inside the middle door. Once, I opened it to explore what was in this mirror, pulled out the drawers and then closed the door without pushing back one of the drawers. The beautiful, beveled mirror ended up with a number of spider cracks that created a psychedelic reflection. On another occasion, in this same bedroom, I managed to climb above the armoire. My brother reminded me of the spanking I received the previous time I played in our parents' bedroom. Of course, I paid no attention to my little kid brother. I jumped from the top of the armoire onto our parents' bed. It collapsed. My brother was in hysterics. I told him not to worry. With his help I managed to get under the bed, propped it up somehow and left it looking more or less as if it were in perfect shape. That night, when my parents went to bed, my repair failed. The bed collapsed again with them in it. I deserved what I got. I was good at destroying things. One year, the Three Wise Men brought my brother a nice horse, probably made of some sturdy cardboard. He was incredibly happy and proud to own such a toy. He did not get to enjoy it for long. I sat on it and flattened it. He cried for days ... and so did I from the thrashing I received from our father.

Not everything I did while we were left alone at home every day for hours was bad or destructive. I knew my mother worked very hard and came home tired. She could not rest, however. She had to do the shopping for dinner and had to cook. To help her a bit, I would sit my brother on top of the kitchen/dining room table, and I would mop the ceramic floors. I always tried to time my domestic chore so that my mother would arrive as I was finishing the mopping. I wanted her to see what I had done and the best time to do it most effectively and with greater impact was for her to see the floor when it was still wet. It shined and it looked much nicer than it actually was. Of course, it could not be too wet otherwise she would make a mess as she came in from the street and leave foot imprints on the wet floor. Timing was everything. I was always elated when she came in, showed satisfaction and happiness and kissed me and Julio as if we were her saviors. I loved moments like these.

There were two periods when even my father was very worried about me and did not pressure me into doing anything. When I was about eleven or twelve years of age, I became ill with a condition that affected my pleura, the tissue that lines the chest cavity and the outside of the lungs. I was very ill and the doctor, who at that time made house calls, came to see me often. Ultimately, after a number of medical treatments, he determined that I needed to be moved to a different climate. With so much humidity, Barcelona did not provide the climate necessary for improvement. So, my father decided to take me to Onda, the Valencian town where his adopted "milk family" lived. They welcomed me as if I were a very valued member of the family. The love they displayed for me was very comforting and the climate was definitely better, but their living conditions left a lot to be desired. They lived in far worse quarters than we did in Barcelona.

Nonetheless, I was happy there. As soon as I got stronger, I went outdoors and played with the neighborhood kids. They made fun of me because I was from the big city. They ran up and down cobbled streets without shoes. I needed shoes. Without them the pain was excruciating.

In the absence of toys, those kids were very creative. They made bows and arrows out of the wires from discarded umbrellas. They sharpened the umbrella metal ribs to convert them into arrows. They built a bull's eye and we all tried to demonstrate our sharp shooting ability. One time I went to get my arrow which was embedded into the bull's eye and as I turned around to go back to the starting point, I was wounded by an arrow that missed my eye by millimeters. But this is not the worst thing that happened to me while I was there.

Part of my diet to strengthen me was goat milk. Most of the milk was unpasteurized. Shortly after I returned to Barcelona, I came down with brucellosis, also known either as Mediterranean or Malta fever. Once again, I became very sick and needed not only medical assistance but constant watching and caring. The doctor determined that what I needed was streptomycin, a drug that, in Barcelona at least, was not easily available. My parents had to resort to the black market. I have no idea what they had to sacrifice in order to afford this medication. Thanks to it, however, I was cured and could resume my normal existence, such as it was.

Perhaps my parents should have placed less faith in new expensive pharmaceutical developments and relied on a revolutionary discovery that gained so much popularity that a song was written praising its miraculous properties. Dad was intimately involved in this period of experimentation. He became a sort of specialized fungus surgeon. People began cultivating a special mushroom, known as the "hongo chino," with supposedly outstanding and wide-ranging medicinal properties. It was not the average, run-of-the-mill mushroom. This revolting thing was a gelatinous semi-transparent, squid-like substance that floated in a solution of tea and sugar that provided it with nutrition to grow and reproduce itself. The top layer of the mushroom could be peeled away, ever so carefully. This is what required the delicate skills that my father possessed. As "newborn" mushrooms were peeled away and given to friends and relatives, the father/mother kept reproducing

My father and me, dressed in the marching band uniforms, and with my mother and sister on Palm Sunday.

Manuel Father, on left, and Manuel Son, right center, Barcelona.

so that more could be harvested. Dad was much in demand. Everyone wanted to have one of these magical fungi. So, he went from home to home to do the required "surgery." He did not ask for payment, but people were so grateful that they gave him tips. Eventually he asked me to assist him in "delivering" the "newborns." The fluid on which the mushroom was floating was consumed by the whole family to fight all sorts or real and imaginary maladies. Dad had a great deal of faith in the curative properties of the "magical fungus" and, of course, we trusted him to do what was best for the family. It was never tried on me when I was really sick, so I have no way of knowing whether I would have been cured. What I do know is that none of us got sick from drinking that kind of slimy potion. Just as this cure-all remedy had quickly invaded our lives and collective consciousness, one day, it disappeared as quickly as it had arrived, as few were ever able to report the existence of any demonstrable miracles. For as long as it lasted, however, no working-class family in Barcelona would have dared to be without one of these "hongos chinos." Once again, this episode demonstrated that my father was willing to do anything to help us and, once again, it allowed me to work side by side with him, as assistant surgeon.

Our parents worked hard, six days a week. There was little time for entertainment in their existence.

Other than visiting some relatives now and then, we went to the movies on rare occasions, and for walks. We led a fairly sedate life. On Sundays my mother usually stayed home all morning cleaning the apartment and doing laundry. While she did, and as to not become a nuisance, our father would take my brother and me for a simple breakfast to the bar where the choir to which he and I belonged rehearsed. Sunday was also the day our father played the drum at the *corridas*, the bullfights. I usually went with him. While we were there, my mother and my brother would visit our grandmother. My dad and I often joined them after the bullfight ended. These visits were not always fun. For some reason that escaped me, grandmother and dad could not stand each other, a situation that embittered my mother all of her life. Attending school could have been a relief, but it wasn't. Either because the teachers were pretty bad or because I was not interested at all in learning, I did not enjoy attending classes.

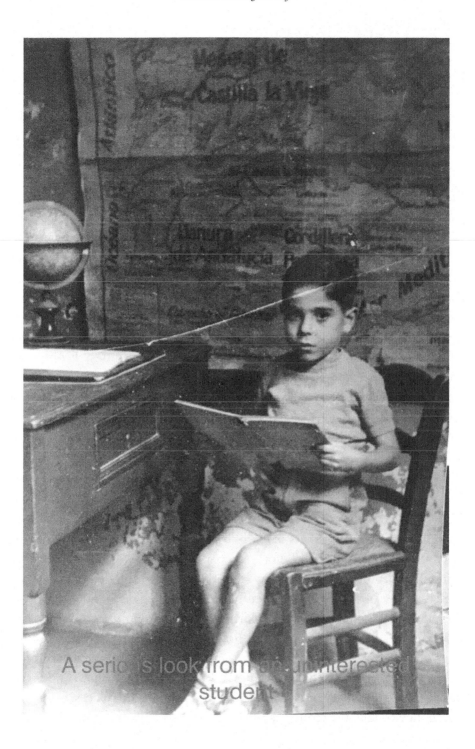

A serious look from an uninterested student

I was far more interested in games of any sort than in studying. I applied myself a bit more to my piano lessons only because my father made sure I devoted sufficient time to this endeavor. I could hardly wait to be fourteen, the age by which most kids could start working legally, to find a job.

I was not much better at the jobs I got than I had been in school. Between the age of fourteen and the time we left Barcelona when I was fifteen and a half, I held a number of jobs. First, I worked for a few weeks for a man who claimed to be a dentist but was only the one who made the dentures, crowns, and other repairs. He knew my father because he was his "dentist". Since my father could not pay for his services, he remodeled his office as payment. I hated the job and disliked the man. So, I abandoned the job after a very short stint. My second job was in the Rambles, in a factory that made mirrors, and glass doors and windows. Everyone working there was old and the atmosphere that reigned was stultifying. I left after a few weeks before they fired me for inattention to my duties. From there I was fortunate to be hired in a prominent audit and management firm, close to the *Mercat de Sant Antoni*, the famed and now restored modernist market in the lower part of the Eixample neighborhood of Barcelona. I worked there for only a few months. I sensed that they were not too happy with my performance. So, I left, again, before they fired me.

Finally, I went to work in a branch office of a German company, at the Rambla de Catalunya, called, if I recall correctly, Orenstein and Koppel. My job there was to file documents and deliver parts to shops in various locations that used products made by the German company. The young boy who had held the job before me had been negligent and instead of filing the documents shoved them behind the filing cabinets. My job consisted mostly of filing all the documents the manager found behind the filing cabinet. I enjoyed the work, other than the filing part. After a while I decided that what had been good for my predecessor was good enough for me. I discovered that filing documents behind the cabinets was much quicker work and less boring. I enjoyed the part that dealt with delivering parts. Since I had to make deliveries to a number of places, they gave me money to take the trolley car. I found ways by planning my deliveries in the most efficient way to walk to avoid using public transportation and saved the money. Since I had to find the most direct ways of going to different addresses to avoid being gone longer than if I had taken public transport, I became very efficient navigating around Barcelona.

There was a young man, about four or five years older than me who was funny and playful. He was also a bit of a bully. I made a serious tactical error in dealing with his bullying. My father had once told me that the manner to deal with bullies is to confront them directly, not to show fear, to threaten them. He recounted a time when it happened to him. He took one of the tools they used at work and threatened the guy with physical injury if he tried again to bully him. So, what did I do? When this bigger, stronger, older young man tried to bully me, I grabbed a pair of scissors and threatened to stab him. He showed not the slightest fear. He did not back down. Instead, he took me by my feet, raised me, and put my head inside a garbage bin. I learned a painful lesson that day. You better be ready to follow through with your threats or pay the consequences.

I probably could have stayed in that job for a longer period of time, but two things happened that put an end to it. One of them was my own doing. At the time I was already fifteen. My parents were somewhat old fashioned and imitated the ways of the middle class. Boys were meant to wear shorts until a certain age and then move to knickerbockers. Which is what I wore at the time. This was a time when I was beginning to pay a lot of attention to girls. They made fun of my funny-looking pants. So, I asked my parents to buy me long pants. My mother was not insensitive to my demand and understood my humiliation at having to ask girls to dance, at the street dances we had in every neighborhood every summer, dressed in those pants. My father, on the other hand, considered the pants I was wearing more than adequate and capable of lasting a few more years. No matter how much I pleaded and begged, he did not desist.

I had to find a way to convince my father. The opportunity presented itself at work. The manager of the office informed us that our company was going to give us a bonus. The problem was that the bonus was not to be granted until the summer street dances would be over. I had to design a way by which my father would agree to buy me long pants if I brought home a bonus and convince the chief in the office to advance me the bonus. This is a confession that I have told my wife only in recent years because I felt so ashamed for the humiliation I inflicted on my father. I was desperate. I could not think of anything else and could not see beyond my immediate need to be "presentable" in front of the girls I wanted to dance with. So, I went to the manager and asked him if he could intercede for me and get me the bonus immediately. I told him that my parents needed the money desperately. He was taken aback and asked me to bring my father so he could discuss the situation with him. I thought I could finesse the situation by telling my father that all he needed to do was say that he was supportive of my request. I could not have been more wrong. The meeting between the manager and my dad went very badly. The manager shamed my father by telling him that if he needed the bonus, he should have been man enough and come to him rather than send his son.

No sooner had we left the office my father cuffed me at the back of the head with violence. I started to run away from him and kept a distance between us all the way home. I thought my mother would be able to shield me from my father's anger. It wasn't to be. I received the most severe but fully deserved beatings. Even though it wasn't very pleasurable to be slapped around, I was actually able to understand and pity my father. I had forced him into one of the most painful and humiliating situations he probably ever faced. I sincerely believe that this incident changed me considerably for the better.

The second reason for quitting this last job was more consequential. My father had always wanted to leave Spain. He dreamed of emigrating to Argentina or Venezuela. The opportunity to do so, however, never materialized. The chance to emigrate, however, presented itself in an unexpected way.

A huge glass factory in Souvigny, France, was in desperate need for different types of expert glassblowers. Headhunters came to Barcelona around November of 1955 and offered jobs to about 20 different master glass blowers among whom was my father. They were promised salaries, far better than what they were earning in Barcelona, including overtime and other odd jobs here and there, good working conditions, and, above all, housing. Most men agreed to accept the job on a conditional basis. They would leave the families behind, work for a while, and determine whether they wanted to stay on and thus ask their respective families to join them. They were all lodged in a hotel where they received room and board. Some decided after a brief period that this town of about 3000 inhabitants, most of whom depended either on farming or the factory, was not for them or their loved ones. But my father, after working there for a while, decided to make a go of it. So, my mother, my brother and I left Barcelona in mid-December and joined him. We, too, stayed at the same hotel for a few weeks, before any decision about housing was discussed.

One of the men in this group, Francisco Ribas, known to all as Cisco, was an acquaintance of my father who had at one time worked with him in Barcelona. At one point, as families contemplated the move to France, the wife of this acquaintance, Vicenta Amorós, and her daughter, Gloria Ribas Amorós, came to our home to discuss details about this momentous change in life. I already knew Gloria. In fact, I had met her on at least three different occasions, the very first time when we were probably eleven or so. Our fathers took us to a wrestling match. The second time, the two families met at a Barcelona beach. At that time Gloria and I must have been around twelve or thirteen. I remember vividly this encounter because Gloria was already a fully developed young woman, and quite pretty. I, on the other hand, was a scrawny juvenile with little if any appeal. The third time, when I had just turned fifteen, was just as memorable as the second, but more painful for me. As I have recounted, summers in Barcelona were great in that whole neighborhood, at different times of the summer, had street dances with live orchestras. A few friends of mine and I used to go from one neighborhood to the next hoping to find girls willing to dance with us. One time we happened to be in the street where Gloria lived. I saw her standing by her father. I went to say hello to her father and, to ingratiate myself with her father and her, asked her to dance with me. She consented. I enjoyed the dance and her and later went and asked her for a second dance. She turned me down. I was hurt and resentful. I wasn't about to forget such a snub. The fourth time was when mother and daughter came to our apartment to seek counsel from my mother about the upcoming trip to France. Gloria looked even more alluring. I kept looking at her, according to her, in a very particular way. She told me much later that I had made her uncomfortable and nervous. I did not see her again, until a few months later in the train station, in Moulins, where our family had gone with Gloria's father to welcome her and her mother.

CHAPTER II

France, December 1955–June 1958

▲▲▲

ONE WOULD HAVE THOUGHT THAT leaving Barcelona would have repre-sented for us a difficult and nostalgic experience. After all, we were leav-ing behind family and friends and a life we knew. We were also going to a country whose language we did not speak, whose cultures were totally unknown to us, and whose living conditions and prospects had not yet been clarified to us. I don't really know how my mother and little brother felt deep inside. I think both of them for different reasons were somewhat uncertain and concerned. I, on the contrary, was quite delighted to explore new possibilities. I felt a certain exhilaration.

Although I had recently become a voracious reader of popular detec-tive novels in Barcelona, I did not feel, nor could I have been considered an educated boy. My studies, such as they were, had had very little impact. Public schools were mostly government propaganda and brainwashing tools. The Catholic church participated as well in proselytizing children, inculcating in them the belief that Spain could only be a successful nation if its citizens were fascist followers and devout and practicing Catholics. My experiences at work had not been much more successful, as I have recounted. It was obvious that I was not serious about my responsibilities, had no discipline and lacked a sense of purpose. Perhaps I did not disagree all that much with my dad's pronouncement that I would not amount to much in life. Somehow, however, my recent very bad experience at my last employment had made a deep impression on me and I felt that something within me was in the process of changing. So I welcomed whatever the future in France held for me.

My dad had found out that one of the younger glassblowers who had been hired was going to Barcelona to spend a few days. He asked him if he would be willing to accompany my mother, my brother and me on his way back. This way, we would be less worried about taking such a long train trip in a foreign land. He was very nice and accommodating and our trip turned out to be rather pleasant. He managed to allay whatever reticence my mother might have had. As long as we were with our mother, Julio and I felt no fear at all.

We arrived in Souvigny a couple of weeks before Christmas. We stayed at the *chaumière*, a combination of hotel, restaurant, and ballroom used by the whole town for celebrations and special events. It was nicely decorated, welcoming, and cozy. During our stay, there were a number of dances to celebrate the Christmas season. My parents, along with many of the other couples, danced merrily. I must confess that I, too, enjoyed the chance to dance. Even at fifteen I was particularly interested in girls and, setting modesty aside, a pretty good dancer already. In Barcelona, one of my friends and I knew a couple of very cute girls from our neighborhood whom we liked a great deal. In order to spend time with them, we were like two little lap dogs that followed them everywhere. They wanted to dance "sardanas," a typical and very particular Catalan dance, something we did not like or know how to dance, but we went along with them. When they wanted to go to the theater to see Catalan plays, we followed them as well even though we probably cared even less about the plays than the "sardanas". All we wished for was the opportunity to perhaps be able to hold their hands, something that rarely happened. So, imagine my amazement at the "friendliness" of a very cute French girl, all dressed in white at one of the first dances I went to in Souvigny. What amazed me the most about this young, beautiful French girl was her generosity. After a few dances she managed to take me away from the dance floor and started kissing me and taking my hands to her wholesome breasts. I had never experienced anything like this. I thought, "is this a great country or what!" The *chaumière* became one of our favorite places. Almost everyone, whole families, gathered there many Saturday nights for dancing. In addition, and to my great surprise, the *chaumière* also became a place for adolescents to hang out. As long as we ordered *un canon*, a glass of wine, we could play pool for hours on end as well as foosball.

Although all the glassblowers who came from Barcelona were not all Catalan almost all of them spoke the language. When they got to Souvigny they were surprised to find two families who had worked at the factory for a number of years and they, too, were Catalan. So, it is not surprising that the *lingua franca* among all of us was Catalan.

Revisiting the "Grand Entrance, Street and Homes" Provided in Souvigny

I don't know whether the first few weeks could be described as euphoric, but if the description fit, it did not last long. We found out that the housing that had been promised to lure us, was still not even under construction. Only two families were lucky enough to be housed in town in relatively decent living conditions. This was not the fate that awaited us. Even though most of us could have said that the apartments we had in Barcelona were modest and rustic, they were almost luxurious by comparison to what was offered to us. By then, contracts had been signed and there was little we could do. We would just have to wait for the excellent promised housing.

What passed for housing was built on a rectangular parcel of land that abutted the factory where our fathers worked and was surrounded by walls made of cinder blocks, as were the "houses" provided. We gained entrance to this "neighborhood" by an opening created by knocking down a bunch of cinder blocks. But, instead of attempting to make it look like an actual entrance, it looked as though there had been an accident and the wall had collapsed unevenly. To top it all, those who lived there dumped their garbage for collection just outside the entrance. Once inside, the rectangle was composed of a series of what appeared to have been single rooms, or cells, that eventually became two such rooms per abode. To call these abodes slapdash would have been a compliment.

The "street," if one could call it that, had a fairly steep elevation so that to go from one cell to the contiguous one there had to be a step. The interior was sparse to say the least. One of the two "rooms" contained a stove used for cooking and heating. The other room was bare. There was no sink and of course no running water. There was not a bathroom either. For water, we had to go to a pump and cart the water in buckets to the "house." For about twenty dwellings there were five outhouses, with holes in the ground. Across from each "house," and on the other side of the path that permitted us to go from "house" to "house," was a very small parcel of land that most of us eventually used to grow some vegetables. There was also a makeshift hut where tools could be kept and some of us also ended up having either chickens or rabbits.

Winters were incredibly cold. Other than the stove that heated the house for at most two hours after we went to bed, we had no other heating. Which heat emanated from it until the fire was out, at most a couple of hours after we went to bed, we had no heating. Our parents slept in one room. My brother and I slept in a folding bed in the other room that was the kitchen, living room, and dining room. We were a bit luckier than our parents because we enjoyed the heat from the furnace. We kept the clothing that we were going to don the following morning inside our bed. When we woke up in the morning we actually got dressed inside the bed. It was far too cold to venture out of it and dress in our frozen clothing.

Our father, who was a very handy man, particularly when it came to masonry and brick laying, quickly made moves to improve our living conditions. First of all, he built a deep sink, perforated the wall and developed a draining system under the path in front of our "house." This permitted us to get water from the pump and store it in this sink. This enhancement to our lodging was seen by other neighbors as a great advantage. My father volunteered to build one for several of our neighbors and friends.

After a few months, we were fortunate that the neighbors next door decided to move. They probably broke the contract and left for Barcelona. This suddenly vacated two "cells." My father went to management and asked that we be allowed to remodel the vacant "house" so that we would get an additional room and the people further up, with a large family, get the other room. This meant that our father had to create a door to have access to the additional room and build a wall to divide the two, now, three room "houses."

Suddenly, my brother and I were able to have our own room, but, of course, we were further away from the stove and thus were even colder than we had been. As soon as this extra room was available, my dad wasted no time in finding a way to rent a piano so I could continue with my piano lessons. I actually attended the conservatory of music in Moulins, a major town about fifteen kilometers from Souvigny.

Gloria and her mother came to join her father in February of that year. It was one of the coldest days of the winter. The fountains in the street were all frozen and the frozen water created all kinds of sculptural shapes that, though attractive, only gave us a greater sensation of acute cold. As soon as I saw Gloria, I remembered her snub and decided then and there that she would fall in love with me. Little did I know that I, too, would soon fall under her spell.

Julio had just turned eleven and it was normal for him to go to school. I, on the other hand, was much older. My parents, however, decided that I would go to school as well. This was rather painful for me. There were two schools in Souvigny, one for boys and one for girls. In the boys' school, there was a married couple both of whom were teachers. The lady, Madame Ronfet, taught the little boys. Monsieur Ronfet, taught the older ones. Unless you were going to go to Moulins to the lycée, all the kids in the school would go to work either in the fields or in the factory at the age of fourteen. I felt totally and completely out of place. There is a photo of all the kids in Monsieur Ronfet's class and I look like some older brother who decided to crash the photo scene. I endured school until the summer.

By sixteen I was ready to find a job. Julio, of course, continued until he received what at that time was called the *certificat d'études*, a diploma that indicated that students had successfully completed the required course-work that normally put an end to study for those boys and girls who were not going to continue on. Gloria, too, stayed in school long enough to be awarded the same certificate.

Very Out of Place Manuel in Souvigny School, 1956

As I have indicated, our father did not want either Julio or me to ever become glassblowers. So, I had to seek employment somewhere else. Souvigny offered no opportunities whatsoever. I had to look for a job where they existed. This meant Moulins, the nearby town. After a very brief spell working in a watchmaker store, I found a job at Chez Raoul, a men's clothing store that in addition to selling upper end clothing had a tailor's shop in the back of the store. I was hired with the possibility of learning to be a tailor. At first, though, I spent most of the time delivering shirts, suits, coats, and overcoats to the store's clientele. I did not care what they had me do. I fell in love with everyone who worked there. They were all very kind and helpful. I was fascinated by one of the young salespeople, called Jean Pierre. I liked how he spoke, the way he dressed, the manner in which he combed his hair, and the stories he told me. I even decided that if ever I had a son, I would name him Jean Pierre.

A budding salesman, Chez Raoul, Moulins, 1957

At times, particularly, before the holidays, when the store was full and the two salespeople could not take care of all the shoppers, I offered my services. It turned out that I was quite adept at salesmanship. The manager was quite impressed with me when I was able to sell some suits that had become *passé* years before.

I had to travel back and forth to Moulins, so I needed some means of transportation. My parents had bought Julio a very nice bicycle. Necessity forced him to lend it to me so I could go to work each day. The trip was not terribly long, about ten miles, but just before Moulins there was an extremely steep downhill followed by an equally steep uphill. This was tiring. I was fortunate after a few weeks of commuting to encounter a young lady, the daughter of the owners of Souvigny's haberdashery. She rode a *mobylette*, a moped powerful enough to drag me along if I held on to her shoulder. We did not coincide each day in our commute, but we did often enough.

Much later, my lot changed for the better. My father had bought a *vélosolex*, a somewhat weird motorcycle with a motor mounted on the side of the front wheel. It was not fancy nor very fast. Although my father was quite proprietary and would not let me use it at all at the beginning, two events changed his mind. He was involved in a small accident. He ran into a lady and, somehow, she ended up placing her finger between the spokes of the wheel and lost part of her finger. This caused a bit of an uproar in town, and it shook him up. After that, my father used the *vélosolex* sparingly. I took advantage of this opportunity to convince him that I should get a chance to use it to go to work. After all, I said, I was helping the family with my salary. Fortunately, he acquiesced. The hills became less of an effort, and I was able to commute at a faster speed.

Bicycles almost cut short my loving relationship with Gloria. She did not know how to ride a bike nor was she interested in learning. I insisted that riding was easy and that we could have a lot of fun riding together around the area, which was rather bucolic and beautiful. She was still reticent, but I promised that I would hold on to the seat of the bike until she had control. We gave it a try on the road just outside the entrance to our "street." Unfortunately, at one point I let go of the seat, she turned to look and saw that she was on her own. She panicked and went straight toward the pile of garbage bags that were right next to the entrance. She wasn't hurt, but at that moment her love for me sank to a very low level. I tried several times over our life together to get her to ride, each with a worse outcome. The last time, in Bakersfield, California, she fell over the handlebars and scratched her face, knees, and hands badly. She has never been on a bike again.

But let's return to the topic at hand: What France meant to me. I loved France immediately. I loved and still love the language, the culture, the Marseillaise and the freedom people seemed to enjoy. I joined the local soccer team. I was not a very good player but enjoyed the camaraderie and the travel to other towns to play. I also joined the town's marching band. I did not want to play the drum, so I decided to learn how to play the saxophone. I have to admit that my rehearsing must have been quite painful to those around me since all the dogs in the neighborhood would start howling as soon as I played the first note. Notwithstanding the opinion of the dogs, I took great pride in learning quickly and being able to march smartly. I had always admired people whose job required them to wear a nice uniform.

Playing in the marching band gave me the opportunity to wear a sort of military uniform. Unfortunately, the one I was given had belonged to someone taller and bigger than me. The first time I wore it I felt quite self-conscious. I thought all eyes were on me. I must have looked terrible, even clownish. I was far too vain for this. I took the uniform to the tailors of the store, and they did miracles with it. The next time I wore it, no one could compete with me. I was the most elegant musician. I was forever grateful to those tailors. These same tailors were generous enough to alter several of the pieces of clothing I was able to buy at the store at highly reduced prices, particularly since some of the items I bought were somewhat démodé. I have a photo of me behind one of the counters in the store wearing a double-breasted coat that makes me look like a bit of a mafioso, but a very elegant one.

Although my father was considered one of the stars at the *Verrerie de Souvigny*, he could not see himself living in this small town forever. At one point, he asked the manager of the factory to consider sending him to a sister factory in Paris. He was turned down, but he did not accept defeat

Manuel A. Esteban

easily. There were probably two or possibly three main reasons why he desired to move to Paris. First of all, he thought that my piano studies would probably improve if I were able to study at a Parisian Conservatory. He also saw it as a necessary move to put distance between Gloria and me. We had fallen in love, and he thought that I was neglecting my piano playing to spend as much time as possible with Gloria. There was also a third and equally appealing draw. At one point he had learned that there was a singing competition in Moulins. He signed up as a contestant. When he and I got there, he was asked what he wanted to sing. He said, Granada, the Agustin Lara's song that had become internationally famous and performed by almost any artist and amateur. The contest organizer hated to have one more interpreter of this song and told my father to sing something else. My father refused. When he finished his performance, with me at the piano, the audience erupted with bravos. He won the competition. For this, he was awarded a beautiful Ducretet-Thomson radio that he still had when he died at eighty-two, in Medicine Hat, Alberta, Canada. This success only reinforced his desire to move to Paris. He thought that he would probably have greater opportunities to display his vocal talents. Thus, he continued to push the manager for a transfer.

Eventually, the manager was persuaded, and granted my father the transfer. My father and I took a train to Paris and from there we went to Choisy-le-Roi, a small suburb southeast of Paris. I had been to Paris on a school organized trip. I loved it. But Choisy-le-Roi was not Paris. The area we stayed in was populated by Fellagha, an Arabic word literally meaning "bandits" which referred to groups of armed militants affiliated with anti-colonial movements in French North Africa. It did not feel very safe. We could hear shootings at night.

Although we had already identified the Conservatory where I would study music, my father soon accepted the reality that he had made a mistake. He had gone from being a star in the factory in Souvigny to being just one more master glassblower in the new position. Reluctantly, he asked me to telephone the manager in Souvigny and ask whether it would be possible for him to go back to his old job. The manager acceded to his request, but dad paid a heavy price for what the manager perceived as a

32

betrayal. Instead of having one of the best jobs when he returned, he was given responsibilities that were well below his capabilities and abilities. He was being punished.

He was unhappy, but I, on the other hand, was overjoyed to be back. So was Gloria. We were both relieved that my father had decided not to stay in Paris. I was so happy, comfortable, and at ease in Souvigny and with my job in Moulins that, at one point, I asked what it would take for me to be naturalized French. I was told that I would automatically become a French citizen if I joined the army. At that time, France was involved in the Algerian War, also known as the Algerian Revolution or the Algerian War of Independence. I mentioned this idea to my father. He told me that I would not need to worry about being killed while serving because if I were stupid enough to join the French army, he would kill me first. That put an end to this scatterbrained idea. Still, I did not give up on my desire to become a French citizen as soon as feasible. Future events changed this hope dramatically.

Both my brother and Gloria lived in Souvigny as long as I did. Neither one of them understood why I felt such admiration and affection for France. They were relatively happy there, but never felt so attracted and drawn into the French culture. I cannot explain it in rational terms. After all, by the time we left France, this time for Canada, we had only lived in France for thirty months. I think Julio really enjoyed his friends and the opportunity to study in a good school, as compared to the one in Barcelona. Gloria had even more reasons to identify with French culture as she joined a theater group, performed in plays, and danced wearing beautiful period dresses.

But once they left Souvigny behind, they moved on. This was not the case for me. Those two and a half years felt like a much longer period and strongly determined the kind of person I was becoming. A person that I liked much better and who became more optimistic about the future and what I could achieve in life, even though very little at the time would have given me any indication that my life could change dramatically. Still, I probably felt more an integral part of the French experience than I had felt part of Spanish life.

Gloria dressed for one of her dramatic roles, 1957

And yet, all of my plans to remain in France and become a French citizen came crashing down. One day, out of the blue, dad received a letter from Calgary, Canada. The letter was from a man called Vicenç Ferrer who had been his apprentice in Barcelona. He had lost contact with him. It turned out that he and his family had illegally crossed the Pyrenees Mountains into France. From there, the whole family had somehow found their way into Québec and later into Calgary. In Calgary he had befriended a fellow Catalan who was an entrepreneur and, upon learning that Vicenç had worked as an apprentice glassblower, convinced him to partner with him and start a glass studio. Vicenç indicated that he had just been an apprentice. For what they had in mind, they needed master glassblowers. I do not know how, but they managed to track my father down in Souvigny. Vicenç's friend proposed to pay our way to Calgary to work for him. My father mentioned this proposal to Gloria's father, and he immediately said that he would be happy to form a team with my father. After a lot of back and forth, because my father was unsure about a move to a country about which he knew practically nothing other than that it was very cold, Vicenç's partner, by the name of Josep Morros, came to Souvigny to convince my father. This clinched it. We were ready once again to become immigrants to yet another country.

My life changed dramatically at the moment mom and dad, and Gloria's parents decided to accept the offer. My father, who had made me swear that I would never work in a glass factory, determined that it would probably be wise if I learned enough about this trade to help in case of need once the glass studio got going in Calgary. So, despite my desire to continue to work at Chez Raoul, I bid good-bye to those people I had gotten to consider as friends and mentors and started working at the glass factory.

When I started my new job, I was amazed by the size of the furnace within which there were at least twelve separate refractory pots, often referred also as crucibles. Seen from above, the set-up would have looked like a huge bicycle wheel with a large axle and twelve spokes that radiated out from the center. There was a platform about two feet above the main floor surrounding the furnace in a concentric circle and twelve corridors emanating from it. Each spoke accommodated a number of employees, anywhere from three or four to as many as ten, who worked on different types of glassware from small cherry glasses to huge lamp shades and coverings for boat lights. Everything created in this factory was for commercial purposes. There was nothing created there that could be considered studio-created ornamental pieces.

My father and his team, for instance, made delicate wine glasses with long stems. The team consisted of one individual who gathered molten glass with a blow pipe, a hollow metal pipe with a mouthpiece on one end and a built-up area on the other end where the molten glass sits. He shaped it on a marver (in the past marvers were made from marble slabs, which is where the name marver comes from), blew some air into it and passed it onto the lead glassblower, also known as the gaffer, who then shaped it some more so it would fit snugly into a mold, blew air into it while turning constantly the pipe, producing a stemless goblet (in other cases, there were specialist gaffers who produced a goblet with its own stem extending out). The glassblower then passed it onto the person who would add the stem to it. When the stem was attached to the goblet it was passed onto the next person, who would add the base or foot, as it was called. Both the stem maker and the base maker needed an apprentice that would gather the necessary amount of glass, shape it slightly and allow those two people to cut as much as was necessary to accomplish their task. I became the apprentice who helped my father finish the base.

There were still a couple more steps before the wine glass could be carried to an annealer, also known as a lehr. First it had to be detached from the blow pipe and then the goblet part had to be cut to the right size. It was then carried to an annealer, an oven used for annealing, which is the process of slowly cooling and hardening glass after it has been worked on by an artist. Glass will crack if it cools too quickly.

I have to say that although I found the work fascinating, I also suffered a great deal. Imagine the heat emanating from the pot where the temperature of the molten glass had to be kept at around 1300 degrees Fahrenheit. The emptier the pot got the closer we had to be to have access to the molten glass toward the bottom of the pot. My left hand, which is the one a right-handed person places forward, ended up with burns that were painful. Blisters eventually disappeared but the front part of the hand, in my case, was always filled with scabs.

There was one very enjoyable part of my job, however. Gloria had also ended up working in the factory after she finished her schooling. And, as luck would have it, she was the one who operated the machine that cut the goblets to the right size. By that time, we were already seventeen. We had fallen in love shortly after she and her mother arrived in Souvigny two months before she turned sixteen. Even though both sets of parents thought we were too young and were not too excited about our courtship Gloria and I were too much in love to heed their rational objections. The guardrails they created for us, particularly Gloria's father, prohibited any physical proximity and I was allowed to go to their place three days a week and for just a couple of hours. This limiting structure followed us well into Canada. Of course, we were creative and found ways of stealing some kisses. But, even then, Gloria was far too afraid of her parents to grant me many advances. She took to heart her mother's governing belief that, as she said, "if you give a finger to a man, he'll take the whole hand; if you give a hand, he'll take the whole arm". She did not need to clarify what else could happen. Although not totally platonic, our long courtship was relatively chaste. We both had to wait until we married at age twenty-two to consummate our relationship. Times have surely changed.

CHAPTER III
Canada, 1958–1970

▲▲▲

Julio, Gloria and I on the Ship Arkadia on
our way to Canada, June 1958

THE MOVE FROM SOUVIGNY TO Calgary was not without its own hair-raising moments. Our first stop was in Paris, where we spent one or two nights. From there we made our way to Le Havre, to board a ship named Arkadia that was to take us to Québec City and then down the St. Lawrence River to Montréal. When we were ready to board, we were asked for some documents from our local *Préfet*, or local magistrate, granting us permission to leave the country. No one had ever mentioned that such a document was needed so we did not have it. Without it, we were told, we could not leave France. We were in a panic. We could not possibly go back. We could not forfeit the tickets that had been bought and paid by our host in Calgary. In our desperation, someone came with the suggestion that we call the manager of the factory in Souvigny. I was not too sure that he would be able or willing to do anything to help us. After all, he was left with a huge predicament. He was going to be forced to replace two of his top glassblowers. To our amazement and luck, not only was I able to contact him by phone but he managed to get the *Préfet* to talk directly to the port authorities. At the last minute, we were permitted to board and undertake our life-changing journey.

The trip was eventful in more than one respect. As the days went by and the sea got increasing rougher, most people got sick and stayed in their respective cabins. My father and Cisco, however, could not pass up the opportunity to eat well and copiously. Often, they were the only people in the dining room. Something important also took place during the crossing: I turned eighteen. The boat trip took almost a week to get to Québec City. There we were able to disembark and walk through the streets of the old quarter of the city. There was no denying it. We were in a different country. And even though we spoke French quite well by then, we had a hard time understanding the French spoken by the Québécois. The trip down the St. Lawrence River was quite beautiful and peaceful. When we arrived in Montréal, we unloaded the few suitcases, a mattress, and my mother's Singer sewing machine and made our way to the train station. It was another three days before we reached Calgary. We really enjoyed crossing most of Canada. The views were magnificent. We were astonished by the immensity of the prairies.

Calgary, 1958–1960

When we arrived in Calgary, Mr. Morros, our host and employer, came to pick us up. My mother and Gloria's mother went with him. The rest of us were driven to our new apartments by my father's former apprentice, Vicenç. When we got to our new lodgings, my mother predicted lean and difficult times ahead for us. Two things caught her attention. First, the heels of Morros' shoes were totally used to the sole. He clearly needed new shoes and perhaps he could not afford them. This perception was further enhanced when the truck stopped and both women had to get out and push it to get it going again. Certainly not the welcome they had expected.

The apartments Morros had rented for us were nice, immensely nicer than what we had left behind. We finally had a fridge and, more importantly and impressively, a shower and a bath indoors. There was plenty of space. Unfortunately, however, there was hardly any furniture. We had two metal beds. My father had had the foresight to bring a mattress and a few blankets from France. My parents slept in the bed with the mattress. Julio and I slept on the metal box spring. Although we placed the blankets under us, the following morning we had a few curious marks on our back and buttocks. Despite these inconveniences, we were happy to have arrived and were looking forward to a different lifestyle and future. It did not take a genius to discern that our fortunes were changing dramatically.

It took very little for our overt optimism to be tamped down. When my father, Cisco and I went to the studio, we knew then that our immediate future and lifestyle was going to be quite different from what we had hoped for and anticipated. The furnace was built with regular bricks, not refractory bricks. The pot inside was resting on regular bricks as well. The furnace was going to be heated with natural gas, which was efficient, but the air to force the gas into the furnace to reach the required 2000-degree Fahrenheit temperature was a home vacuum cleaner. We knew that this home-made set up was not going to work at all. To top it all, a batch of glass is prepared from the reagent-grade chemicals such as floated silica sand, sodium carbonate, calcium and other chemicals. None of these were to be found anywhere in the studio. We were bewildered. How were we going to create molten glass? We were told that we would melt down mostly discarded and broken milk bottles. So, each day, Morros and I became scavengers looking for enough broken and discarded milk bottles to produce a batch. It did not take long for me to cut myself on both hands. My hands began to really hurt, and it was soon obvious that I had a serious infection. Morros thought that I was exaggerating and a bit of a namby-pamby. One night, however, the pain became unbearable. We called Morros to see if he could take me to the hospital. He grumbled but drove me to the hospital, nonetheless. As soon as we got there, doctors determined that I was seriously hurt and was beginning to develop gangrene. They inserted tubes into different locations in four of my fingers and started the process of draining whatever was accumulating in both my hands. To this day, I can still see the scars left as a reminder of this unfortunate experience.

The glass that was produced by recycling milk bottles was almost impossible to work with. My father and Cisco did what they could with what was available, but the quality of the glass was so poor that even their greatest attempts to mask it by speckling the clear glass with a variety of different colors failed miserably. We carried on, nonetheless, and produced a number of vases, fish, paperweights, and other ornamental pieces.

My father and Cisco predicted that the business was in danger of going under. The regular bricks were beginning to melt. First, the bricks holding the pot allowing the fire to heat the bottom and the pot itself, collapsed and the pot dropped onto the floor of the furnace. Before long the whole furnace collapsed as well. Morros did not have the resources to rebuild the furnace properly, this time. Morros was very unhappy and blamed us for not having done enough with what he had created. He even told us that we would now learn what it is like to be in Calgary without a sponsor. He predicted that we would rue the day we had not tried harder to make a go of the business he had created for us. Of course, there was very little we could have done differently. It was not our fault that he had no idea as to what was necessary to have a viable glass studio. We did not part in the friendliest of terms, as could be expected. In any event, a few weeks after our arrival, we found ourselves unemployed and with very few resources to survive.

The two families were forced to move from the apartments that Morros had rented for us. Gloria and her parents moved to a modest but affordable apartment not far from where we ended up living for the next two years. Our new residence was the upstairs suite where my dad's former apprentice lived with his wife, son and daughter. It was an older house. It was never meant to accommodate two separate families. Once past the front door, there was a staircase that led upstairs. No door separated the two residences. Upstairs there was a long, open hallway from which we accessed a small and rudimentary kitchen, two small bedrooms, and one bathroom. From one of the bedrooms, we could step onto a tiny terrace from which we could see, diagonally across, the grand entrance to the Calgary Stampede Grounds. Although we had no money to spend on rides or any of the shows that attracted thousands of people every summer from all over the world, Julio, Gloria and I were truly excited about the opportunity to just wander through the grounds, which at that time was free, and take in the contagious western atmosphere that pervaded the immense expanse that was the grounds.

Our first Stampede, Calgary 1958

There was also the Calgary Stampede Parade. It was a spectacular show, and it was free. We had never seen anything like it. It was as if we were watching a Hollywood movie set. We were treated to hundreds of cowboys and cowgirls riding beautiful horses, horse-drawn wagons of all sorts, west stagecoaches, military marching bands, and, most impressive of all for us, as Europeans, lots of indigenous people in all their colorful regalia and native dresses, followed always by the Royal Canadian Mounted Police. Although we were to watch other Stampede Parades, this first one was without a doubt the most memorable.

Angela and Vicenç were incredibly generous people and treated us as if we were family. Julio and I felt as if we had been adopted. In fact, the very first Christmas we spent sharing the house with them was very special. I don't recall what present I got but my brother got one that he valued for many years not for what it was but for what it represented. Not only did it show him how much he was loved by this wonderful couple, but it was also something that typified Canada: a pair of ice skates.

Vicenç and Angela were also great hosts. Every Friday night, they welcomed a large group, mostly men, to watch boxing. It was thanks to some of these men that we were ultimately able to find jobs. My mother, Vicenta, and Gloria were the first to find employment. Gloria got hired at Holy Cross Hospital, working in the kitchen. She loved it because almost all the workers were young women more or less her age who came from all over Europe. They got along exceptionally well. This made the transition from France to Canada a bit easier for her. My mom and Vicenta found employment at a factory that made windows.

My father, Cisco, and I were less lucky when it came to seeking and finding employment. Some of the Spaniards told us that there was so much construction going on in Calgary that all we needed to do was to go to a construction site and ask for work. They wrote phonetically for us to say: "we are looking for a job." So, each morning, instead of each one of us venturing out individually, which might have been a bit more effective, the three of us went seeking employment. It was a pathetic situation. I was designated as the one to speak because, supposedly, I pronounced better. The question was easy. Understanding the answer was far more difficult.

If the foreman said no, it was very easy to understand. If the answer was longer and did not contain the word no, we had no idea what the man had said. So, we waited. After a while, we realized that there was nothing for us there. We moved on to the next construction site. Now, these were major projects. There was little that any of us could have contributed. But we were naïve. We continued our search the next day with the same depressing result.

We had become so depressed that after several futile attempts we realized that we needed something to give us a boost of happiness. We learned that for thirty cents per person, we could go to the early afternoon movie sessions that offered a double feature, almost always of western movies. I think that over a period of time, we must have seen every conceivable western ever filmed. Of course, we did not understand any of what was said, but it wasn't too difficult to follow the rather simplistic plots. It was also at this same time that, because I had so much free time, I began to read every book I could lay my hands on, mostly books I bought cheaply at the Salvation Army stores. I did not understand much of what I read. Sometimes, I understood each word in a sentence but did not get its meaning. It was disheartening and dispiriting, but also exhilarating to discover that, slowly but surely, I was making progress. I did not read for content. I just wanted to learn English. Thus, any book would do. In fact, I did not select the books, the books selected me as they were the only ones that were available.

As had been the case with Gloria, Vicenta, and my mother, once again, it was a fellow Spaniard who helped us find a job. It turned out that there was a French-Canadian woman, who had enjoyed some success as an entertainer, who invested her money in acquiring properties that she rented out. She needed some handymen to clean, repair, and ready the houses whose renters had vacated before she could rent them again. Since she spoke much better French than English, I was, once again, assigned the task of translator. We worked for her for a few weeks. We did a lot of cleaning, some of it rather disgusting, and lots of small repairs, mostly painting, laying linoleum flooring, and carpeting.

Marie, that was her name, had a lover, a Lithuanian. He owned a painting business. He had just got a contract to paint a two-floor motel. He needed more painters. He convinced Marie to release us from our duties so we could go work for him. We joined his crew, made up of a German, a Russian, a Croatian, and a Serbian. It was a motley crew to say the least. The German was the one who seemed to be the best English speaker. The three of us were happy that we had finally found a steady job. We worked on this project, and we were happy. However, at the end of one of the weeks, we did not get paid. It turned out that our Lithuanian had gone broke. The project was never completed. We found ourselves unemployed again. Fortunately for us, the German invited us to follow him to what I realize now must have been something like the Better Business Bureau and place a collective claim against our failed employer. As Spaniards, the three of us had no faith in anything to do with the government. But lo and behold, somehow, we were paid and started to receive unemployment benefits as well. Not only were we pleasantly surprised, but quite impressed with the generosity of the Canadian government.

Needless to say, we were not happy to be idle. We knew that unemployment benefits for us would not last long. We had to find a job. Our efforts, however, came to naught. When we were at our most depressed stage, there was a knock on our door. One of the painters, Nick, the Serbian, informed me that he and his Croatian friend had formed a painting company. They had acquired contracts to paint a number of houses and they needed some help. He asked me to join them. I told him that my father would be most upset and insulted if I got the job rather than him. Nick told me that he needed someone young to whom he could teach the trade. He did not think that my father or Cisco would be as adaptable and willing to take orders from him, a much younger man. I discussed the situation with my father who reacted as I had predicted but informed him that it was better for one of us to bring a salary home than to fall prey to pride. So, I went to work for Nick and Walter.

A few weeks later, Nick and Walter realized that they needed more help. They asked my father and Cisco to join them. Everything was going rather smoothly. It did not last long, however. One day, Cisco and my father mixed together several cans of partly full paint cans of the same color. We then painted the outside of the house. The following day, when Nick came by to check on us, he realized that the walls had blisters and peeling areas. He was puzzled until he realized that we had mixed latex and oil paint all together. We had to scrape the walls, sand them, and repaint them. Nick was not happy. He told me that henceforth I was to be responsible for my father's and Cisco's work. I told him that I could not possibly tell my father what to do. He replied that it was either this or he would have to fire them. When I conveyed this conversation to my father, he was furious. In the end, it was either accept this new reality or end up without a job. So, in a way, I became their foreman. At last, we entered what appeared to be a period of tranquility. Everything was going relatively well. We all had jobs and were able to lead a normal existence.

Something happened in our first winter, however, that could have been incredibly tragic. To heat our upstairs part of the house, we had an old gas heater. One night, I heard a tremendous noise. I got up and saw dad on the floor. I called my mother only to realize that she was groggy as well. It did not take me long to realize that I was not too stable on my feet either. I called out to our friends, downstairs. They came up and saw us all in bad shape. The gas furnace had malfunctioned. Had my father not fallen down and awakened me, all four of us might have died. I will never forget the fear I experienced on that day. We were all badly shaken up.

After this event, life went on rather normally. My brother was doing well in school. He and I became good friends. By now he was fourteen and we could share a lot more with each other. We also did not have many other friends. So, we got to be a lot closer. For the first time in our life, we did a lot together. This close relationship became stronger and has lasted to this day. My brother and I love each other as brothers, of course, but are also the best of friends. Each one of us has always been there for the other when the need has existed. In fact, there is absolutely no doubt that he has been, is, and will always be my best friend.

There was one activity that my brother truly disliked: that of chaperone. Gloria and I could be together only in the presence of her parents or accompanied by my brother. The assumption of Gloria's parents was that we would not attempt to do anything improper in his presence. Of course, we did not. Nonetheless, Julio disliked this role and tried to avoid it as often as possible. The only time Gloria and I managed to spend time alone was when I went each working day to walk her home from Holy Cross Hospital. Her father knew exactly how long it would take to cover the distance. He would either be at the window looking for her to arrive or sometimes he seemed to find it necessary, just by accident, to be outside at the time we arrived. Gloria followed to the letter her mother's advice not to grant too much access to men. I did have access to "her finger and hand" but she put the brakes on to her "arm" and beyond. We both felt somewhat frustrated, but Gloria was pleased to know that her mother would have been proud of her.

There were four or five single Spaniards who always teased me about my relationship with Gloria. They could not believe that she resisted my advances so much. They felt sorry for me. At one point, they confided that every Sunday they "invited" a number of young ladies to visit their apartment to satisfy their physical needs. They encouraged me to join them, if I felt the need. I was horrified. I could not imagine indulging in such a personal and private activity in the presence of others. They had a hard time understanding my reticence.

As we were finishing our second year in Calgary, something happened, once again, to change the course of our life. One of our fellow Spaniards noticed, while at the unemployment office, a job posting for one glassblower at Altaglass, in Medicine Hat, a town about three hours by car from Calgary. Since we did not own a car, he volunteered to drive my dad to visit the glass studio and determine whether he would be interested in the job. My father and Cisco decided that they should both go and offer to work as a team. There were a lot of creations they could do together but not individually. The original idea of the owners of the studio was for one person to replace the helper who had recently left. However, when my father and Cisco demonstrated what they were capable of creating, they were both hired on the spot.

This created a bit of a dilemma for Gloria and me. I was more than willing to move to Medicine Hat with my parents and brother. Gloria had other ideas. By now, we had been in our courtship for three years. Gloria proposed that since both of us had decent paying jobs we should get married and stay in Calgary. I could not even imagine marrying at twenty. Gloria was mature enough and ready to put an end to what she viewed as a never-ending courtship. I was anything but ready for such a momentous and life-changing decision. Despite my reluctance, I had a conversation with Nick to let him know that I would probably leave with my family. He told me how happy he was with the manner and responsibility in which I performed my assigned duties and offered me a substantial increase in salary to two dollars and ten cents per hour. This was a very respectable salary and one which, when added to what Gloria was paid, would have allowed us to lead a comfortable life. Even though Gloria was very attached to her parents, she was ready to live apart from them and to settle into married life. Her arguments made a great deal of sense. They were rational. But I was in no mood or ready to assume the responsibilities of marriage. Frankly, I guess I was afraid though I would never have admitted this reality to myself or to Gloria. In the end, and to Gloria's great chagrin, both families moved to Medicine Hat. One of the virtues of being poor and having little to our name was that moving was relatively easy. We had practically nothing to move.

Medicine Hat, 1960–1965

Gloria found employment rather quickly in the local hospital in the sterilization department. She also made a friend for life, Erica, an immigrant like her, but from Germany. In time, she and her boyfriend, Bert, also a German immigrant, became very close to us. We have been friends for over sixty years.

Unlike Gloria I did not have as easy a time getting a job. Medicine Hat is called the Gas City because it has a lot of natural gas. This cheap and available natural resource permitted a number of factories, from fertilizer to tire and brick making, to establish their businesses there. I thought I would be able to find employment in one of them. I did not. The owner of the glass studio still did not have a helper because my father and Cisco were a team. When he found out that I could be his apprentice, he hired me.

I went from leaving a job that would have paid me two dollars and ten cents per hour to earning one dollar and a quarter. Gloria quickly understood that such a salary was insufficient for us to consider living independently of our parents. Though quite distressed, she accepted, for the moment, to continue with our routine courtship.

Altaglass, 1960

Despite what I considered a miserly salary, I enjoyed working with Cisco and my father. I did not work directly with them. My responsibility, at least at first, was to aid the owner of the studio. I also found comfort with life at home. We lived in a nice apartment in a peaceful neighborhood. Julio did not like the public school to which he was assigned, even though it was practically across the street from where we lived. Without consulting with any of us, he went to the nearest Catholic school and enrolled himself there. While we had not been brought up in a religious home, he felt much happier in the environment provided there. By this time, he was sixteen and I was twenty. We got along incredibly well together. Each provided the other much-needed support to adapt to an entirely new environment.

My father was elated to be doing what he loved, particularly since the work at Altaglass rewarded creativity and initiative. My mother was relieved to find a job in the local hospital in the laundry department. We clearly needed more than one source of income to make ends meet. Dad made about $75 per week. I don't remember how much mom made, but I doubt it was more than I did, which was $35 per week. For my full participation I got a pitiful weekly allowance. Though not satisfied with the situation I did not complain. The three salaries together did not permit us to do much more than lead a simple and frugal existence but given my parents penny-pinching tendencies, we felt that, for the first time ever, we could live without financial worries.

Our collective lives flowed smoothly. Gloria and I continued to spend as much time together as we were allowed. By the time we moved to Medicine Hat Gloria's parents were not able to go everywhere with us. Vicenta had recently had a stroke and was somewhat paralyzed. She recovered over time but was limited in movement. This gave Gloria and me greater independence, but I was still expected over at their house three times per week. I still remember our Sundays together. At that time, television was limited to one channel. So, after dinner, Gloria and I sat together at the sofa separated by a safe distance, and we watched the Ed Sullivan show followed immediately by Bonanza. Immediately after Bonanza, it was clear that my time there had come to an end. Fortunately, they allowed us to go out alone as long as it was in the presence of my brother or with friends. We were clever enough to adapt to changing circumstances.

I have always enjoyed physical activities. Over the years I have played tennis, racket ball, squash, and pickleball. For over twenty years I ran about seven miles a day. In those years in Medicine Hat, I had not yet dedicated myself to any particular activity. My brother participated in some sports at school. One of them was the high jump. I trained with him. We had a small garden in the back of our apartment which I quickly proposed as a place for us to train. We got two poles, ran another pole horizontally from one to the other and voilà, we were almost ready. Since we did not always land well, we needed something to cushion a fall. So, we dug up a good portion of the grass and turned it into soft dirt. Mom and dad were not particularly happy, but the damage was done.

Since I was overflowing with energy, I also joined the local soccer team. It was made up of men often referred to by Canadians as DPs, or displaced people. There were two Dutch brothers, one Italian, a Slav, and the rest of the team members were all Germans, with the exception of yours truly. We were not exceptional players but managed a few wins. Besides, the team travelled to various towns in our region, and we always managed to have fun. One of the German players, Bert, became Erica's boyfriend. By the way, the two Dutch soccer players were the two most important musicians in the band at the German club where Bert, Erica, Gloria and I went to dance almost weekly.

Another physical activity was swimming at the local pool which happened to be just a couple of blocks from where we lived. The lifeguard at the pool was our next-door neighbor. He was in between Julio and me in age. He was called to play a pivotal role in my future as I will recount further on.

My role at Altaglass changed considerably over time. At first, I just helped the owner with his work, making beautiful swans, candle holders, and some ashtrays. But, since he was also the person who built the furnaces, the lehr, many of the molds, and some of the tools, I was left to occupy myself with menial tasks. Instead, I chose to start making some pieces of my own creation. I could never have competed with my father, Cisco or the owner. They were good at what they did. There was no point in duplicating their work. Instead, I became very good at working with solid glass. I started to make ducks, penguins, paperweights, and unusual ashtrays for cigarettes and for pipes. I also made some ornamental pieces that imitated some of the work that has made Murano glass famous.

I can actually say that glassblowing has been one of the jobs I have loved the most. To this day I still dream about it. But at that time, I could not see myself making enough of a good living nor did I think that this job could fulfill my intellectual needs. To try something totally new I enrolled in the local Business School. I took night classes in book-keeping. I did very well and was quite excited about the options that this might open for me. Full of confidence, I applied for a position at the local branch of the Bank of Montreal. When its director found out that I was fluent in French he told me that, if I got the job, I would probably be sent to Northern Alberta where there were quite a few French-Canadian communities. I discussed it with Gloria and asked her if she would come with me. Of course, she said yes, as long as it was as a married couple. I was given an exam at the bank that required me to reply to some questions to check my ability in English; there were also some mathematics problems, as well as a couple of other questions. There was nothing about bookkeeping. I remember feeling quite inadequate and unprepared. I had no idea how I had done. The response came back quickly. The manager called me and told me that I would not get the position. I did not possess the requisite level of education. Someone important had just said that I was an uneducated person. I was devastated and humiliated as well. My hopes had been painfully dashed. I came to the conclusion that there was a certain restlessness within me that needed an outlet that could only be met by some intellectual activity. To a large extent, this turned out to be a moment of significant importance. I knew that I had to do something. I just did not know exactly what that something was going to be.

It was around this time that the lifeguard, our neighbor, asked me to consider going to college. I had to confess to him that I had the equivalent of about grade seven or eight. He was surprised, he said, because he always thought that I was rather smart. He then informed me that the government of the province of Alberta, where grade twelve exams were the same throughout the province and were taken also at the same time, had passed a provision that allowed people over twenty-one who had not been able to complete high school for whatever reason, to stagger the exams over a period of time. He suggested that I think about what this could mean for my aspirations. I thought about taking advantage of this opportunity and discussed it with my brother. He reasoned that this was perhaps too big a mountain to climb for someone who had the equivalent of a grade seven or eight education, none of it anchored in what was expected of a Canadian student. It was difficult to argue against the reality proffered by Julio. So, I decided to heed Julio's advice.

By this time, I had turned twenty-one. Gloria gave me an ultimatum. If I was really in love with her and I had any intention of marrying her, the time to decide was now. Otherwise, she said, the best course of action for her, if not for us, was to split up and go in our own different paths. I was in love with her and had always thought about marrying her ever since we started to go out together. For some irrational reason, perhaps, I had decided that I was still too young. We both agreed to marry the following year. Gloria wanted to be a June bride, an important month for weddings at that time. I agreed as long as it was after the twentieth, which was my birthday. This way I would be twenty-two. Unfortunately, as we would find out, there were no openings at the church before the beginning of July. Gloria was greatly disappointed.

We now found ourselves in a quandary. Neither of us had any money. How could we prepare for the expenditures normally associated with becoming independent, renting an apartment, and furnishing it? Both of us agreed on a strategy. We would inform our parents of our upcoming wedding and ask that they allow us to keep one of the two payments we received each month. To my surprise, my father accepted my proposal. So, for one year, Gloria and I saved every penny. We were determined to have a good start and not to depend on our parents for any financial help. Once I accepted the reality that I was going to be a married man, I assumed my responsibilities with pleasure and discipline.

Our wedding was a small and low-cost event. There were no more than thirty people, including all our family. By this time, my parents had sponsored the legal immigration of my mother's middle sister, her husband, and their two children. They were all at the wedding party, of course. My cousin, Montserrat, was the flower girl. Beyond the family we had Vicenç and Angela, of course, two Basque friends who came from Lethbridge, one of whom was Gloria's maid of honor, our Medicine Hat friends, Bert and Erica, the owners of the glass studio, and a few others. Julio was my best man.

The wedding day itself, 7 July 1962, which happened to be my mother's birthday, was very hectic for Gloria and me. We could not count much on our parents for anything other than physical preparations. Their English was not sufficiently fluent to do anything too elaborate. On the morning of the wedding day, my father cut my hair as he had done since I was a kid. He saw no reason to spend money on barbers when he could do it himself. I did not look my best with a fresh haircut that was anything but professional. We did not have a car. We borrowed the one our friend Bert had, a beautiful Mercury Monarch, and Julio and I, with the help of Bert and a couple of other people, adorned it with paper flowers as was customary at the time. When this was accomplished, Julio and I went to the flower shop to pick the flowers Gloria and I had selected and took them to the church to decorate the altar. Back home, we all got dressed quickly and drove to the church. I remember only two things about the ceremony. The first one was Gloria's appearance. She was beautiful and glowing with happiness. The second was how monotonous and downright boring the priest who performed the ceremony was. He almost put everyone to sleep.

I do not think I actually noticed this when we came out of the church but upon seeing the photographs outside the church, I was shocked how provincial most of our relatives looked. For some reason they had all chosen to look elegant by wearing hats.

Neither men nor women looked comfortable under them. It seemed as though someone had just dropped them haphazardly on their heads. I think that Gloria and I looked quite handsome and happy, though.

Manuel Esteban and Gloria Ribas Wedding Day
With our Parents, July 7, 1962

PROOF
JUL 7 1962

We had rented a locale to hold the luncheon but the festivities that followed, in order to save money, took place at my parents' apartment. We had lots of fun, nonetheless.

I had promised Gloria that we would have a honeymoon that she would remember forever. I delivered on my promise, but what made it so memorable was not in the least what I had planned and hoped for. We wanted to go south to the USA, to Coeur d'Alene, Idaho close to Medicine Hat but for us who had never gone anywhere by ourselves it represented a great adventure. And an adventure it became. Of course, we needed a car. Since neither of us had a car, we had to ask our parents to let us borrow one of theirs. My father found an excuse to say that I could not have his, even though when he bought the car, he promised me that I would have access to it. Gloria's parents were more magnanimous. We took theirs. I should perhaps mention that both our parents bought the same model car. They were modestly priced and cute. They were, however, unusual. The DKW Junior was a small front wheel drive, two-stroke, three-cylinder car that sounded more like a sewing machine than a real car and could reach the maximum permitted speed limit on the road only going downhill. None-theless, this was the only car we could get, so off we went.

In order for us not to get lost, I had gone to CAA, the Canadian version of AAA, to get a map that would take us to Coeur d'Alene without incident. The agent there was very helpful and accommodating. I left the office with a beautiful map with the routes well highlighted. I had also made reservations at a nice motel in Lethbridge where we would spend our very first night together.

Before we left our family, friends and guests, we changed into some-thing more comfortable than Gloria's wedding dress and my spanking new suit. Gloria still looked beautiful and appealing in a very nice navy-blue dress. We said goodbye to all, got into the almost toy car and off we went. When we got to the motel, in Lethbridge, we awkwardly prepared our-selves for bed. Someone had given Gloria as a present the nightgown for her first night of marriage. Even though I had other thoughts in mind about the sartorial nature of her gown, I did notice that it was a rather garish yellow that was so transparent that it left absolutely nothing to the imagination. I did not find it sexy. I would have wanted to be able to ex-plore on my own rather than have an unimpeded view. I will not get into a lot of details but let us say that our first night was close to a total disaster. We were both unprepared and inexperienced. For reasons that we found out the following night, we were unable to consummate our marriage. Though clearly disappointed and somewhat embarrassed, we went to bed and told ourselves that it was nothing but nerves.

The trip from Lethbridge to Coeur d'Alene was a trip to hell. The agent at CAA was nice but knew nothing about roads. The directions we were given took us through the mountains on roads that were not paved. I still don't know how we managed to make it. It was a harrowing experi-ence. We were afraid that the car would fall apart from all the bouncing up and down over all kinds of trenches. Eventually, however, we did make it to a normal road that took us to our destination, although a bit later than anticipated.

We wanted to have a fancy dinner before retiring. The city then was rather small. Its culinary offerings were quite limited. We did eat somewhere but the restaurant did not serve liquor of any kind. We were not used to drinking but we thought we would celebrate with some wine our new freedom to be out alone. When we left the restaurant, we searched for a bar where we could at least have a beer. We had never been in an American bar and did not know what to expect. When we entered the bar, we were shocked at how poorly illuminated the interior was. It looked as though people there were in the dark because they did not want anyone to recognize them. The patrons looked at us as if we were aliens from another planet. We quickly left the premises and went to the hotel. So far, we were not too pleased with the manner in which our honeymoon was developing. Things were still going to get worse, much worse.

When we went to bed, this time determined to successfully and fully consummate our marriage, the difficulties from the previous night reappeared again. Gloria was inaccessible, to put it nicely. The more we tried the more pain she experienced. When the deed was more or less accomplished, Gloria began to bleed profusely. We were both in a state of panic. What in the world was happening? In the middle of the night, I had to take her to the nearest hospital. When the doctor checked her he had a smile on his face. He patiently and delicately explained to us something we should probably have known. Gloria's hymen was determined to put up a great fight. The doctor said that in a couple of days making love should not be such a difficult combat. I could not even imagine what would have happened if Gloria had not been so protective of her virginity before our marriage. How would we have explained her profuse bleeding. I sweated just thinking about having to call her parents from the hospital. Chastity was never better rewarded than on this occasion.

This was not to be our last travail. A few were rather comical. The first funny one is recorded in a photograph. The hotel where we stayed had a pool. I wanted to show Gloria what an excellent swimmer and athlete I was. I went up to the highest plank and dove from there. The photo of me in mid-air clearly indicates that I was to have an embarrassing and painful belly flop that left part of my chest and stomach as red as a tomato. The following day, I dove with such force and bad angle that I ended up scraping my palms and knuckles bloody. The more serious incident resulted from our wanting to prove to ourselves that we were now adults and could do adult things. We went to buy beer and had a picnic by the side of the lake. It was a nice setting. Since the cans of beer were not cold, we placed them by the shore, in the water. As we waited for the beer to get cold, a speed boat went by creating big waves, which arrived at the shore with such force that they dragged our beer far into the lake. There appeared to be a conspiracy against our happiness. To forget about all our recent troubles, we took a hydroplane ride over the city and the lake. It offered us a great view and to our relief, the plane did not crash. It landed nicely and safely on the calm waters.

After a few uneventful, but peaceful and enjoyable days, we started our trip back to Medicine Hat. We were going to spend some time on the other side of the U.S. border, in Waterton, Alberta, a quaint area known particularly for its lakes and national park. We had not made any reservation but did not expect to have any difficulty finding adequate lodging. Lodging we did find but not what we had hoped for. We reached the Canadian border at dusk. As much as we had enjoyed seeing part of another country, we were very happy to be on Canadian soil again. Not too far from the border I lost control of the car. We found out later that a tire had exploded. The car ended up on the side of the road, on its roof and it kept on rotating while we were inside. Both of us recounted to each other that we were able to view what was happening as the car was flipping over as if we were in a movie.

Despite not having seat belts we were not seriously injured, a miraculous situation given how it had happened. Gloria had been covering her legs with my jacket. The jacket ended up under the roof of the car. One of her sandals had been ripped off her foot. She did have a nasty cut on her upper arm, but nothing else. What were we going to do now with the car inoperative and in the ditch? To top it all, we did not have any flashlights. It was already very dark. This was before cell phones, so there was no way to communicate with anyone or call for help. I asked Gloria to wait by the car while I ran back to the border.

I had lost the notion of time and was under the impression that we had just recently crossed the border. I decided to run for help. Because the car had spun around while on its roof, and probably because I was in shock and disoriented, I started to run in the wrong direction. Fortunately, after a while, a car facing me must have noticed my distress and stopped to ask where I was going. I explained what had happened. They informed me that I was going in the direction of Waterton, not the border. They took me back to the car, where Gloria was waiting full of fear. Then they took us to town and to the Mounted Police office. A young officer took us back to the car so we could retrieve our suitcase. When we got back to the police station, we were told that there was a convention in town and all accommodations were full. We would have no choice but to sleep in a cell. The world came down on us. We both felt like crying. How could something like this happen to such a young couple filled with joy and the exhilarating feeling of freedom. Was this what freedom would mean for us? The young officer took pity on us. He called his wife, explained what had taken place and the predicament in which we found ourselves. She told him to bring us home with him.

I suppose it was part of the shock, but I was unable to sleep. Instead, I spent the whole night vomiting. I was also quite worried about how I was going to break the news to Cisco. His car was basically a total wreck. The following morning, the young couple treated us with kid gloves, prepared for us a scrumptious breakfast and convinced us that all would be okay soon. This sad episode would be in the rearview mirror, and we would be able to start our married life on solid footing. More than anything, they gave us a deep sense of what type of people Canadians were: generous, compassionate, and spiritual. I don't know what we would have done if we had had to spend the night in a cell. Our honeymoon had already provided us with enough negative incidents to last us for a long time.

We had to call home and talk to our parents. They were shocked, of course, but were relieved to learn that though a bit roughed up, we were safe and sound. We left the car behind to be taken to Medicine Hat. It would either be fixed, if possible, or considered a heap of bent metal. Gloria's father was extremely nice to me. No reproaches of any type, for which I was eternally grateful. I know my father would have been far less tolerant. When we were told later that the car could be repaired, Cisco asked that the car be painted red. He had always wanted a red car. He told me:

"you see, something good emerged from your terrible experience." What a nice father-in-law.

Back in Medicine Hat we settled into our rented apartment. It was a block away from the hospital where Gloria worked. She could get there on foot. I would be picked up by my father and taken to work. We furnished our basement apartment with taste but with few and inexpensive pieces of furniture. As close as both of us had been to our families, we immediately functioned as an independent unit. We did not rely on our parents for much and they were cognizant of our desire for freedom and left us to our own designs. As reluctant as I had been about getting married too young, I immediately assumed my responsibilities. Our weekly pay was insufficient. So, I went to the daughter of the owner of Altaglass, who ran the business side of the studio, and asked for an increase in salary. I argued that in the two years I had been working there I had demonstrated amply that I was worth far more than the measly salary they paid me. I demanded one dollar fifty per hour. She granted me the request. I wondered whether I should have been more aggressive in my demand.

As I have mentioned, we did not have a car. Sooner or later, we were going to need one. Our savings, however, were too meager to hope for much more than adequate transportation. Across from the Altaglass studio there was a car dealer. Each noon, on our break, I would go look at second-hand cars. I fell in love with one of the largest cars there. It had everything! Buttons everywhere, automated everything, and a powerful engine. Without consulting with Gloria, I put down a small down-payment and bought it. I took it home and proudly called Gloria to show it to her. She liked it, of course. What was there not to like? It was beautiful. That was her first reaction. But Gloria was not going to be a typical, subservient Spanish wife. She was full of recriminations. How could I have possibly taken such an outrageous step without at the very least consulting with her? I was crestfallen. It had never crossed my mind that I did not have the absolute power to make such decisions without consulting her or anyone else. After all, I was the man of the house.

We made peace and that weekend drove to Elkwater Lake, about thirty miles away, to have a picnic. The drive there revealed two realities. First,

I was not that great a driver and the big car wandered a bit all over the road. Second, when we returned and had to gas up, I calculated that the car averaged fifteen miles per gallon. What an incredible drain on our meager resources. We agreed to downgrade. On Monday we went to the same dealer and convinced the salesperson to let us exchange the car for something less ostentatious and smaller. Without realizing what we were doing we bought the car that made Ralph Nader famous: the Chevrolet Corvair 1960, the car he branded as "unsafe at any speed." He was right. What an incredible lemon it was. We could never drive from Medicine Hat to Calgary without having one mechanical problem or another. I was clearly batting zero for two. This time, however, Gloria could not blame me for anything. We had made the choice together. A very bad choice, of course, but a collective one.

The man who owned the house whose basement we rented was a builder. By 1963, my parents were ready to move from their rented apartment to a house. Our landlord was charged with building their house. The lot they had bought overlooked Kin Coulee. The view from the backyard was not spectacular but it provided a rather panoramic view of part of the city, the railroad tracks, and the coulee itself which contained a nice park. Gloria and I wanted to build our own home next to the one being built for my parents. Gloria and I wondered whether we could save enough money for the required down-payment. We knew we could not afford the monthly mortgage. We came up with a brilliant idea. We asked Gloria's parents whether they would be interested in living with us and help us with the monthly payments. They were delighted. So, we bought the lot next to where my parent's house was to be constructed. The total price for the house was $12,900. The constructor and I came to an agreement. I would paint the house inside and outside if he reduced the price by $500. He agreed.

I must admit that the painting turned out to be of the highest quality. The house looked great. There was a lot of work to be done outdoors as well. The backyard was sloping a lot. We wanted to have a flat area to have a luscious lawn. We ordered loads of rocks to build retaining walls. In fact, to ensure stability, we built two retaining walls, one down from the other, separated by a romantic path. We levelled the ground, covered it with good mulch and quality soil, and seeded it. We were incredibly proud of what we had accomplished. In our opinion, what we had done had increased considerably the value of both properties. It would probably have been true, but two events came to disrupt our dreams of property ownership.

Days after seeding the lawns we had a tremendous downpour that washed away most of the seeds and created all kinds of ruts. The yards looked terrible. Our attempts to repair and restore were unsuccessful. The yards looked like someone whose hair was beginning to thin in uneven ways. But at least, we convinced ourselves, the yard was flat. Even that was to change. A couple years later, we woke up one morning to an incredible sight. Half the backyard had collapsed. The retaining walls we had built had made their way to the bottom of the coulee. We had a large crater that ate up half of the yard. To avoid the danger of falling down the crater, we had to build a new fence. We were beginning to wonder whether there was some evil spirit that wished us ill.

Although I was very happy working as a glass studio artisan, my restlessness and intellectual curiosity had not abated. I remembered what our lifeguard friend and neighbor had said regarding the high school provincial exams. The summer of 1963 I decided to start the process. I chose to take the French exam, even though I had not prepared for it. When I got the results, I was surprised, impressed, and vindicated. I received 85%. What a great beginning, I thought. My brother was quickly able to lower the level of my euphoria. I had done well in French, of course. After all, I knew the language better than most if not all the students who took the exam. But, what about all the other required courses? How was I planning to prepare for them?

I was not about to accept defeat. Was it going to be a quixotic quest? I did not dare think about the challenges. I just decided to forge ahead. Julio was about to enter his academic year 1963-64, his grade twelve. He was highly respected by his teachers, in particular Sister Patrick Ann and Father Larry. I entreated him to talk to his teachers, present my particular circumstances, and ask them whether they would be willing to help me by allowing me to complete the same assignments as other students, write the same exams, and have them correct all of them. With the same generosity that I had already ascertained in other Canadians they acquiesced. Julio thought that I was about to enter some sort of chimera. I assured him that I would give it all I had. If I failed, at least I would have tried. If I succeeded, worlds of new opportunities would open up for me. Julio became my teacher, which was good training for him as he was determined to become a teacher.

Julio and I decided that I should take three courses: Physics, Social Studies, and English. If I managed to pass them, I would need two more: math and a science course with a lab. He was allowed to borrow all the required textbooks that I would need. Since he would be taking the same three courses, he would be able to help me if I had any difficulties, which, of course, I was bound to encounter. I could only study at night, of course. Life was going to get a bit more complicated. Discipline and dedication were going to govern my life if I were to achieve success. Gloria was incredibly supportive. I needed her support and encouragement. I was about to embark on a journey that would leave little time for anything but work and study.

In the middle of this exciting period something tragic happened that shocked the world. I was finishing the touches on a beautifully artistic glass sculpture when the son-in-law of the owner came running toward me to tell me that something horrible had just taken place. President Kennedy had been assassinated. This was November 22, 1963. I remember having to sit down immediately. My legs did not want to support me. I was probably one among millions of people who had fallen in love with what President Kennedy represented. A breath of fresh air, an unbridled optimism, a modern way of looking at the world, hope for the unprivileged, a savior to many. I believed that something important had just been broken, possibly forever. In the midst of the optimism, I enjoyed because of my decision to push forward with my chimeric goals, this tragedy drove me into a sudden and lasting funk. It would take a long while before I could push this horrific event out of my mind. I did and resumed my studies under the guidance of my teacher/brother.

I found all three subjects daunting. Whereas regular students had had a number of previous courses that allowed them to build upon them, a background against which to place their grade twelve studies, I came into them without any preparation whatsoever. Everything was new to me. At times I felt like I was falling freely into an abyss of information without points of reference or benchmarks. There were plenty of times when I wanted to give up. But there was always a little voice within me that urged me to just carry on. I did. Julio helped me a lot as did the teachers who, through him, provided feedback and words of encouragement. When time came in the Spring of 1964 to take the provincial exams along with all of Alberta's twelve graders, I braced myself for whatever fate wanted to deliver to me. Passing grade at that time was 55%. I was elated to receive 57% in Physics, 60% in English, and 75% in Social Studies. That coupled with the 85% in French, provided a serious boost to my confidence.

Around February of 1964, we found out that Gloria was pregnant. We had a daughter whom we named Jacqueline, following the agreement that we had reached in France that if we had a son, he would be named Jean Pierre and if we had a daughter, Jacqueline. Our daughter was born in September of 1964. This welcome addition to our family was going to make studying a bit tougher, particularly since I would need to go to night classes. Julio was to enter his first year at the University of Alberta, Calgary, in the Fall. Gloria would be called upon to assume even greater responsibilities and work. But Gloria was so pleased with the results of my studies, the seriousness with which I confronted the challenge that she urged me on.

The summer of 1964 was long and arduous. I had the equivalent of grade seven or eight math. There was no way that I could face grade twelve math without lots of preparatory work. The task seemed insurmountable. Again, I urged Julio to prepare me. He was after all going to be a math teacher. I told him that we had a couple of months for him to get me up to the point where I would not embarrass myself in class. So, we did grades nine, ten, and eleven in two months. Did I feel ready to tackle grade twelve math? Not in the least. But what could I do? I enrolled in two, night classes, math and biology. Most of the students were people who, for one reason or another had not finished grade twelve but, because they were now over twenty-one, could attempt to make up for what they were missing. Only two of us were immigrants and a bit older than the rest. The other one was a Greek guy. Most of the students dropped out little by little until very few of us remained, among those, the Greek guy and me.

I found math very difficult. On the other hand, I adored biology. The grades after the exams made this patently clear. I received 59% in math and 87% in biology. My high school average grade was a respectable 70.5%. The doors to the university were wide open for me. Who could have even imagined, given that I was such an uninterested and poor student in Barcelona, that such a possibility was even remotely imaginable?

One of the first decisions was determining what career I would choose. Since I had taken courses in bookkeeping, I thought about accounting. I had been supplementing my salary at Altaglass by giving private classes in Spanish to the daughter of our family doctor and also to the daughter of the most prominent chartered accountant in Medicine Hat. I went to talk to him to seek his advice. He persuaded me that a career in accountancy would be a bad choice. According to him, new machines called computers were going to replace members of this profession. Of course, he could not have been more mistaken, but I trusted him and did not know any better. I frankly did not know that much about what could have been a good fit for me since my knowledge about the many offerings at a university was incredibly limited. I decided that since my brother was going to be a teacher so could I. But what kind of a teacher could I be? I had loved and done well in biology, so I would pursue a teaching career in biology. With this decision, I had eliminated one of the concerns.

There was a major concern that had to be resolved though: the economic one. It was clear that Gloria could not come with me to the university in Calgary. We could not manage without her salary. If she was to continue working, then she needed someone to help take care of our daughter. Gloria's parents were willing to help in whichever way helped us the most. Had the price of higher education been what it is today, I would never have been able to afford it. Before making any final decision, I went to the owner of the studio and informed them that I was contemplating attending university. I could only consider such a daring move if they could assure me that I would be able to continue working during the Christmas break and the summer months. They looked at me somewhat condescendingly. They obviously did not think that I was university material. But they humored me. They told me that I could count on such employment and could in fact return to full time work if I failed in my endeavor. They did not believe for a second that I could possibly succeed. As insulting as I considered their response, I needed to have their assurances. Gloria and I were going to need every possible penny in order to make ends meet. The physical separation barely three years into our marriage was going to be painful. The fact that I was leaving her behind with an almost year-old baby girl made it all the more difficult. In retrospect, what I was asking of Gloria was tantamount to heroic.

Before leaving for Calgary, I felt I had to do something. I went to the local branch of the Bank of Montreal and went to see its director, the one who had told me that I was not educated enough for the job for which I had applied. I asked him if he remembered me. He said he did. I told him that I wanted to inform him that I had completed my grade twelve exams and that I had been admitted to the University of Calgary. He seemed surprised but wished me well. I was happy not to have gone to a forgotten, northern Alberta branch of the Bank of Montreal as he had originally predicted. The future seemed far rosier than it had been a mere three years before when I had had such a humiliating experience.

I should add that just before I left for college, I, along with Gloria and our two families were granted Canadian citizenship. This was a very much anticipated, welcome, and happy day. At that point, I think all of us realized that we would never go back to Barcelona, certainly not to live. We all felt that Canada was now our home. We had what we could have only considered a dream in Spain. Though we had modest homes, we were homeowners for the first time in our lives. We also had cars. And, to top it all, Julio was already a university student, and I was about to become one. We were living the American dream in Canada, the land of possibilities.

University of Calgary, 1965–1970

The main cost for college was not going to be tuition but housing. Once again, I was able to count on my brother. Julio had been rooming with a friend at his home, but he decided to join me. We found room and board for a very reasonable price at the home of Mrs. Ike, an American lady who had immigrated to Canada. She was quite a character. Another fellow Medicine Hatter also joined us. We each had our own room, of course. It was, by the way, the very first time in my life that I was not going to share a bed. It was clear to us that Mrs. Ike made a fair amount of money on us. She fed us some of the worst meals we had ever had. Everything she served was clearly cheap. Sometimes we did not even recognize what we were served. Ken, our friend, ate everything as if it were prepared by the best chef in the world. Julio and I were a bit more discriminating (finicky, he called us). At times we left everything on our plate and had a hamburger or something equally unhealthy but tasty at the university or at our local beer parlor. Ken was happy that we seemed not to be hungry at times. He ate our portions. But whenever he did not, Mrs. Ike always managed to repackage and camouflage whatever was left of our meals into something even less appetizing. Then, unbeknownst to us, Mrs. Ike decided to sell her house. The house was bought by an Italian family. Those who took possession of the house had just arrived from Italy. They spoke not a word of English.

My brother and our fellow-border, Ken, delegated me to be the translator. I had never studied Italian but had learned a bit from listening to the Italian arias and popular Italian songs my father loved to sing. So, I understood some of what they said and managed to convey our wishes and needs. If Mrs. Ike's food had been full of surprises, we were in for a few more surprises, some of which turned out to be rather memorable. Of course, most of what they served was typical Italian fare, spaghetti, pasta of all sorts with lots and lots of tomato sauce. At one point we expressed our desire for some variety. This is when we had the biggest surprise of all. They served us a rather smelly, and totally unappetizing fish-like dish. Julio and I tasted it but pushed our plates out of reach immediately. Ken, as usual, ate it all. When the nice couple asked what was wrong, I asked if they could show me what they had bought. They were eager to show me. The food had come from cans: it was cat food! When I explained by imitating the sound of a cat, they were horrified. They apologized. Ken, however, maintained that it had not been so bad.

As I first walked onto the campus of the University of Alberta, Calgary, I was reminded of a joke I once heard. A man asks to be shown the university. He has never seen one. His guide takes him to the campus, shows him the Arts and Science buildings, the Engineering building, the administration building, the library, and so forth. The guide asks for the man's opinion. The man looks puzzled and says, this is quite nice, but where is the university? I felt a bit like this man my first time at the University of Calgary. The only university I had even seen, from the outside, was the one in Barcelona. It was a splendorous turn of the 19th century architectural beauty. What I was seeing now did not in any way resemble that august building. Still, I was most impressed with the whole complex of structures and the incredible expanse of land that comprised the land owned by the university. I also learned that no matter how huge a campus is, the building that houses one's own program of studies quickly becomes your home.

Julio was a student in the School of Education. I chose to be in Arts and Sciences. When I enrolled, the University was called University of Alberta, Calgary, an important satellite campus of the University of Alberta, in Edmonton. At the beginning of my second year, the university became an independent campus. By that time, however, I had already bought a beautiful, warm jacket with the emblem University of Alberta, Calgary. I still have it. I actually preferred the one my brother had from the School of Education. It was a beautiful dark blue. Mine was a loud green. But I wasn't about to change faculties just to have a nicer jacket.

I was very happy to have Julio there. In his sophomore year, he was already an experienced university student. He became my guide and helped me with registration, and all the other bureaucratic hurdles that one has to clear. As I said, I wanted to study biology. All first-year biology classes were filled to capacity. I was directed to elementary zoology. In addition, I took a second year Spanish, a survey of English literature, an introduction to psychology, and French. These were all year-long classes. I did well in Spanish and French, as could have been expected, but had a more difficult time with psychology and in particular with zoology. I had never had a single day of chemistry in my life. There was a fair amount of chemistry in the zoology course. I felt incapable of overcoming my lacunae in an area of study as essential as chemistry. So, I had to accept the reality that I could not continue with my dream of a degree in biology.

I truly enjoyed my English literature class. The young instructor who taught the course was exuberant, enthusiastic, and his obvious love for literature contagious. I spent a lot of time preparing my first paper for this class. When I was done writing it, I asked my brother to read it and make whatever changes he felt were necessary. He read it and told me that it wasn't good at all. I had thought that it was rather good, well-reasoned and not badly written, despite my limitations in this, my fourth language. I was crestfallen, but it was too late to make any dramatic changes. I had to submit it as written. The class had about twenty-five students. All of them were freshmen, of course, and young. I was the oldest. Sitting on the desk near me was a young nun. I have no idea how old she was but seemed somewhat older than the other students. Before the instructor returned our essays, he said that he had never seen such poorly written papers. I was petrified to see the grade assigned to my work. He said that there were two exceptions. He first returned the work to the nun and praised her obvious talent. He then came to me and returned my work. It was covered with red markings and corrections. Yet, the grade was quite good. He then proceeded to shame all the other students asserting that they should be ashamed to have a foreign student write so much better than they. I could hardly wait to get back to my brother and show off.

Having realized that biology was out as a major, I wondered what subject would be best for me. Someone actually helped me make a life changing decision. Well into the second part of the English literature course, the instructor approached me and told me that he thought I should consider majoring in English literature. He further encouraged me not to settle for being a teacher but to consider a Ph.D. I told him that this was a bridge too far for me to even contemplate such a momentous decision. Besides, I replied, I would always speak English with an accent, and I would always feel too self-conscious. He then suggested I do Spanish literature. I offered an argument that made little sense. I said that most people would think I had taken the easy way out, as if a Ph.D. in Spanish was something that every Spaniard could easily get. He was not about to let it go. What about French, then? After some reflection, I thought that this seemed to be as good a choice as any. I loved France, the French language, and everything to do with French culture. As I have pondered about it during my later years, I have often wondered how I could have taken such an important decision on the spur of the moment? The problem was that, at that time I did not know enough about university studies to contemplate any other option. I have never regretted my choice but more than once wondered whether I would have chosen some other career had I been better informed and more knowledgeable of all my options.

My path forward appeared settled. What was settled also was the never-ending process of learning. This revelation reminded me of Newton's Third Law of Motion. It states that for every action there is an equal and opposite reaction. What this means is that pushing on an object causes that object to push back against you. The exact same amount, but in the opposite direction. This is the way I felt about studying. The more I learned, the more I realized how little I knew. The harder I tried to master some subject the more the subject pushed against me. I quickly understood that this was going to be my future, one in which I would be constantly attempting to fill voids of knowledge, never fully filling them and never satisfied with the insufficient results. But it was a constant battle worth fighting.

A lot has been written in the last few years about grade inflation. I don't recall this being a concern back in 1965, when I started. My personal experience was that one had to work extremely hard for one's grades. My discipline and hard work paid off. I did considerably better in my freshman year than I had done in the high school exams. My sophomore year was even more successful. At the end of that year and into my senior year, I was granted a number of prizes and awards. All of them gave me a sense of accomplishment and pushed me to do even better. But, from a very practical point of view none of these were as important as the Province of Alberta Scholarship, which was awarded to me each subsequent year. Thankfully, it provided a monetary stipend that covered the cost of tuition. After that second year, I never had to worry about tuition. I was very fortunate to receive a number of important scholarships that, financially at least, made my life easier.

In my third and fourth year, the grading system had been changed from percentages to letter grades. I did my best work in Latin. Half of the course was devoted to grammar. The second introduced us to Latin authors. I had never been so happy reading excerpts from Caesar, Cicero, and Virgil, to highlight just three. I received an A grade in this course as I did in all the rest with the exception of Philosophy. Divided, like all other courses into two often distinct halves, the Philosophy course I chose to take in my third year concentrated solely on philosophical concepts. I did well there. I felt confident I would complete the course with an A grade. The second part, however, studied logic. I had always considered myself to be logical and in possession of a fair amount of common sense. The study of logic tested my logical mind. Logic proved to be a serious challenge for me. The fact that I ended up with a B indicates that I did not rise to the challenge.

My fourth year was very satisfying. I had three French literature courses and two Spanish. I was fortunate to have several very good professors. I would be remiss if I did not credit two of them for providing not only excellent preparation but for modeling what a professor ought to be. Serge Zaïtzeff, a Frenchman born in Versailles, was my favorite Spanish professor. He also became one of my very best friends. Henri Mydlarski, also French, a specialist in 17th century literature, was without a doubt the most demanding but also the best prepared professor in French. He was so good and thorough that his teaching came to my rescue when I took my Ph.D. comprehensive exams at the University of California, Santa Barbara. I had a question on what in France became known as *La Querelle des Anciens et des Modernes*. This was a polemic literary and artistic fight that originated in the prestigious and overpowering *l'Académie française*, that pitted those, led by Boileau, who believed that the better course was to continue to imitate Greek and Roman writers, artists, and thinkers because they were the epitome of perfection. The *Modernes*, led by Charles Perrault, maintained that modern generations could improve on the classics because the essence of the arts is constant innovation. That had not been covered in any of the courses I had taken at UCSB. Fortunately, Professor Mydlarski had made passing reference to it in one of his classes. Even though it was only superficially covered, as he did with everything he taught, he made sure we understood its significance. I obviously took him to heart. I was able to answer the question harkening back to his brilliant explanations. Many years later, during the ceremony granting me the honor of distinguished University of Calgary alumnus, I had the opportunity to tell him in front of many of his colleagues how important and valuable he had been to me.

I do not wish to make it sound as if the five years I spent studying at the university were nothing but hard work. One of the things I learned upon arriving at the University was that there were intramural sports that one could be involved in. No one could live in Canada and not learn to skate. What else could one do during the long winters? Of course, I learned how to skate. But I had serious limitations. I could only turn fast, one leg over the other, when moving right to left. I never managed to apply the same technique to turning right. I was also unable to make sudden breaks. My approach to coming to a sudden stop was to come crashing against the boards. It was not very elegant nor practical if one wanted to play hockey. Julio was a far more accomplished skater than me. However, he was very reluctant to join an intramural team. I insisted and he gave in. When we sat at the bench waiting for our shift on the ice, Julio refused to jump in. Even though real body checks were not allowed there was plenty of body -contact. The other guys were big, fast, and ferocious looking, at least to us. I wanted to show that I was not afraid. I took my turn. I think I must have been on the ice less than ten seconds when I got squashed against the boards. I left the ice with a very fat lip. That was the extent of our organized hockey career. We decided from then on only to go out to the ice rink outside Mrs. Ike's house for a few pick-up games with little kids, all of whom ran circles around us. I had fun, though.

Of course, one could not be a university student and not join fellow students, Friday nights, at the local beer parlor. This too was fun and relaxing at the end of demanding weeks of study. I was fortunate to be involved in an activity that afforded me an opportunity to make friends and be further immersed in extracurricular acts.

One of Julio's friends told him that he might be interested in joining a campus organization called World University Services (WUS). One of the goals of this organization was to facilitate student interchanges between Canada and other countries. Julio found out that the following summer the country chosen by the WUS was Chile. He joined and immediately applied to be one of the exchange students. He was selected and was sent first to Mexico for an extensive orientation and then to Chile for most of the summer. When he returned home and started his next academic year, he learned that the student who had been the president of the organization had graduated. A replacement for him needed to be identified and selected. Julio was asked to assume the presidency. He accepted. This position did not demand a lot from him, but it taught him about international organizations, how to plan for student exchanges, and how to recruit new students. Notwithstanding the danger of being accused of nepotism, Julio asked me to be his vice president, a post I accepted readily. We were going to be working together, something I valued. In addition, I, too, learned a great deal. We both made some good friends, some of whom were from other countries. Overall, it was a valuable experience.

For the first two years, Julio and I went back to Medicine Hat for Christmas and during all the summer months. I had to work. Our trips back and forth, particularly at Christmas time, were not always uneventful. At that time of the year, it was usually very cold, and roads were almost always filled with snow and ice. On one of our trips to Medicine Hat, we left Calgary under incredibly difficult conditions. There was so much snow on the road that it was often almost impossible to determine where the road ended and the ditch on the side started. Julio had bought a second-hand British Vauxhall. It was narrow and tall. For some reason, I was driving it on that day. We knew it was going to be a long trip because of barometric conditions. When we were about twenty miles or so from Medicine Hat, we started to sing. Snow clearing machines had begun to clear the road of snow and we could see the end of our journey. We could relax, we thought. Then I hit a patch of ice and the car skidded across the road and we went down the embankment. The car overturned, landed on its roof, and, luckily, it turned itself back onto its four wheels. There were a few minor scratches, and the car was now a few inches less tall. The roof had collapsed a bit. We were very lucky that one of the trucks clearing the road came to our aid. The driver attached some chains to Julio's car and pulled us for a long distance inching our way back to the road without causing our car to roll down the ditch again. Before we even got home to our family, we took the car into a local garage, asked them to spray paint some of the scratches and jack up the roof of the car. It did not look as good as before the crash, but it functioned well, and we had spent practically no money.

Gloria, Manuel, and Jacqueline 1966

On another occasion, when Gloria and Jacqueline were already living with me and we had gone to Medicine Hat to spend Christmas with the family, we had another hairy experience. The temperature was around 30 degrees Fahrenheit below zero. We bundled up our Jacqueline, who was about one year old, and took off. But the door on the passenger's side would not lock or even close. Gloria had to hold on to the door for a few miles before the car warmed up enough for the lubricant in the door to thaw. In retrospect, I shiver thinking what could have happened to us had we had any type of problem with the car. It was so cold that we could not have survived for long. But such were conditions in winter in Alberta at the time that we had very few options but to carry on, regardless of risk.

Before Gloria and Jacqueline came to live in Calgary, my trips back to Medicine Hat were essential. I had to work. We desperately needed to replenish our purse so I could continue living in Calgary while studying. It was the time in between these stays in Medicine Hat that I missed Gloria and our little Jacqueline. Gloria and I exchanged letters all the time. We did not speak on the phone. It was far too expensive. Whenever Gloria was able to convince her parents to take care of Jackie for the weekend, she took the bus and came to see me. Of course, we were very eager to be together, though our much-desired encounters were not all that satisfying. I had a very small and uncomfortable bed. Our love making required the flexibility and agility of a contortionist. It was awkward and unsatisfactory. The usual postcoital sleepiness that should have followed was disrupted by the discomfort of the miniscule bed. The following day we both felt strange. Gloria claimed that I did not pay enough attention to her and did not understand the obstacles she had to overcome each time she came to visit me to convince her parents, spend long hours in a bus, and eventually leave me somewhat disconsolate because I had not shown enough appreciation and love. She was right. As soon as she was gone, I wanted to be near her again. I promised myself that I would be more affectionate, but each visit ended basically the same way. Things changed the moment I was back in Medicine Hat and resumed our normal married couple routine.

At the end of my second year at the University, we both came to the conclusion that our separation was not good for our marriage or for the well-being of our daughter. We had to make serious changes. Gloria would have to quit her job at the hospital. In Calgary, she would not be able to work since she would not have her parents to babysit while she was at work. We certainly could not continue to pay the expenditures associated with owning a house. We had to take things one step at the time. First, we informed Gloria's parents of our decision to move to Calgary and that this would require us to sell the house. This was painful for them. They were incredibly attached to Jackie. The separation from her was going to be difficult and painful. We were still coming back to Medicine Hat for the Christmas break and during the summers since I needed to continue working at Altaglass. Our having to sell the house meant that they would need to move. They reacted as well as we could ever have hoped for. They found and bought a tiny little house. It had two bedrooms, one bathroom, a small living room, and a miniscule kitchen that barely accommodated a small dining table against one of the walls. The rooms were so small that the doors had to be accordion type as there was no space to have a regular door that could open either toward the bedroom or the living room. It did have a basement with a low-ceiling room that allowed family gatherings from time to time. Cisco was happy though, because he had a very large backyard where he could have a vegetable garden.

Just before the beginning of my junior year, Gloria, Jacqueline and I moved to Calgary. We rented a two-bedroom apartment. To help us defray the cost of rental, Julio, who was about to start his senior year, agreed to move in with us. This was a fun year. Jackie loved her uncle and was very happy. Gloria and I spent many hours playing cards with Julio when our studies allowed.

At this time, we still owned our Corvair. One day, Julio and I decided to go see a football game at the university. When we got to the car, it would not start. There was complete silence. Nothing was moving. Even though neither one of us knew anything about cars, we did manage to lift the hood in the back, where the motor was located. It did not take a mechanic to realize that the battery of the car was missing. When I called a garage, I was informed that the 1960 Corvair had a rather unique battery. Unique enough to tempt someone to steal it. Then and there Gloria and

I decided that as soon as our economic situation allowed it, we would need to get rid of this "unsafe at any speed" car. Then, at the end of my junior year, we gave up our apartment and went back to Medicine Hat. Although we did not know it at the time, this was going to be the last time that I was going to work at Altaglass.

For the first time in three years, I began my school year without having my brother as a fellow student. He had taken a position as a math teacher in Medicine Hat, at the same school where he had been a student. He was happy but he knew that he would be coming to Calgary often to visit us. Or should I say that he would come to stay with us while visiting his girlfriend. A year earlier I had introduced him to a female student in one of my upper-level Spanish classes. Her mother was Italian and her father Dutch. He was a Shell Company geologist. His company sent him to oversee work in various foreign countries. The whole family had recently moved to Canada from Central America. Nory spoke perfect Spanish. My brother was rather shy around girls but liked Nory immediately and they fell in love rather quickly.

Gloria and I had to find another apartment in which to live. We rented the upstairs suite of a house owned by an Italian family. I don't recall exactly why, but I had found this place and rented it without Gloria having seen it. When we moved in, we realized that it was very filthy. The walls in the kitchen were splattered with spaghetti sauce. It looked as if the previous renters had had food fights. The linoleum tiles on the floor were coated with so much dirt that it took us days to scrape them clean. While cleaning the window over the kitchen sink, Gloria ended up with a thick wood sliver embedded in one of her fingers. I had to take her to the hospital to have it removed. The physical pain was severe but the psychological was probably worse. Gloria was overwhelmed by all the filth, so much so that she broke into tears. Eventually, and after a lot of work and effort, we were satisfied that we had cleaned as much as it was humanly possible.

My fourth year was a happy one. Not only were Gloria and I happy to be together again enjoying seeing our little Jacqueline grow, but we also enjoyed a much richer social life. Barbara Zaitzeff, my Spanish professor's wife, became very close to Gloria. We started to invite each other to dinners and card playing at our respective homes. At first, Serge and I were uncertain as to how we should address each other in Spanish, which has a familiar *tú* and a more formal *usted*. We had always used *usted* in class and in the department. As the two couples got closer it seemed artificial to address each other as if we were just recent acquaintances. Still, we did not know how to change. So, for a while, we both avoided addressing each other directly. Finally, Barbara indicated that it was ridiculous to continue to avoid using the familiar *tú* instead of *usted*. It did not take long for both of us to adapt. At the university, however, we continued to keep the normal relationship between professor and student.

Gloria and I, being a married couple and older than other students in the Romance Languages Department, were invited to parties organized by younger faculty. We valued their friendship but both Gloria and I always felt somewhat out of place among professors. These gatherings were interesting in a number of ways. Not only were all the professors vastly cultured, as could be expected, but so were their spouses. In addition, the parties were like reunions in the United Nations. There were Belgians, Swiss, French, British, but few Canadian born ones. The languages spoken at these parties were mostly French and Spanish. The conversations were exhilarating. We learned almost as much at these gatherings as I did in class. One of these professors was Brian Gill, an Englishman, a professor of French who joined the faculty, if I remember correctly, in my third year. Because we were roughly the same age, we became friends. It was from him that I bought Beethoven's complete symphonies. They were contained in a nice box. Brian had used the back of this box to create a chess board. So, for the price of one I got my very first exposure to classical music and a chess board! We also attended parties organized by students. We danced and laughed a great deal. We had never had so many interesting acquaintances and friends. We were happy.

During my fourth year, I was advised to apply for a very prestigious scholarship, The Woodrow Wilson Fellowship. I do not know how many Canadians were eligible to be considered, as this was an American national program offering full support for Ph.D. work in the arts and sciences to 1000 Fellows each year. I did not need to know the details other than learning that I could and should submit my candidacy. The annual selection process, including a very rigorous interview by leading academics, provided a yardstick for academic excellence and, in many ways, a model for other fellowship programs. After submitting the written part, I was invited to be interviewed in Vancouver. I had been promised a difficult oral interview. It was. I must have done well enough, however, as in 1969 I was awarded the Woodrow Wilson Fellowship. This program had started in 1945, after WWII, and it came to an end in the early 1970s. I was, therefore, one of the last people to be so honored.

This fellowship opened a lot of academic doors for me. I have no doubt that it made me a better candidate for the Province of Alberta Graduate Fellowship, which I received at the end of my fourth year. The understanding was that I would have to attend graduate school in order to receive the fellowship and the generous monetary provision that came with it.

As the fourth year came to an end, I had to choose a university to continue my studies. I thought that new professors and a new academic environment would be a welcome change, and access to different methods, approaches, and ways of viewing and critiquing literary works. Gloria and I wanted to remain in Canada and not too far from our parents. With this in mind I chose to apply to the University of British Columbia, in Vancouver. As a fall back I also submitted my application to the University of Calgary. I was quickly accepted at both. There was a major difference between the two institutions, however. Whereas I could complete a master's degree in one year in Calgary, it would have taken two at UBC.

This posed a serious dilemma. I was already twenty-nine years old. Gloria and I wondered how many more years of privations we were prepared to withstand before I was fully and gainfully employed so we could lead a normal life. A move to Vancouver would imply more expenses, an additional year of study not counting the several more years if I decided to pursue a doctorate. Gloria left the decision to me. She did not want to become an impediment to my chosen course of studies. Whereas I would have preferred UBC, I was a practical person and, after pondering the ramifications of selecting one institution over the other, I declined the offer from UBC and chose to stay at UC, in Calgary.

The summer of 1969 was important in other ways. Julio and Nory got married in August. Jacqueline was a month short of her 5th birthday and as cute as a button. Her uncle and future aunt wanted her to be the flower girl at their wedding. She discharged her responsibilities with aplomb and grace. We were all very proud of her. I brought a bit of color to the ceremony. Nory, despite not being a traditionalist in most things, could not hide her reproaching look when she saw that, as best man, I was wearing a very striking pink tie. She did not seem overly pleased, but I thought I looked striking and debonair. After their wedding and a short honeymoon, Julio and Nory went to Medicine Hat. Julio continued in his teaching post and Nory also found a teaching position. They seemed settled, while Gloria and I were still fabricating a new life for us.

Gloria and I decided that it was too disruptive both for us and for Jacqueline if we kept going back and forth each winter and summer between Calgary and Medicine Hat. It was better just to remain in Calgary. This meant that I had to find employment. I was able to locate Nick, the person for whom I had worked as a painter. I asked him for a full-time job for the summer and part time during the academic year. He was happy to see me and come to my rescue.

Working during the summer did not represent a departure from what I had been doing for the last several years, except that it was painting rather than glassblowing. The challenge was working during the academic year while taking a full load of courses and writing a thesis on top of it all. Nick said that he would try to accommodate my schedule. I was successful in taking courses in the early afternoon. Other than attending a few parties and hosting some dinners for our few friends, our life became rather routine. I worked from six in the morning till noon each day. The afternoons were devoted to my classes. Later in the academic year two major activities absorbed most of whatever free time I had. First, I needed to select the subject of my thesis, carry out the necessary research, and submit it for examination and approval. Second, I had to determine which universities would be best to pursue the Ph.D.

Every time our existence became rhythmic, events beyond our control shattered our peace of mind and threw us curve balls, so to speak. In the last year in Calgary, we learned that Gloria was pregnant. Our first reaction was one of joy. We had never really discussed how many children we wanted to have, but two seemed a good number. Perhaps we would have a son. Upon some reflection, however, I came to the painful conclusion that if ever there was a bad time to have a second child it was at the precise moment when we would probably have to move again, possibly to the United States. Would we have the economic resources for a family of four? I did not think so. I mentioned this to Gloria. She was taken aback by what she considered too materialistic and transactional pondering. I felt chastened and dropped my reservations immediately. I felt even worse, having had such thoughts, when, about eight weeks into the pregnancy Gloria had a miscarriage. Little did we know that our chance to have another child would evaporate a few months hence.

Despite the traumatic experience that had jolted us, I could not allow myself to be depressed or despondent. I had to persevere. So, I plunged into my studies. I loved submerging myself in the works of famous poets, playwrights, and novelists. I also found each period and literary movement fascinating. But over time I came to detect preferences in what I chose to read. I placed poetry a few notches below theatrical works and found those less engaging than novels. Of all the periods and literary movements, I leaned more and more towards the works that represented two of these movements, realism and naturalism. The more I delved into these works, though, the more I found serious differences between the two, that pushed me to prefer the one over the other. I regarded novels emblematic of the realist movement to be akin to the work of a filmmaker who would leave the camera running and record whatever happened to come in front of it, without commentary. To me this smacked a bit of superficiality. Naturalists, on the other hand, to follow the same line of thinking, were cinematographers who not only depicted life as they saw it but entered into the homes and lives of the characters depicted and intended to understand and document the environment in which they lived, the social forces that shaped their experiences, and the forces that undergirded their attitudes, beliefs, and behavior. Perhaps because of my working-class upbringing I discovered a greater affinity with naturalist authors and in particular with the most representative of this movement, Emile Zola, and more to the point, the Zola of the series of novels that featured the *Rougon-Macquart* family. In a way, I did not find a project. It found me. Professor Tony Greaves, a Zola scholar, agreed to guide my effort. All I needed to do, then, was to propose my research project.

During one of my many sleepless nights, I came upon a topic that would combine my love of Zola and my attraction to Blasco Ibáñez, a Valencian novelist who was often called the "Spanish Zola." My focus was to study aspects of Zola's influence on the Valencian novelist. Whenever the question of Zola's influence on Blasco Ibáñez was analyzed, three types of critical reactions occurred. A group of critics subscribed to the principle that Zola's influence on the Spanish novelist was undeniable; another claimed that any detectable influence ceased to exist towards the end of the nineteenth century; still another asserted that any possible affinities were due to their being members of the same Naturalist school. Whichever attitude critics favored however, their analyses were limited to Zola's *Rougon-Macquart* series and, in general, to Blasco's Valencian cycle. My goal was to offer a brief synthesis of these varied critical attitudes, show the influence of Zola's *Germinal, La Terre,* and *L'Assommoir,* on Blasco Ibáñez four *novelas de rebeldía,* and, in addition, demonstrate that, contrary to the general critical view, Blasco drew inspiration as well from Zola's *Les Trois Villes* and *Les Quatre Evangiles.* In composing his four novels of rebellion, Blasco's ideas on Christianity derived from Zola's *Paris,* and his attitude towards social problems and social justice was suggested from his reading of Zola's *Travail.* It seemed appropriate and justifiable to assert that by the time Zola ceased to write, his influence on Blasco had evolved and progressed from purely artistic to ideological as well.

Once I had imagined what I was going to write and how I was going to proceed I did not allow any distractions and worked tirelessly until the work was complete. By August of 1970, the faculty of graduate studies approved my thesis. The unimaginable had become a reality. Five years after completing the requirements that permitted me to enroll at the university without ever having had an official diploma, I was granted a Master of Arts degree. Our sacrifices had been rewarded. I do not exaggerate if I say that Gloria and I began to awake to a new dawn.

My education journey was not yet complete, though. My ultimate objective was to be a professor at a Canadian university. When I consulted my professors, almost to a person, they all advised me to attend American universities. According to them, Canadians valued an American Ph.D. more highly than a Canadian one. Although I would have preferred to remain in Canada, I applied to a number of American universities, among them Harvard, the University of Michigan, the University of Wisconsin, and, on a lark, the University of California, Santa Barbara. All these universities had one commonality. They all had famous, Zola, specialists. I also sent an application to the University of British Columbia. All but this latter one accepted me. It was obvious that the Department of French remembered that I had declined their offer to do a Master there the year before.

I did a lot of research on all of the universities that had accepted me. I must confess that I discarded Harvard because I was afraid that I might not be sufficiently prepared academically for such a prestigious institution. After much soul-searching I also discarded the others, primarily because in addition to the four languages that I had already mastered I would still need to learn another one, in most cases either German or Russian. I do not know exactly why I resented having to learn either one of these two languages, particularly Russian. I do know why I had an aversion to German. Hitler's German armies had bombed Guernica out of existence and had helped a despot like Franco tyrannize a whole nation. It was probably childish and immature to refuse to study the beautiful language of Goethe, Günter Grass, Bertolt Brecht and others because I hated what Hitler had wrought on the world. However, the University of California, Santa Barbara would allow me to fulfill the language requirement by taking Portuguese instead of either German or Russian. Furthermore, the French Department had a renowned Zola scholar. Needless to say, Gloria was not unhappy to leave behind the very cold winters of Alberta for the sunny and warm weather of California.

Although our economic situation was not going to be an easy one, we were lucky that I had been granted a Canada Council Doctoral Fellowship for four years with a yearly stipend of $4000, to be paid quarterly. I also secured a University of California Doctoral Fellowship that would cover tuition for the duration of my doctoral studies.

With our friends Serge and Barbara, we undertook a trip south with Santa Barbara as our final destination to explore the university and ascertain what our new life there was going to be like. We left Jacqueline with her grandparents and off we went. We visited San Francisco, Las Vegas, San Diego, Tijuana, and finally Santa Barbara. Gloria and I were like kids. Other than our memorable but almost tragic honeymoon trip, we had not been on any extended voyage anywhere since we came to North America. Everything was new and exciting.

In San Francisco we did not stay downtown. It was far too expensive for us. We got rooms at a modest hotel in some neighborhood I could not find now, even if I tried. Not far from it there was a decent-looking restaurant-bar that advertised some sort of entertainment. The young lady who came to take our order was scantily dressed. Imagine our surprise when she suddenly went up on a small stage and shed the scanty clothes she was wearing. She ended up fully naked. She danced and showed her body in all her splendid beauty. As soon as she was done, she came to our table, still in her birthday suit and served our orders. All four of us were speechless. Serge and I thought that we had made a tremendous choice in coming to this restaurant. Though somewhat shocked we enjoyed the titillation. I still remember vividly that day but have no memory at all of what we ate. In Las Vegas we slept in a campground and almost melted in the extreme heat. Since we did not have money to spare, we just walked around and went to every conceivable venue where we could enter for free. San Diego was a much smaller city than it is now, but the weather was wonderful. Tijuana proved to be a lot of fun and cheap. We ate very well, had lots of margaritas, and went to a few shows that featured beautiful *señoritas*, one of whom seemed to take a fancy to Serge. Barbara thought the situation funny. Serge loved the attention and glowed with satisfaction. Gloria and I just loved what we considered our first vacation in years. In Santa Barbara, I went to the department of French and met the few professors who remained on campus for the summer. The campus was beautiful and its setting near the ocean spectacular. We were very surprised, however, that the University was not in Santa Barbara, despite its name, but in Isla Vista, a sort of student ghetto. Overall, it was a great trip and a splendid preamble of good things to come.

When we got back to Calgary, we said our goodbyes to my brother and Nory, who had tendered their resignations to their respective schools in Medicine Hat and moved back to Calgary. Julio wanted to pursue a Master of Arts degree in French literature. We also bid adieu to Vicenç and Angela, with whom we had renewed our almost family ties, thanked Nick for all his support, and had a difficult time leaving behind our dear friends Serge and Barbara. We promised that we would do everything in our power to keep in contact and visit them as often as circumstances would permit. We gave up our apartment and headed to Medicine Hat to bid farewell to our parents. This was a very difficult separation. We knew that the physical distance that would separate us was significant. We would not be able to see them for every Christmas and summer, as we had done the past five years. We were all very conscious that this was a major move. Their only grandchild, who was deeply attached to them and they to her would be growing up far from them. They understood that my future career made this move necessary but clearly resented the impact this imposed distance would have on all of us. We left with deeply felt sorrow and tears in our eyes. We were embarking on yet another sort of immigration. Would we ever be able to settle down?

CHAPTER IV
University of California, Santa Barbara 1970–1973

▲▲▲

Gloria at UCSB campus. The three of us near married student housing.

ONE OF THE ADVANTAGES OF not having accumulated much over the years is that we had little to take south with us. We were able to fit everything into our Datsun. In Santa Barbara, we were scheduled to be lodged at the university's graduate student housing. But, because we wanted to become acquainted with the city and the new surroundings, we got to Santa Barbara almost two months before classes were scheduled to begin. Graduate housing was not available to us when we arrived. We were forced to find an apartment until our assigned housing would be available. We found one in Isla Vista, of all places, on Picasso Street. The young manager was very kind and helped us get settled. The apartment was badly furnished but habitable. We explored Santa Barbara, went to the beach, walked in front of the recently burned down Bank of America in one of the many demonstrations against the Vietnam war, and, above all else, enjoyed the fantastic weather.

I was very surprised to receive a communication from the university indicating that I owed money to cover fees. It had assumed that the graduate fellowship I had been awarded by UCSB would cover all costs. But it did not. Fees were separate and not inconsequential. I panicked. I went to see the department head and asked him what options were available to me. He indicated that I could be a teaching assistant and that this would more than cover this additional expenditure. I said that under the conditions of the Canada Council scholarship I could not have any paid employment. I suggested to him that, if he agreed to it, I would function as a graduate teaching assistant but would not receive the stipend associated with it, as long as part of that money was used to cover the cost associated with the fees. We made an agreement.

This arrangement worked out for me in another way. The two instructors who managed the graduate teaching assistants were exceptionally good at preparing us to be effective teachers. I learned a lot from them and there is little doubt that without their constant attention to our performance I would not have become as good a teacher as quickly as I did.

This issue regarding the fees was not the only surprise that awaited us. Shortly after our arrival I woke up one morning with an unbearable pain at my lower abdomen and down to my testicles. I went to see the University clinic doctor. I don't know how competent he was in general but when it came to his diagnosis of my pain, he was laughable. He told me that I should not wear briefs. They were too tight, he proffered. This was the cause of my pain. The pain disappeared for a while but one night I woke up again with even more pain than the previous time. I was almost delirious. I was also vomiting uncontrollably. Gloria managed to get me to the car and take me to the nearest hospital. I was quickly diagnosed. I had a stone lodged at the entry of my left kidney. Unless I underwent immediate surgery, the doctor indicated, I would lose my kidney.

Nowadays, kidney stones are obliterated without surgery. A few years after I had mine, my brother underwent the same type of surgery. He has a three-inch scar. My surgeon almost dissected me in half. I ended up with a thirteen-inch scar. I have never again had any problem with my kidneys, but the scar has remained a constant reminder of one of the most memorable and painful welcoming experiences in Santa Barbara.

When we moved into married student housing, we had no furniture. We furnished our two-bedroom apartment with whatever graduating students were leaving behind, and whatever we could buy at places like the Salvation Army stores. We made bookshelves out of bricks and wood boards. The sofa bed we found was cheap, somewhat attractive, but unbelievably uncomfortable. The only piece of value was a wonderful solid wood desk that we bought for ninety dollars at one of the Salvation Army stores. This is the only piece of furniture that came with us when I got my first faculty appointment in Michigan. The environment, though, was quite welcoming. Other graduate students and their families were nice and friendly. Many of us shared a common backyard where we often shared barbecues. There reigned a joyous atmosphere that made a strange place to us less depressing.

It did not take long for us to meet some fellow students who became good friends. On the first day Gloria and I took the elevator up to the office of the Department of French and Italian, we coincided with a newly married couple, David and Bianca Bernstein. We immediately became close friends. There was also another fellow student, Joseph Bayot, a native French speaker from Louisiana who became an instant friend but left UC, Santa Barbara after only one year. He did not like any of the professors or the French program as a whole. We met other people who became friends for life. At the very first social gathering of the department we immediately connected with a brand-new faculty member, William Ashby and his wife Gaye. We are still close friends to this day.

Jacqueline turned six that September. We wanted to enroll her in first grade, but the teacher noticed that we spoke to her in Catalan and that Jacqueline did not say that much in English. Of course, she did not say much because she was painfully shy, not because she could not speak English. Nonetheless, the teacher insisted that she be placed in primary first, a sort of pre-first grade. We should have objected but did not because we were not familiar with the American system and had faith in the teacher. We should have objected more forcefully after realizing that the teacher was not very worldly and probably had some prejudices against foreign people. She advised us to speak English at home. Jacqueline, according to her, would be handicapped in school if she found herself constantly battling a bilingual environment. I told her that Gloria and I spoke four languages each, and that, linguistic experts agreed that being multilingual offers tremendous advantages over being monolingual. Still, Jacqueline was kept back in school because of the teacher's ignorance.

Probably because we had uprooted Jackie from her beloved grandparents and taken her to a foreign environment, she had a hard time adapting to school. Gloria and I walked her to school each morning. She did not really want to go in. She got so anxious and nervous that she vomited each morning on the same flower bed. I was amazed that the flowers actually survived such a consistent attack. To give Jackie a bit of joy, we bought her a very cute bike. She loved it. Her happiness was brutally interrupted shortly after though, when she fell and broke her wrist and arm. She was in a cast for a long time. We were sad and heartbroken. We wondered whether it had been a good idea to give our little, skinny girl a bike. Of course, her arm healed but she continued to be extremely shy and retiring for many years.

We seemed destined to go from one medical mishap to another. Not even a year after I had my kidney operation and Jacqueline had broken her wrist and arm, I found myself having to rush Gloria to the hospital's emergency department. Her menstrual cycles had become erratic and heavy. We realized that this one time was far worse than usual, and it did not seem to abate. Doctors determined that she had to have a hysterectomy. She recovered but was weak for a while and moody for some time. She felt sadness and a sense of loss. As time went by, however, we all seemed to fall into a pattern and our lives became more peaceful.

I found the French and Italian Department quite different from the one I was used to in Calgary. At UCSB there was a clear pecking order. Teaching assistants were, of course, at the lower rung of the ladder. They were followed by instructors, who taught most of the lower-level courses, then there were the untenured full-time faculty. One step above the last group were the tenured faculty, distributed by rank: associate and full professor. Even among those at the top of the ladder, there were clear distinctions, according mostly to the celebrity status they enjoyed as published authors, not as teachers. Then, even among this latter group were those I would refer to as the peacocks. They walked around as if they were the gods of the department. They were not necessarily the best teachers nor the most approachable and helpful to students, but they let everyone know that to be close to them was tantamount to being near the pinnacle of success in the profession.

Most of them were very knowledgeable. If we could stomach some of their posturing, arrogance, and theatrics, we could certainly make good progress and learn how one should approach research and transform this into cogent arguments. It did not take long for me to appreciate that I had made a mistake in choosing to work with Dr. Philip Walker, the Zola specialist. He had the reputation of being an inept teacher. I never took a single course from him, because he did not teach anything that could have advanced my project. He saw Zola and his novels as examples of his hidden and personal understanding of Christianity. This is not at all what had attracted me to Zola, as I have indicated earlier. We seldom met and when we did, I left his office depressed and disheartened. This situation was not sustainable, I thought. Eventually, I took the unusual step of approaching Professor Delattre, a Balzac expert who was an excellent teacher and with whom I quickly developed a good relationship. She immediately put a stop to my veiled pretense. She informed me that Dr. Walker had never had the opportunity to direct a Ph.D. student and would be deeply hurt if I abandoned him. She would not help me do it either.

This drawback did not keep me from enjoying my course of study. The family had adapted well to life in our new environment. I managed to successfully mix my course work, our social life with new friends and fellow students, and a lot of sporting activities. I swam every day with my new friend, Bill Ashby, a professor of French linguistics. After five years of toiling away without much respite, I must have convinced myself that I deserved some fun. At the married student housing there was always someone who seemed ready to organize games, mostly volleyball. I signed up for everything. At times this meant neglecting my studies more than my attachment to discipline should have allowed. Gloria and I played tennis with David and Bianca, while our poor Jacqueline occupied herself playing on the other side of the courts. She was incredibly patient. Not many children at that age would have been so accommodating. We took her everywhere with us. There were good moments for her and some incredibly boring ones. Gloria never really felt integrated. She was surrounded by Ph.D. seeking friends who, with the exception of David and Bianca, seemed to look down on her, particularly the women. It seemed that to them she was merely a wife and a mother. She was hurt. She was made to feel almost like an intruder. Fortunately, she knew who and what she was and was comfortable in the role she played in our family. She was conscious that I valued her participation and that without her unflinching support, love, encouragement, and years of sacrifice I would never have succeeded in my academic pursuit.

Fortunately, we spent our summers happily and she had a chance to put aside her hurt feelings because our parents came to visit us often and for long periods of time. We did not have enough space in our small apartment to provide much comfort to them, but they were used to rough conditions. Gloria's parents slept in our bedroom, and we slept in a very uncomfortable sofa bed that we had in the room that functioned as living, dining, and kitchen. Gloria and I put down the cushions from the sofa bed on the floor of this multipurpose space. The apartment looked like a gypsy settlement. We showed them the area and even took them to Tijuana. Since they were not at all demanding in any way, they just loved being with us and enjoyed gleefully whatever we provided in terms of entertainment.

Our parents had always been very loving and generous. At this time, they could have been tremendously helpful to us in one very specific way. Our car probably needed new points, but we had no money to take it in to be fixed. In order to get it started I often had to park on a downhill slope. It seldom started just by pressing on the start button. Inertia would sometimes suffice to get it going. When it did not, our parents and Gloria had to get out of the car and push it until it started. You would think they would have asked what was wrong with the car and how they could help. They did not. It never crossed their mind to give us some money to get it fixed. Neither Gloria nor I asked for any help nor did we ever bring this up with them in later years. We just continued pushing the car downhill until we could afford to take it in.

Before the 1970-71 academic year got going, our Calgary friend Serge called us to tell us that he would be spending a semester in Merida, Mexico, for a research project. He proposed that we meet him and his brother, Michel, in Guadalajara. He had a car and was planning to drive all the way to Merida, making a number of stops to explore different cities along the way. Because my scholarship was from Canada, we were paid in Canadian dollars which, at the time, were more valuable than the greenback and went a long way in Mexico. We could do a lot at a very low cost. We made it to Tijuana and from there by bus to Guadalajara. The five of us visited the city, of course, went to Lake Chapala, and took off on an adventurous trip. We stayed in a number of wonderful towns and cities. We visited Mexico City, Oaxaca, Tuxtla Gutiérrez, Campeche, as well as the archeological ruins of Monte Albán, Palenque, and Chichén Itzá. The highlight of the trip was San Cristóbal de las Casas. As we were driving up to the mountain it was incredibly cloudy. We had very limited views. Suddenly, we rose above the clouds and, as if an apparition, saw the town from a distance under sunny skies. It looked otherworldly. We stayed at a beautifully preserved old hacienda with all its rooms around a splendid courtyard. We had never seen such colorful indigenous people. They were shy and did not want us to take photos of them. Fortunately, I wore blue pants and a pink shirt and was, to them, more colorful than they were to us. While they were distracted looking at me, Serge and Gloria took wonderful pictures of them.

We ended our trip in Merida. Compared to what we had witnessed to this point, Merida looked drab. We managed to visit seaside villages, where we had wonderful fresh seafood meals. Perhaps not all were fresh, come to think of it. Gloria got food poisoning and got quite sick. I, too, ended up with severe diarrhea. Despite our great discomfort, we visited the ruins of Chichén Itzá. Back in 1972 one could go up all the way to the top and sit next to the sculpture. What a glorious sight and view from atop the pyramid.

Barbara, Serge's wife, was supposed to meet us there, but she called Serge to tell him that she was not going to come. She was leaving him. We were all shocked beyond words. Jacqueline was particularly affected as she loved Barbara and was looking forward to spending time with her. We never saw her again. For Jacqueline, this recent disappointment came on top of all her suffering during the trip. Serge had to stop the car suddenly and exit like a bullet because Jackie had to vomit, quite regularly. She hardly ate and had practically nothing to drink. Water was out of the question. She did not like milk much and managed to knock the glass over almost as a daily ritual. Serge, who never really liked kids or knew how to even talk to them, suffered the entire trip never knowing when Jackie would vomit. I don't think Jacqueline has many fond memories of this trip. We made our way back to Santa Barbara by train and made a week-long stop in Mazatlán. The very first thing we did when we crossed the border was to go have hamburgers and fries. As much as we loved our time in Mexico, we were very glad to be back in the US.

I resumed my studies, of course. Gloria, who had become out of necessity an excellent seamstress, got busy making clothes for her, Jacqueline and me. Almost everything Jackie wore was made by Gloria as was most of what she wore herself. I was also the beneficiary of her talents. She made me two leisure suits, some tennis shorts, and a number of disco shirts that were fashionable at the time.

The summer of 1972-73 we had visitors from Barcelona. One of Gloria's first cousins, Benedicto, his wife, Ramona, and daughter, Silvia, decided to come visit the United States. I think they thought that they could see the whole country and part of Canada in a month. They spent some time in New York and then flew to Los Angeles. I don't know where they thought they were going but they brought very large suitcases full of items easily available in the States: cologne, soaps, and other toiletries. They wanted to see many parts of the country. We told them that everything was very far apart and that we needed to limit our choices. Gloria and I were also very concerned that they had become rather well-to-do while we were still living on a very modest budget. We took them to visit Los Angeles, Hollywood, Tijuana and San Diego. For some reason, Benedicto had come to believe that Canada was the dream land. I sincerely believe that he had imagined himself leaving Barcelona to seek his fortune in Canada. He was in a hurry to leave Santa Barbara to go to this imagined paradise. I told him that neither Medicine Hat nor Calgary would correspond to whatever image he had created in his mind. I could not dissuade him.

We packed our car as best we could, and the six of us began our long trek up to Medicine Hat. We had decided that we would see as much as possible along our way north. We first went to Las Vegas. Now this city was the epitome of their concept of America. They loved it. I stayed home with the two girls, and Gloria, Benedicto, and his wife, Ramona, went to a show. The following day they could not stop marveling at what they had seen. The real America. After a couple of days, we continued. It was the middle of the summer, and the heat was almost unbearable. We had no air conditioning in our car. Everyone was sweating profusely. About fifty miles from Las Vegas our car broke down. I asked the five of them to wait under an underpass where it was shady while I would get a tow-truck to come get us. We had to go back to Las Vegas and spend the night there while the car was being fixed. We were not hungry but drank gallons upon gallons of water. We were all dehydrated.

The next day we made it to Salt Lake City and went to see the Mormon Tabernacle. Benedicto wrote his name and address in the visitor's book. Little did he know that one day he would receive a visit from a pair of Mormons at his home in Barcelona. Then something happened when we were driving through Montana that Gloria and I had never seen, nor have we ever seen since. As we were driving, we saw two police cars by the side of the road. Some of the police were pointing their guns at a group of men who were sitting down and were manacled. The scene seemed taken straight out of a western film. Of all the places we had taken them to visit and of all the things we had done with them, years later, they could only remember and talk about four things: Universal Studios, Disneyland, Las Vegas, and the police scene. Those represented America to them. Everything else seemed trite and uninteresting.

When we made it to Medicine Hat, Benedicto and family had a difficult time hiding their surprise and disappointment at seeing the type of humble house Gloria's parents lived in. There is very little a tourist would see in Medicine Hat. We visited Altaglass, the glass-blowing factory where our parents worked, walked around the small and basically deserted downtown, went to Elkwater lake for a swim and a picnic, and to the Medicine Hat Stampede. They liked the latter because it was like watching a western movie. After a few days, we took them to Calgary from where they would fly to Barcelona. In Calgary we visited all the important sites, went to visit my brother and family. We also took them to Banff, in the middle of the Rockies, a destination for tourists from all over the world because of its inspiring and majestic natural beauty. After a few hours, they said once you have seen one mountain you've seen them all. So much for trying to impress city-dwellers. Finally, we visited the Calgary Tower, at that time the tallest building in Calgary. From the very top, the views were magnificent. One could walk around the glassed-in top and have 360-degree views. This would have been spectacular in and of itself, but, as luck would have it, we were treated to an unparalleled show. There was a storm and the whole city went dark. The skies were pitch black when lightning began. We were all in awe. It was a most unexpected and beautiful send off.

Upon our return to Santa Barbara, I began to question the assumptions under which we had operated to this point. I had anticipated that the four-year Canada Council fellowship would suffice to complete my Ph.D. During the summer, I took stock of what I had accomplished so far and what it would take to complete all the required work in the two remaining years. Other than the actual coursework, I had done practically nothing on my dissertation. I had to admit that I had probably squandered valuable time enjoying what extracurricular activities were available. Something had to change. I was further seriously concerned about what would happen if at the end of the four years I was unable to land a teaching position and was therefore out of a job and without any financial recourse. A change of strategy was required.

I calculated the inherent risks and made a decision. I would seek employment beginning with the academic year 1973-74. The Modern Languages Association met annually in New York between Christmas and the new year. It was mostly during that short period of time that colleges and universities conducted their initial interviews of those under consideration for teaching positions. This deadline forced me into action. I wanted to go back to Canada, but I could not limit my searches. I had to consider options within the United States. After exploring all the available positions in both countries, I became dismayed at how few of them were available for someone with a specialty in the nineteenth century. Our entry back to Canada seemed to lack doors or even windows. Whatever jobs were available in French in Canadian institutions of higher learning were by now mostly limited to expertise in French Canadian literature. I had none. The job market for professors, particularly in the Humanities, had pretty much dried up everywhere. The competition for whatever positions were posted was brutal. I applied to all the ones that seemed remotely within my competencies. Though they were all in French, I highlighted my ability to teach also Spanish. I also thought that the number of fellowships I had garnered over the years and the very positive letters of recommendation that I was certain would be written by my professors would make me a very competitive candidate. I was, however, applying as a foreigner. I did not perceive this as a handicap, but it definitely was for most small colleges and universities, which, by and large, did not possess the staff to carry out the legal and administrative work needed to hire a foreigner. If they hired me, these institutions would need to demonstrate that I was uniquely qualified to merit a green card.

Right after Christmas a group of us from UC, Santa Barbara, boarded a plane for New York. We were not necessarily competing for the same jobs so there existed among us a sense of common misery and comradery. I was extremely nervous and apprehensive. Besides, I was battling a huge hangover. Serge and his new bride Nelly, a French speaking Egyptian woman, had come to visit us on their way to Mexico. We had celebrated their nuptials with wine, probably cheap. I was battling more than a hangover, however. I was very apprehensive. I did not know how I would react to the inherent pressure of responding to the many questions that would be directed at me knowing that so much of our future life depended on the success or failure of my performance. An unfortunate accident had made me even more indecisive. A bottle of shaving lotion had exploded in my suitcase. All my clothes were impregnated with the smell of the lotion. Even though it was the dead of winter and incredibly cold, I had no choice but to open the hotel room windows as much as possible in a desperate attempt to aerate the clothes I was to wear the following morning. I didn't know how successful my efforts had been, but no one mentioned anything or received me with any apparent nasal reaction.

I do not recall how many interviews I had lined up. It did not take long, however, to come to the realization, after meeting with members of the respective search committees, that they were just going through the motions. They had no real interest in me. Fortunately, however, two responses were very promising.

The committee of three faculty members from the University of Michigan, Dearborn, made a positive impression on me. They obviously liked each other and conveyed contagious enthusiasm. From what they explained, the job was not what I had hoped for. Still, if they finally offered it to me, I would consider it. The second interview went very well. I believe that the person who spoke to me was the dean of the college. Unlike what normally occurred in these initial interviews, that is, a follow up campus visit, I was offered the position right on the spot. The position was ideal. It represented what I had always imagined I would want as a professor. To top it all, it was one of the best private colleges in the east coast, Colby College. Who could ask for more? There was a caveat, however. Three people would be hired on a one-year contract. At the end of the year and based on the overall performance of each one of us, only one would be hired into a tenure-track slot. The other two, I learned, were American women. I was not afraid of the competition, but I wondered how I, a foreign student, could compete successfully with those two other candidates at a time when affirmative action was already a focal point for many institutions. I also did not know whether these other candidates would already have their PhD. or would be like me, an ABD, an "all but dissertation" postulant. I promised that I would seriously consider the offer and asked for time to think about it and discuss it with my wife.

At every turn I found myself in uncharted territory. Everything seemed to be moving at vertiginous speed. Everything was new and challenging. I did not want to make the wrong turn and live to regret my choice. I felt the heavy weight of responsibility. Our life was about to take a dramatic turn of events. I could not fail Gloria and Jacqueline. I had to think quickly and create as many open avenues to the future as possible. Before leaving New York, I asked to meet with the three faculty from the University of Michigan, Dearborn to let them know that I had received an offer. I informed them that I had asked for some time. If they were really interested in me, I would urge them to schedule my on-campus interview as soon as possible. Not long after I made it back home, I received a formal invitation. Things were moving in the right direction.

Upon my return to Santa Barbara, I sought the advice of those professors with whom I had the best relationship and whose counsel I valued the most. Dr. Walker was not one of these, but as my dissertation director, I felt a responsibility to inform him of my plans and seek his input. Nothing at all came of our conversation. In fact, much later I learned that either his father or his grandfather had been the President of Colby College. Why he did not reveal this will forever remain a mystery to me.

Some of those willing to provide some guidance shared my concern about the three-person competition for a single position. Others urged me to stay at UCSB until I had my Ph.D. in hand. They argued that this would make it more competitive. Still others indicated that, given that the market for professors of literature was shrinking rapidly, it was difficult to predict the future and thus, as they said, "a bird in the hand is worth two in the bush," tantamount to saying grab what you can now and wait for better times for a more ideal position. Had I been single I might just have waited. But as a married man with familial responsibilities and about to turn thirty-three years of age, once again, I leaned toward what appeared to be the most practical route.

I went for the U of M, Dearborn interview in February. Coming from sunny Santa Barbara, Dearborn was anything but an attractive city. It was cold, gray, and depressing. The campus itself, basically a commuter campus, lacked atmosphere and was drab. The University was clearly organized differently from any other I was familiar with. Its administrative structure was unique. French, Spanish, and German were part of the Department of Humanities which, in addition to these three disciplines, included English, Linguistics, Philosophy, Religious studies, Art, Music, and Theater. It was a department that in any other university setting would have been a full-fledged college. It formed part of a much larger unit, the College of Arts, Sciences, and Letters, CAS&L. All other departments were structured more or less along the same lines, with many disparate disciplines within each one of them.

Interestingly, I liked most of the people I met. These interviews were conducted at times by small groups of the Department of Humanities. In fact, they were attended by some professors from departments outside of CAS&L. I was bombarded by so many different questions covering so many varied topics that I had to draw upon not only my formal education but all of my life experiences. It was at once frightening and exhilarating. When Gloria asked me how it had gone and whether I felt I would be offered the job, I had to confess that I did not have any idea. Within days, however, I received a letter expressing the hope that I would accept the position at U of M, Dearborn. I wrote back immediately with my acceptance. At the same time, I informed the dean at Colby College that I was honored that he considered me worthy of joining the faculty at his college but that I had to decline his offer because I had accepted a permanent position at another university.

With this momentous decision behind us, I concentrated all my energy and time on the courses that remained and on the preparation for the grueling comprehensive examinations, including the oral qualifying test. When the final results were in, I was gratified and proud to have received all A's but one. Madame Delattre, my favorite professor, had assigned a

B to the work I did on Stendhal. Given how rigorous and demanding she was, I showcased that B grade with pride. The only things that remained were to continue to enjoy the last few weeks in idyllic Santa Barbara, bid farewell to our friends, particularly David and Bianca Bernstein and, above all, Bill and Gaye Ashby who, to this day, continue to be among our closest friends.

Finally, I informed the Canada Council that I would not be needing the fourth year of the fellowship and thanked them profusely for their generosity. Without it my dreams of a higher education would have remained just that, dreams. Thanks to the Canada Council, these dreams had become a reality. I also professed my extreme disappointment at not securing a position in Canada. I felt deeply indebted to Canada and had hoped to repay it by devoting all of my talent and acquired knowledge to educating Canadian students.

CHAPTER V

Michigan, 1973–87

▲ ▲ ▲

GLORIA AND I HAD LEFT Barcelona in 1955. We had not been back to our native city in eighteen years. Jacqueline, born in Canada, had not grown up in a Catalan environment. She was about to turn nine. We felt that it would be a good time to introduce her to our city and to all the close relatives that we had left behind. We had a few months between the time I completed all the requirements for the non-official ABD, and when I was to report to U of M, Dearborn. I was still to receive the last installment of my third year of the Canada Council allocation. We could just as well spend this money in Santa Barbara, Dearborn, or Barcelona. It was an easy decision to make. We decided to go to Spain for a few weeks.

Before leaving, though, we made the relatively easy move from Santa Barbara to Dearborn. All the furniture we had accumulated over the three years was not worth much. We packed all of our books and our few personal possessions, packed our Datsun, and headed east. When we arrived, we stayed with Paul Crapo, my future colleague in French. We dropped by his apartment with most of our possessions and then headed for Barcelona.

In Barcelona we stayed for a few days with my cousin, Carme, her then husband, Antonio, and their two boys, Toni and Jordi, in the small condo they owned in Bellvitge, a compound of many high-rise buildings each uglier than the next. It was a conglomeration of people from all over Spain who had come to Barcelona for a more prosperous life. They may have thought that they had improved on their previous living conditions but to us, this city within a city looked exceptionally crowded, barren, and uninspiring. What we saw was not at all what we had imagined would be awaiting us in our return as prodigal children.

My cousin and her husband had planned a trip to Andalusia, the province from which Antonio originated, with many stops along the way. This was not going to be a four-star voyage. We would camp all the way, would eat whenever possible at the campsites, and only splurge with restaurant meals when absolutely unavoidable. Antonio worked for the car company SEAT, a subsidiary of FIAT. He had bought one of the larger cars SEAT produced. But under no circumstances was it equipped to carry the luggage, two camping tents, all the necessary camping gear, and seven people. Four of us sat in the back on the sleeping bags and inflatable beds. Antonio and I sat in the front. At different times, I placed between my legs one of the three kids. These were pre-seat belt times. It was pure folly and totally irresponsible behavior, but this was Spain in 1973. A sort of free for all with few rules and those that existed were meant to be flouted and ignored.

Despite these conditions, we loved the trip. When we had lived in Barcelona our family had seldom ventured outside the city. On this outing we visited Granada, Sevilla, Nerja, and a number of smaller towns, including the one where Antonio had been born. The three little cousins had a wonderful time together and so did the adults. We managed to stay at campsites that provided entertainment, dancing, and good, cheap meals. The only painful though somewhat funny incident involved Gloria. After a long luncheon with lots of sangria on a very hot day, Gloria began to feel sick in the car. She asked Antonio to stop the car so she could vomit. He did so in a hurry, but with such lack of precision that when Gloria opened the door and jumped out of the car with tremendous force she ran right smack into a tree. She was not seriously injured, but she knocked herself out. We laughed a lot later but, at the time, we were all concerned and worried. The rest of the trip was enjoyable and memorable.

Jacqueline got to meet a lot of our relatives whom she had only heard mentioned up to that point. She was delighted to know that she had many cousins, uncles, and aunts. She also realized that there were a lot of people beyond her immediate family who spoke Catalan. She had a much more difficult time with those who only spoke Castilian Spanish, a language she barely understood and did not speak at all. Then and there I told her that, once home, I would teach her Castilian, a beautiful and very useful and practical language. This, not always to her liking, we did until she was fifteen. Each day was a battle. Finally, tired of all the battles and having faith in her promise that she would continue to read in Spanish on her own, I surrendered. Of course, she did not keep her word. But I must say, she had acquired a solid foundation upon which to build.

As much as we had valued our reconnecting with family and loved not only Barcelona but the parts of Spain, we were fortunate to visit, we had no interest whatsoever in going back to our native city to live permanently. We would try to go back as often as possible but, ultimately, we longed to go back to Canada. We viewed our stay in the US as a temporary necessity.

When we got back to Michigan, we took advantage of Paul Crapo's generosity and stayed at his apartment while he was visiting his folks back east. The most natural thing would have been for us to live in or very near Dearborn. Instead, mostly because many U of M, Dearborn faculty lived in Ann Arbor, near the main campus and with easy access to U of M's fabulous library, we chose to rent an apartment in Glencoe Hills in Ann Arbor, a beautiful complex that included a swimming pool, tennis courts, and a few other amenities. Gloria and Jacqueline found our new digs a great improvement over the married student housing we had left behind. The weather in September was still pleasant. There was no reason to miss Santa Barbara's glorious temperatures. It did not take long, however, for the weather to turn ugly. Gloria had a very difficult time adapting to such a dramatic change. Her mood changed as the winter set in. She became somewhat dejected and had a hard time hiding her displeasure. I, on the other hand, had little time to worry about the weather. My new job was both thrilling and terrifying.

U of M, Dearborn was undergoing rapid expansion, which was surprising at a time when other campuses had ceased to grow because of an economic downturn. Throughout the country, jobs for academics had dried up considerably. This presented a boon for a growing campus. It was able to hire young professors with incredible academic pedigrees, many of whom came straight from some of the best public and private universities, including Ivy League Schools. Many of these ended up in the Humanities Department. Their friendship made my integration much easier than it would have been otherwise. Theirs was a friendship that was rewarding and uncomplicated.

The same expansion that attracted incredible academic talent caused a different type of problem. As a graduate student at UCSB, I had a grand office that I shared with a fellow student. He was seldom there, so I had it practically all to myself. At U of M, Dearborn I was shown what was to become my office for a number of years. What a disappointment. It had probably been a relatively spacious classroom now converted into a five-person faculty office. We managed to create some privacy by strategically placing metal bookcases that shielded each one of us and the students who came to see us for counsel. It was neither ideal nor acceptable but here was no point in complaining. This was our fate until a new building was erected and we moved to much better conditions.

This was my first disappointment but certainly not the last. In my first year I taught both first and second-year French and Spanish classes. With some exceptions I found the overall preparation of students, inferior to that of those I had had both at U of Calgary and at UCSB. I found it difficult to admit it to myself and I certainly did not dare confess it to anyone, including Gloria, but, deep down, I felt that the job was beneath me. Yet, at the same time I was ashamed to even contemplate this reaction. My recent colleagues with their impressive academic accomplishments did not seem to share my dejection. Did I think I was better than them? Had I forgotten my humble origins and beginnings? Had I become an elitist? Was I now so arrogant that I would look down on students who, for whatever reason, were limited to attending a commuter campus? Were they less deserving of higher education than I had been? Following a period of introspection and soul-searching I came to see that my role and responsibility was to give my very best to these students and help them realize their dreams as some of my teachers and professors had done for me. There was no time for self-pity. I had a job to do. I would do it to the best of my ability. I was also determined to make the best of what, at the time, seemed like an undesirable situation.

The first few departmental meetings left me literally speechless. Most of the dominant figures of the department were professors of English. When they spoke, I was amazed at the elegance, clarity, and command of their English. I could almost visualize the structure of their phrases, including the commas, colons, semi-colons, and periods. There were times when I felt like participating in the discussions and debates. But just the thought of speaking in their presence froze the words in my mouth. Whenever I was able to battle the actual fear and said something, I blurted it out; it came out in a torrent of indelicate utterances. I quickly gained the reputation of being one of the most direct and least tactful members of the department. In time, of course, I became less easily intimidated and was able to speak in a controlled manner and express my thoughts, perhaps not as diplomatically and beautifully as the most senior members, but effectively and even convincingly. But this did not happen overnight. It took time.

As a young campus, there were many opportunities to become involved in the development of an institution of which we could all be proud. Paul Crapo, my closest collaborator in French and a member of the search committee that hired me, Chris Dahl (who had been hired the very same year I was) and I, in particular, quickly jumped at the chance for valuable involvement. In a way, it was enthralling and intoxicating to provide what we viewed as an incredibly important contribution. The three of us, along with a couple of other new faculty, were hired as instructors, not assistant professors. All of us were ABDs. We were expected to complete our doctoral dissertation in a timely manner. Consciously or unconsciously, we fell prey to our sense of self-importance, so much so that we neglected this requirement and became even more engrossed in our service to the cause. We experienced a strong sense of empowerment. All of us succeeded in convincing ourselves that what we were contributing with our input was of such value and necessity that it was well worth postponing work on our dissertations. We were basking in our self-perceived accomplishments. Sooner rather than later we would pay for our self-indulgence and arrogance.

While all of this was going on, there was a rather urgent matter to deal with. I could not remain at the university for more than two years unless

I secured a green card. The U of M had an excellent legal office, and its attorneys were accustomed to the paperwork that it was necessary to file in order to obtain permanent status for foreign faculty. In my case they needed to demonstrate that I had qualifications that made me unique and essential. Being able to demonstrate that I could teach French and Spanish was not sufficient. The decision was made to add Portuguese and Catalan to my areas of expertise. I thought that moving forward would be a mere formality. It turned out to be far more complicated and certainly stressful. At one point I was summoned to the office of legal counsel and informed that there were quotas for Canadian citizens. I would probably need to go back to Canada, spend a couple of years there and then reapply for the position. This was not a realistic option. There was no way that my position would be held for me. I was good, but not indispensable. Gloria and I went into panic mode. As I said, though, the attorneys were good and creative. They discovered that they could make a better case for me as a Spaniard since there were no quotas for that group. They asked me whether it would be acceptable to me if they proceeded on that basis. It was an ironic situation. I had never considered being a Spaniard an asset. But lo and behold, in this instance it was a life saver. We were granted green cards. A major obstacle had been cleared. I could concentrate on some of the others that still awaited me.

As soon as we learned that we could stay in the US, we started looking for a house to buy. We found one that was small and old but had potential. It was not too expensive. The required down-payment, however, amounted to $8,500. We had managed to save around $1,500. We contacted our parents and managed to borrow $4,000 from Gloria's parents and $3,000 from mine. They agreed to be repaid on a bimonthly basis, one payment per month to each. With the purchase of the house out of the way, I could concentrate more fully on my situation at the university.

There was no major in any of the foreign languages we taught. Our role was always going to be secondary, an adjunct to other more important and established lines of study. I was lucky in that Paul loved to teach lower-level courses. This meant that I had the privilege to teach some literature courses now and then. I would prepare these courses with great anticipation. Reality always came crashing down on my expectations. Students could hardly follow the plot of any novel or short story I had selected. The language was too difficult for them. So, I often ended up having to explain the most basic aspects of whatever it was that we were studying. I was never able to teach literature. But literature is what I had hoped to teach. I would have to find one way or another a means by which to accomplish this. Our situation also created other more serious challenges for us. Unlike those professors in graduate programs who were able to articulate their teaching with some of their research, we would never have this ability. Our teaching and our research would never be combined, they would always be bifurcated, on two distinct tracks, rendering our expected output in publication all the more onerous.

As the number of students in our classes increased as the campus grew, Paul and I, along with the person responsible for Spanish, came to the conclusion that our students deserved to have more variety in instructors. To achieve this goal, we needed to free up some courses the three of us taught. I volunteered to ask the English section to allow me to teach some of their introductory literature courses. Over the years I taught *Introduction to World Literature, Introduction to Fiction, Introduction to Drama, Introduction to Humanities, Western World Literature I, and II.* I could not be happier while at the same time we were able to hire part-time instructors with incredible credentials. We convinced a young woman, Susan Nisbett, whom I had met in Ann Arbor and had degrees in French from Yale, to teach some of our courses. At another time, we also hired David Bernstein, my friend from UCSB who had recently moved to Michigan. When time came that neither one of them could continue teaching for us because Susan became a journalist for the Ann Arbor newspaper and David took a full-time teaching position elsewhere, we hired a French woman, Marie-José Bayoff, who turned out to be an excellent colleague as well as a friend. Eventually, we also added a new part-time instructor in Spanish. Though the actual growth in enrollment was not that dramatic, we managed to give the impression that we were flourishing in foreign languages. Paul, in particular, was determined to make French a model program. He became very involved with the Alliance Française, an organization that proved to be a great source of information and help. This association opened several opportunities for our students. Paul also organized trips to Québec. We rented a van and the two of us took groups of students to Québec so they could practice their French and be exposed to a French culture.

In time, we had to admit that we needed to become more creative if we wanted French and Spanish to really flourish. We contacted management in both Ford and General Motors, headquartered in the Dearborn region, and asked them to tell us what we could do to prepare some of their present and future employees when it came to their foreign language needs. They basically informed us that they wanted and needed people who could speak business French and Spanish. So, with their guidance, we developed a series of courses that led to a minor in the pertinent language with a clear emphasis in business. Ford asked me to teach courses in Spanish for their engineers and business leaders assigned to work in Mexico. I found the interaction with such people revealing and was amazed at the little respect they demonstrated toward Mexicans and their culture.

As self-glorifying as we were because of our successes and involvement in the evolution of the College, reality came crashing down on us in a most inglorious way. Even though we were instructors, we were still subject to the seven-year period during which we either received tenure or we were terminated. At one point I came to the realization that I could not afford to procrastinate any more. I started working seriously on my dissertation. As I had done with my thesis in Calgary, I devoted myself to this task with discipline and purpose. I sent Gloria and Jacqueline to Medicine Hat to spend part of the summer so that I could work without interruption on my project. At the beginning of the 1976 school year, I submitted the final draft of my doctoral dissertation, *Zola and the Democratization of the Concept of Decadence*. The main thesis of my dissertation was that in trying to discredit and belittle the works and beliefs of the main proponents of the Decadent Movement, namely, Félicien Rops' body of work, Baudelaire in his *Fleurs du Mal* and Joris-Karl Huysmans' *A rebours*, to mention only a few, Zola's own works displayed some of the very same elements that characterized the Decadent movement. They shared an aesthetic ideology of excess and artificiality. Their movement was characterized by self-disgust, sickness at the world, general skepticism, delight in perversion. Zola expropriated some of the most extreme elements of their movement, in an attempt to show their tendency to dehumanize and distort in the name of pleasure and fantasy, and by burying them into his own novels proceeded to democratize them. UCSB granted me the much-awaited Ph.D. and I ceased to be an instructor to become a very proud Assistant Professor. I had finally accomplished something unimaginable even eleven years earlier, when I attended my first university class.

The first winter we spent in Ann Arbor reminded us of the years we endured cold winters both in Calgary and Medicine Hat. Unlike the latter two places, where although very cold winters were mostly sunny and snow was white for long periods of time, Ann Arbor offered cold, icy, gray, and dirty snow. Gloria became quite despondent. I had promised her that as soon as I was granted the Ph.D. I would attempt to find a teaching position in sunnier and warmer climates. In the spring semester of 1977, I secured an interview at Scripps College, a private liberal arts women's college, a member of the Claremont Colleges known for its extensive interdisciplinary core curriculum and historic campus. I was very much attracted to this College precisely for its interdisciplinary curriculum. The preparation for the visit took a lot of work. All professors had to teach a particular course that included philosophy, history, art, and literature. I would be expected to demonstrate that I was capable of discharging this expectation. To prepare for it I read Bertrand Russell's *History of Western Philosophy* from cover to cover. The interview went exceptionally well. I became very impressed by the setting and the beauty of the campus and even more by the quality of its students. I had breakfast with a group of young ladies who taught me that teaching at Scripps College would be a learning experience for me as much as for them.

I was shown to the office that I would be allocated were I to be offered the position. Just outside the office's window was an orange tree whose oranges were easily within my reach. So far, everything seemed almost too perfect. When I was interviewed by the president, a very charming and cultured youngish man, he told me what the expectations were for faculty. Unlike many typical research colleges and universities, one could achieve tenure even if you hadn't published a book. All I would need to show was that it had been accepted for publication. I must confess that this frightened me. It had only been a few months since I had completed my Ph.D. I had published a couple of articles already but had not given a second's thought to the possibility of undertaking such an ambitious project as writing a book. Nonetheless, I was so very much impressed with the College that I asked for some time to ponder the offer.

Before revealing what happened with the Scripps offer, let me describe my situation in Ann Arbor. By 1977 Gloria and I had already bought a cute, old house in an established neighborhood, just a couple of blocks from some of our new friends. Since the house was old and the previous owners were an elderly couple who had not taken good care of it for a long time, Gloria and I devoted months of work to fixing it up. We removed old carpets to discover beautiful wood floors that only needed polishing. We removed layers of glued, old and stained wallpaper to give the house an air of modernity. We built our own bookcases, dining room and stereo cabinets. Further, we modernized much of the kitchen. The basement had been a disaster. Over the years, humidity had eaten into the cinder blocks that formed the foundation of the house. I had to strip all the scaling build-up of rot from each and every cinder block and use plaster paint to protect the walls against further deterioration. Gloria and I also changed the roof in our garage. Gloria's father helped me put up a fence all around the backyard and, at the ripe age of 75, climbed up a huge apple tree we had and without telling us trimmed its branches to the point that it looked more like a bush than a tree. My father also came to use his expertise in brick and concrete working. All together we replaced a backyard that looked abandoned, overgrown with bushes and other unseemly plants, and turned it into a very pleasant and inviting picnic area.

During the fourteen years we lived in Ann Arbor, we went back to Medicine Hat and Calgary to visit our parents and my brother, and his family as often as other responsibilities permitted. In fact, one year, I was very happy and fortunate to replace a colleague and friend of ours, Brian Gill, to teach a course to teachers of French. I truly valued the opportunity offered to me by Brian, who thought of me to teach a course somewhat outside of my competencies, and by the University of Calgary. I enjoyed preparing for the course and my efforts were rewarded by very positive evaluations. I was also fortunate to spend all five weeks of our visit with my brother and his family. Gloria, Jacqueline, and I were starved for familial love. These almost annual visits fed our needs. Jackie, in particular, loved to spend time with her grandparents. She knew they loved her unquestioningly, and she, in turn, ensured that she devoted as much time to them as possible, always conscious that the two sets of grandparents kept track of how much time she spent with each of them. Once Gloria's father became semi-retired, Gloria's parents came often to spend a couple months with us during the summer. My parents came less often, as did Juiio and family, but in all instances, we valued their visits immensely. What filled us with satisfaction was that they all liked our friends and our friends treated them as if they were family. Consequently, they felt right at home when they came to spend time with us.

As I mentioned, Gloria and I had also built a cadre of exceptional friends who made us forget the ugly winters and the muggy, mosquito-filled summers. We got together with them often for dinners either at our home or theirs, not just two couples but often in groups of as many as ten people. Our close-knit group was made up primarily of three couples and a single friend. Each one of them was impressive in a multitude of ways. Chris Dahl, a professor of English but steeped in biblical and Christian theology, went on to be a successful chair of the Humanities Department at Dearborn, Dean of the College of Arts, Humanities, and Social Sciences, at Millersville University, and Provost and then, for over twenty years, President at SUNY, Geneseo. His wife, Ruth Rouse, was an attorney who hated law and became a prominent social worker; Richard (Dick) Nisbett, at that time a young faculty member, was already a star of the Psychology Department in the Ann Arbor campus, has gone on to shine even more brightly. Malcolm Gladwell recently stated in the *New York Times Book Review*, "The most influential thinker, in my life, has been the psychologist, Richard Nisbett. He basically gave me my view of the world." Richard's wife Susan, at times an instructor of French, as I have mentioned above, became a journalist covering dance and eventually the editor of the newspaper she worked at. She was and is an accomplished pianist and chef. Harvey Hamburgh, a professor of Art History and film studies, went on to become the heart and soul of the Arts Department at Montana State University, Bozeman and his home the intellectual center of the community of artists and movie buffs. His wife, Robbie, who was a school counselor when we met her, went on to be principal of a school and the force behind and principal also of a brand new one in Bozeman. She has also become a published author. Ron Morash, a professor of mathematics, was the successful author of several advanced mathematics textbooks, a great conversationalist and my running and racket-ball partner. These incredible people were our friends. We could not believe how fortunate we were to be around them. Gloria and I were in a constant state of awe and wonder.

To these regular dinner guests were added now and then others who also brought into our social and gastronomic gatherings diversity of thought and conversational richness. One of these other couples lived in Livonia, about 30 minutes from Ann Arbor. Alan Baum, an MIT Ph.D. in applied mathematics, was a professor at U o M, Dearborn but ended up working at the Ford Motor Company in the technological and innovation area. His wife, Lonna, co-owned a physical therapy clinic and later in life has become a renowned author of books for children. Paul Crapo, my dear colleague and friend, whose commitment to French language and culture was recognized and rewarded by the Alliance Française as well as the French government itself with a series of honors, came to our dinners often as a single man first and later with his wife, Katie, a pre-business advisor with whom I would end up working closely a few years later. Paul eventually left UM-Dearborn to become chair of the Department of Foreign Languages at the University of Georgia. There were a few others, but I will conclude the list with Neil Flax, a professor of German and comparative literature whose interests favored modern literary criticism. He and I spent countless evenings arguing about how best to approach literature and what were the best schools of literary criticism. He preferred the structuralist approach and also loved Jacques Derrida's work. I almost abhorred these critical approaches, and I certainly did not think that teaching them to undergraduate students could possibly have any enduring effect.

We did not see eye to eye on much when it came to these debates, but we certainly had to dig deep into our intellectual reserves to convince the other. Given this cast of characters one can only imagine the stimulating, educational, multidisciplinary, and entertaining discussions we always had around the dinner table. Our daughter, who was always an integral part of everything we did, always told us that she'd rather be with our friends than with those of her own age. She explained that she learned far more from them than she did in her classes at school.

After almost four years in Ann Arbor, we were well established and, frankly, as happy as we had ever been. Gloria had started to work as a seamstress at a select women's store. Shortly afterwards she was hired to be in sales as well. Before long, she was asked to be assistant manager. The dejection that she experienced at the beginning of our stay in Ann Arbor was slowly dissipating. Our friends and the satisfaction that her job provided more than made up for the inconveniences created by the weather she so much despised. As we contemplated leaving to take up the Scripps offer, we wondered whether we were ready to leave behind friends and jobs that by now provided rewards and satisfaction. There were other factors to take into account as well.

I found myself going through a process similar to the one I used when determining whether to stay at the University of Calgary or transfer to UBC and spend two years, rather than one, for the same degree. At that time, I had opted for the quickest, most practical, and least disruptive option. Now I had to decide what was the shortest and most direct path to tenure at one or the other institution. I was convinced that at U of M, Dearborn I would be awarded tenure and thus job security before the age of forty. I was uncertain as to my chances at Scripps, where the expectations for research and publication were much greater. There was also the issue of annual salary. The salaries at both institutions were basically the same. But, at Dearborn, I was able to teach a course each summer that was well remunerated. I decided to take a risk. I would go to my department chair, indicating that I had an offer from Scripps College, that I was willing to accept it, but would gladly reconsider should my salary be increased. The strategy worked. In a way, the decision was made for me. I would stay. In retrospect I wondered whether I chose to stay based on the salary and those practical reasons I had outlined for myself or fear of possible failure at a college that expected superlative teaching and research. Future developments in my career would confirm that this was the right choice and that it was wise to listen to my instincts.

The belief that U of M, Dearborn represented an easier path to promotion and tenure was anchored on past history. This was about to change in dramatic fashion. Normally, all final decisions on promotions and tenure had to be approved by the President at the main campus. But heretofore this had been pro forma. Only rarely were decisions overturned. Then, Harold Shapiro was appointed Vice President for Academic Affairs at the main campus. He visited Dearborn and met with a select group of administrators and faculty. I was one of those faculty. He let us know in no uncertain terms that though a distinct campus with different responsibilities and expectations, we were all the University of Michigan. He would, of course, take into account that our teaching load was slightly higher than on the main campus, but henceforth all promotion and tenure decisions would need to go through him on its way to the President. Our work, particularly in the area of teaching, but primarily in research and publication would be expected to be at a level commensurate with the reputation and prestige of the University of Michigan. A new era began right then and there. I, for one, took to heart his words and became aware that as important as service had been it would never replace or make up for a sterling record of publication. The rules of the game, so to speak, had changed. My focus, therefore, had to change as well.

I calculated that I had roughly two years during which to accumulate a sufficiently impressive record of publication to be considered for promotion and tenure by 1979, six years after I joined the faculty. So, I got busy. In 1974, before I had completed my dissertation, I published a paper on the French poet Eluard and the Catalan painter Joan Miró. Then there was a hiatus of almost four years before, in 1978, I published a paper on "Baudelaire Judged by Emile Zola," followed the next year with one entitled "Zola's Democratization of the Concept of Decadence." In 1979 I also published two articles, one entitled "Arch Enemies: Zola and Barbey d'Aurévilly," (the latter famous mostly for one single work, *Les Diaboliques*), and another "Zola and Blasco Ibañez: A New Look." During this same period of time, I presented talks at different national conferences and published book reviews. I had published on French, Spanish, and Catalan literature and had done it in four different languages confirming the case that had been made by legal counsel at the University of Michigan that I merited the green card.

With a generous Fellowship from U of M Rackham, in 1979, while Gloria and Jacqueline were in Barcelona, I headed for Paris to carry on research on Zola as well as on Georges Feydeau. I had recently signed a contract to write a book on the latter and needed to become more familiar with his life and plays. I met with Feydeau's son, Alain, an actor who played key roles in his father's own plays. He shared a lot about his father with me and provided me with a number of documents, photos, and anecdotes that, though not essential for my work, made me see Georges Feydeau not only as a playwright but as a person. I also met with Henry Gidel, a professor at the Sorbonne who had just published a seminal two-volume study on Feydeau. This, too, proved to be a very positive experience. It was not always common for competitors – after all, I was about to enter into the terrain that he had plowed conscientiously and conclusively – to share information and ideas. He was tremendously helpful and gracious. By the end of my stay in Paris I had done sufficient research. I was ready to start writing. I was also ready for some leisure. Michel Zaïtzeff, who lived in Lille and taught at the conservatory of music in nearby Roubaix, had decided to come down to Paris to spend a couple of days with me. He wanted to show me a good time. The first day we just spent visiting parts of the city I still did not know well. The second day, however, he decided that we were going to have dinner at an Arab restaurant and then go to the famed Harry's Bar, one of the most famous bars in the world. By the time we left the restaurant I was already a bit tipsy from all the wine we drank. At Harry's, Michel insisted that we have a drink, a specialty of the house, called *pétrifiant*. What that drink contained I will never know. What I do know is that when we left the bar I decided to walk. I walked for a very long time because I knew that if I went to bed, I would be sick. It was all to no avail. Despite my best efforts to clear my head and sanitize my stomach I spent the night as sick as a dog. When I got up, I could barely function. I looked at myself in the mirror and I could barely recognize myself. I looked jaundiced. This outing with Michel had been a colossal mistake. Gloria was to arrive that very day.

When Gloria's cousin, Benedicto, learned that Gloria wanted to join me in Paris he proposed that he and Ramona drive her there and that after a couple of days we take a trip together culminating in Portugal. So, all three knocked on my door while I was still cursing myself for my weakness and stupidity. Gloria noticed immediately that I did not look normal. I had to confess my folly. She forgave me but none of them took any pity on me. They had come to Paris to do touristy things and I was to serve as their guide. We spent a few days in Paris and departed on our trip. We had a marvelous and comfortable voyage with them, particularly since they drove a Mercedes. We all loved Lisbon. But one of the main highlights was our meal at a restaurant that had been recommended to me that looked straight out of a 1940s Hollywood movie. It had several levels separated by three or four marble steps. If we closed our eyes, we could see Fred Astaire and Ginger Rogers dancing all around us up and down the marble floors and steps. Beyond the beautiful and elegance of the setting, the food was fantastic and the service impeccable. What pleased us the most, however, was the price. It turned out to be so inexpensive even for our cousins who were calculating the price in pesetas, that Benedicto and I decided that we would cap the meal off with cognac and a cigar. On our way back to Barcelona, we made a few stops along the way. What impressed us the most was our stay in Coimbra, a beautiful city and a university library that is a masterpiece of architecture.

After a very productive and relaxing stay in France, Portugal, and Spain, I was ready to continue pushing forward in my career. Given all these presentations and publications added to my almost six consecutive years of excellent yearly evaluations in the three areas under consideration, namely, teaching, research, and service, I was confident that the time had come for me to submit my candidacy for tenure and promotion to Associate Professor. Imagine my surprise when I received a letter from the chairman of the department indicating that the committee had decided not to put my name forward for promotion. I could not believe it. It did not make any sense. How could I have gone from six straight years of incredibly positive annual evaluations only to be turned down? It was unfathomable. I learned later that two of the heavyweights of the Department, both professors of English, had argued that my record did not justify promotion after six years. Their arguments, I was told by some who formed part of the committee, had been specious to say the least, but they were two powerful people who made a point of intimidating their colleagues. The two people in question who lived together claimed to be cousins when almost everyone knew that they were a gay couple. Supposedly, my colleague in Spanish, someone I had pushed to hire and who became a good friend and frequent dinner guest at our home, had let them know that in my published works on Zola and the Decadent Movement, I had displayed a certain homophobia. I knew that I still had one more chance to be considered. But, if the result were to be the same, I would be released because the seventh year was the final year. If not granted tenure I would be given a terminal year. At that point I could not keep from wondering whether I had decided properly in not accepting the Scripps College offer.

It was so distraught that I confided in my friend and colleague, Neil Flax. When he learned of the supposed true reason why the two senior faculty blocked my promotion, he made it a point, without telling me, to come to my defense and convince them, with whom he was close, that they were totally wrong. When the following year I, once again, asked to be considered, the department voted unanimously to tenure and promote me to Associate Professor. Gloria and I were invited to celebrate this event at the house of the two faculty members who had previously led the move against my promotion. I had to coexist with them, so I pretended not to know what had happened the previous year. In time I forgave them. Gloria never did. When all was said and done, I had achieved what I had hoped would occur: I was tenured by the age of forty.

By this time, I was well on my way to becoming an important and integral part of the administrative structure of the College, as a faculty representative. I was a member of a number of important committees among which was the Executive Committee of CAS&L, the one that met weekly with the Dean of the College. After 1980 I entered a period of sustained activity in the area of professional development. I published a considerable number of articles, made presentations nationally and internationally, was awarded a number of grants and fellowships, was an active member in professional organizations, became a reviewer for *Catalan Review, Nineteenth Century French Studies, Philosophy and Literature,* and, in 1983, published a book on the French playwright, Georges Feydeau.

In the fall of 1982, I was granted a sabbatical and another generous Rackham grant. I had the option of half a year at full pay or one full year at half pay. Gloria and I chose the latter. Back then the US dollar was mighty, and we believed we could stretch the grant and my reduced salary to last for a full year if we went to Barcelona. My objective was to do research on Mercè Rodoreda, Catalonia's foremost writer. We rented a spacious and elegant apartment two blocks from where my cousin, Carme, and her family lived. As soon as we got settled in, we developed a daily regimen that combined work, exercise, and pleasure. I went to the main library each day from nine in the morning to about one in the afternoon. Went home, changed into running gear and went for a strenuous run up and around the Montjuic hills, where later the 1992 summer Olympics would be held. After that, we waited for our daughter to get home from school and ate, as is typical in Spain, a late lunch. We devoted the rest of the day to exploring Gloria's and my native city. We had bought a book called *Barcelona paso a paso* (Barcelona step by step), and with this guide in hand we discovered parts of the city heretofore unknown to us. We visited whole neighborhoods, admired most of the turn of the century architectural gems, went to concerts, museums, and theaters. We became such experts on Barcelona that our relatives asked us for tips and guidance.

One of the most personal reasons for spending our sabbatical year in Barcelona was to allow our daughter to imbue herself with the language and culture of her parents and grandparents, to reacquaint herself with the relatives she had met a few years earlier, and to give her an academic preparation that would make her transition to college easier and richer. We could have waited until the end of her senior year and postponed our trip to 1983-84. She would hear none of that. She was adamant that she was ready and willing to leave after her junior year. This meant that she would complete the work of some grade twelve courses by correspondence while in Spain and while she attended school full time in Barcelona. She was undeterred.

We enrolled her in a private academy where she was expected to study math, literature, history, philosophy, and philology. Some of the courses were conducted in Castilian Spanish, while others were in Catalan. Jackie spoke Catalan relatively well, read it with some difficulty and did not know how to write it. She could read Castilian relatively well and had a rudimentary knowledge of the written language. So, she was handicapped in both languages for the level at which she was expected to function. Her first two months at the academy were pure misery. She came home crying almost every day. But suddenly, she started to go out dancing, to parties, and to skiing trips with friends. Overnight she changed from a painfully shy person to an outgoing, gregarious and self-assured young woman of eighteen, a birthday she celebrated shortly after we settled in. I helped her a bit at the beginning, but soon she no longer needed my support. Gloria and I were extremely impressed with the grades she got at the end. Where I needed to come to her rescue was one of the subjects for her high school diploma: poetry. She just could not get it. When I explained to her what the poet was trying to convey her reaction was "Well, if this is what is meant, why doesn't the poet say so?" She was quite literal. I would remember this when, a few years later, she wondered whether she should pursue a Master's in French literature. I advised her then to study something more in tune with her intellectual interests. She chose business.

When she turned eighteen, we asked her what she wanted as a birthday present. Her answer surprised us. She wanted us to take her and her favorite classmate and friend on a trip through France, Italy, Germany, and Austria. Since we had rented a car for the year, and since we have always been unable to deny her much of anything, and since she was doing so well adapting herself to a totally new life, language, culture, and family, we granted her wish. We all had a wonderful time filled with lasting memories.

Since Jackie was very responsible and old enough to stay in the apartment on her own, Gloria and I took a number of trips during the year to discover new regions of Spain. We had a great time. We had not been by ourselves since our honeymoon. These lengthy outings were meant to celebrate our twentieth wedding anniversary.

We happened to be in Spain at a historic moment. Franco had died in 1975 and since then Spain had become a democracy, with King Juan Carlos as titular head of state. But then, in 1981 there had been an attempted *coup d'état* headed nominally by the infamous Colonel Tejero of the Guardia Civil. It failed to a large extent because King Juan Carlos opposed it. Many were those who feared a return to military dictatorship. In October 1982, while we were there, we witnessed Spain's final steps towards democratic norms. Felipe González, a socialist, won the election. He became the third prime minister since the restoration of democracy. Whether left or right leaning, there was cause for celebration. One year after a failed *coup d'état*, Spain, against all odds, had become a solidly democratic country. For those who had been in exile for over forty years or even for those of us who had left Spain in tatters, this return to full democracy was an existential change. We were elated to have seen the process unfold and celebrated its historical importance.

In time, our daily routine became anything but routine. As we neared the end of my sabbatical, we spent a lot more time just exploring. We all did a lot with our cousins on both Gloria's side of the family and mine. With them we travelled around Catalonia, spent time at a beach resort, in Ametlla de Mar, and went to Valencia, where my cousin's aunt, my mother's first cousin, lived, to see the famous Fallas Festival, which takes place in March. It is a festivity that combines tradition, satire, and art, and culminates in incredible fireworks.

Our otherwise placid stay was punctuated by two almost comical events. About four months into our sabbatical, I don't know how but I discovered that because we were there as Canadians our legal stay in Spain was limited to three months. When I realized that we had become illegal "aliens" I decided immediately to visit the US Consulate. I explained our situation and they told me there was nothing they could do as we were not

US citizens. I pleaded with them. After all, I was a professor in an American university doing US sponsored research that would redound positively on the reputation of the university. They told me to seek help from the Canadian consulate. They gave me a contact person. Well, there was no Canadian Consulate to speak of. The person in question was a businessman working in Barcelona who functioned as part time consul. He was empathetic but said there was little he could do. The solution was to go back to the States and re-enter Spain for another three months. We panicked. We could not afford such an expenditure for the three of us. He then suggested something somewhat sneaky. Why not drive to Perpignan for a day, cross back into Spain and make sure the border patrol officers stamped our passports. This would allow us three more months at the end of which time we could repeat the trick. We considered this a great suggestion. After spending a wonderful day in Perpignan, we made our way back to Barcelona. At the border they waved us through. I stopped and asked them to stamp our passports. They became suspicious. Why did I need the stamp, they asked? I responded that we wanted to show our friends back home how many countries we had visited by displaying our passports full of foreign stamps. They looked us over, spent some time wondering about us, but they finally made us happy. After this experience we decided that we would risk being in Spain illegally. After all, who was going to think of us as foreigners? We looked like the rest of the people and spoke Catalan.

Before we left Ann Arbor, I had done some research and read somewhere that, if we were going to be traveling through Europe it would be wise to be in possession of an international driver's permit. I submitted all the required documentation to some agency and received a beautiful and official-looking permit. We only had to use it once, but I did it caused tremendous confusion. On one of our exploratory trips through Spain, I was stopped by a Guardia Civil on a powerful motorcycle. Apparently, I had done something illegal. He asked to see my driver's permit. I gave him the international one. He has never seen such a thing. He wanted a real one. I submitted to him my Michigan one. He was puzzled. He wanted to see the car's registration. I told him that we had rented the car for a year from my aunt's friend. I could show him the letter she had written to demonstrate that I had not stolen the car and was driving it with her permission. He was getting a bit frustrated, it was obvious. Then he asked whether we had any other documentation, like a NDI, National Identity Card. I said no, but we had our passports. He asked to see them. The rest of the conversation went something like this:

> Police: *I see that you have a Canadian passport, but you were born in Barcelona, correct?*
> Me: *Yes, sir.*
> Police: *So, you are Spaniards, correct?*
> Me: *Well, not really.*
> Police: *What do you mean, not really?*
> Me: *Well, you see, we became Canadian citizens in 1965 and gave up our Spanish citizenship.*
> Police: *But didn't you say you are a professor in an American university doing research here?*
> Me: *Yes, sir.*
> Police: *Ok, let me see if I understand this. You are both Catalan, I can tell by your way of speaking Castilian. You are living in the US but are Canadian citizens. You are driving a car that isn't really yours, although you have a letter that you yourself could have written. For all I know, you could have stolen the car. On top of this, your driver's permit is not recognizable to me. Have I got it right?*
> Me: *I guess you have it nailed down.*
> Police: *Give me some time to sort this out.*

With this, he took the passports, the two driver's licenses, and the letter indicating that I had a right to drive the car. From my sideview mirror I could see him shuffle the papers going from one to the other, not knowing what to do with them. He scratched his head for a while and walked back to my side of the car. He gave all the documents back to me and simply said: *Drive carefully.* And, with that, he got on his motorcycle and left. We could have ended up in trouble but instead Gloria and I had a good belly laugh.

While in Barcelona we also hosted visitors from France and back home. Michel Zaïtzeff came in February of 1983 to spend a few days with us. February of that year turned out to be one of the coldest months ever. We even had snow, a very unusual sight in Barcelona. Our apartment did not have a heating system. Consequently, as temperatures dipped, we got colder and colder, so much so that we decided to get a propane heater. I guess we were not the only ones to have had this brilliant idea. By the time Michel and I went to get a propane tank most places had sold out of them. We spent hours going from place to place with the same sinking feeling: every store was sold out. Finally, after many hours of walking we were lucky to find a place that had one left. We took it home as if it were one of the greatest treasures we had ever discovered. It did not heat the apartment, of course. But we were able to huddle together in front of it and be warm for as long as we sat there. Going to our respective bedrooms at night, however, was a different story. We used every conceivable piece of cloth to pile on top of our beds to keep warm. Fortunately for all of us, the cold spell lasted only for about ten days, but while it lasted, we suffered tremendously. For the first time since we had left Ann Arbor, we missed our home. Not that our home in Ann Arbor provided us with exceptional warmth during Michigan's very cold winters. The house had no insulation at all. But our fireplace and the heating system functioned well, and we did manage to feel protected against the cold. Gloria, Jackie, and I laughed and said that this episode would be just one more experience that would make our year-long stay in Barcelona unforgettable.

Besides Michel, we had several other guests. Jacqueline had her best friend from junior high come stay with us for a couple of weeks. She was happy to function as a guide and show her the city that she was beginning to love as if she had been born there. Our friends Chris and Ruth also came for a few days, explored Barcelona with us, ate fantastic meals in historic restaurants, and we introduced them to our relatives, who referred to them as the giants, since both are well over six feet tall. We then took a wonderful trip through the Pyrenees Mountains, stopping along the way at quaint little mountainous villages, on our way to Madrid, where Chris' sister lived with her Spanish husband, Alfonso. From there we went to

Cuenca, famous for its *casas colgadas*, or hanging houses, and into the town where Alfonso, Chris Dahl's brother-in-law, was born, Carrascosa de la Sierra. We spent a few days there in an environment that seemed to take us back to an idyllic and remote time. We were woken up each morning by the sound of cows rumbling along the main street. The overall impression could not have been any more bucolic. Alfonso also took us to the surrounding mountains where we found a large piece of tourmaline crystal that I kept for many years.

While we were basking in the glow we experienced almost daily, I received a letter asking me to consider being the Humanities department chair. I had been acting chair for a few months the previous summer and some colleagues must have thought I managed the responsibilities well and nominated me for the post. I thanked them for placing their faith in me but informed them that I had no interest in administrative responsibilities. Truth be told, I did not have a very high opinion of the administrators with whom I had to deal. To me, more than a few were more interested in self-aggrandizement and in feathering their own personal nests and the nests of their own departments than in supporting faculty and in providing the best environment for the education of our students. Over the years, however, I have learned that one should never close doors. Adaptability and flexibility are good qualities to have.

When we got back to Ann Arbor, we were happy to be surrounded by our friends, of course, but all three of us agreed that 1982-83 was the best single year of our lives. Neither our daughter's nor our opinion has changed one iota in the intervening years. In fact, the three of us were reminiscing recently and we all still agreed that that year could never be duplicated. Our incredibly positive experience, however, carried serious drawbacks as well. Jacqueline, who had left as a girl and came back home as a woman, found that her first year at the University of Michigan was a disappointment in every respect. Her social life was dismal compared to the joyous times she had lived through in Barcelona. Her classmates were less worldly and interesting. The courses themselves were less demanding. She got used to her life back at home, of course, particularly when she found a Puerto Rican boyfriend. She would now have a great opportunity to showcase her newly acquired mastery of Castilian Spanish.

For her part, Gloria opted not to go back to work at the women's clothing store. Instead, she registered at Eastern Michigan University in bookkeeping and accounting courses. After completing the work there, she took a position in a local bank. As I will recount later, this new job did not lack excitement.

Like Jacqueline and Gloria, I, too, was not immune to this sense of loss for what we had left behind in Barcelona. I could not see myself doing what I had been doing before the sabbatical for the rest of my working life. I questioned the value of my publications. What kind of an impact could they possibly have? How many people read them? How much did I add to the body of knowledge on any particular author or topic? Would I have to continue teaching French and Spanish language courses sprinkled with the occasional Introduction to literature ones that I was able to "borrow" from the English Department? These questions kept nagging at me. Of course, I had little choice but to continue and I did so quite successfully. But I cannot say that I was content or happy at work. My doubts persisted. In my heart of hearts, I felt a certain emptiness. Was this just the aftermath of a year filled with wonder and happiness? I hoped so.

Despite my hesitation and doubts, I continued to be active in the three areas on which we were evaluated on a yearly basis. Year after year I was praised for my teaching, service, and scholarship. I continued to be an active researcher. Between 1980 and 1988 I published a number of articles on French, Catalan and Spanish authors as well as on comparative literature. Furthermore, I had two entries that appeared in *The Book of Days*, a publication out of Ann Arbor, Pierian Press. I also authored seven reviews published in four different professional journals and made numerous presentations at conferences in the US and Europe.

CAS&L now had a new dean, Victor Wong. He had been a Physics professor at the Ann Arbor campus who, somehow, moved or was moved to the Dearborn branch. He was full of new ideas, among them, the digitalization of many of the activities and functions we still conducted the old-fashioned way. He also thought that the College was not doing enough to advise, guide, and counsel students, particularly entering ones, many of whom were first generation. He appointed an associate dean to oversee this important function. Gene Grewe had been the chair of the Humanities Department, and an ex-military man whose main asset was to keep the trains on time, so to speak. He inherited an office that was composed of several women, some more experienced than others, but all with great passion and dedication to students. He held this position for two years from 1982 to 1984.

When he retired, he came to see me. He said that he had observed how I discharged my responsibilities first as a member of the College Executive Committee and later as acting department chair. He thought that I would be an excellent replacement for him and, if I was willing to consider the post, he would speak to the dean and would recommend me. I was more than surprised. I was stunned. I thought I had made it clear that I wasn't interested in administration. Besides, I considered the job he held as a dead end, without any appeal whatsoever. Still, I remembered the advice I had given myself never to say never and always leave a door open, just in case. I inquired about the specifics of his responsibilities and, in passing, about the salary that would accompany the job. It was a twelve-month appointment against the nine-month one for faculty. But there would still be an opportunity to teach a summer course, which I had been doing for several years to supplement my annual salary. I learned that I would be making about $8,000 more per year. This seemed like a fortune to me. Suddenly, the job did not seem as stultifying as I had supposed. I told Gene that I would need to give his proposal some serious consideration.

When I got home Gloria and I had a good discussion and, as usual, she indicated that she would support any decision I took. Consequently, I made a list of the pluses and minuses of leaning in one direction or the other. I also decided to seek the advice and input of some of the friends and colleagues I trusted the most. Almost to a person they warned me that this position, particularly as defined, was a dead end. Why, they proffered, would I want to assume a responsibility that represented little more than running an office made up of women whose sole responsibility was, as they put it, to direct the traffic of students. This was clearly a put-down on the job these professional women did, and I felt insulted on their behalf. What my friends did not know because I had not shared my sentiments with them, was that I needed to try something else in the hope of coming out of the funk into which I seemed to have fallen. There was also the economic side to it. Both Gloria and I were tired of always having to worry about our finances. I decided that the next logical step was to have a conversation with the dean. I wanted to know directly from him what he expected from me if I accepted his offer. He did not seem to have a clear vision beyond following in the steps of what Gene Grewe had determined needed to be done. I found his response uninspiring but understood that he would basically leave me alone to do the right thing. I would be called the associate dean but my main responsibility, as Gene Grewe's had been, would be primarily to ensure that the student advising was done effectively, efficiently, and successfully.

I began in my new role as associate dean in the 1984-85 academic year. I held this position for two years. But rather than be satisfied with what had been established by my predecessor I shaped the job to respond better to perceived needs and to expand my portfolio. I assumed that if the dean was not satisfied with the way I interpreted my role and what I was attempting to accomplish he would have plenty of opportunities to have a chat with me.

It took but a few weeks for me to discover that keeping the trains running on time was necessary but not sufficient. Much more would need to be changed and improved to make the office of Advising a smooth running, well-oiled, efficient operation. In my humble opinion, student advising could not and should not be limited to what the women in this office were able to achieve. Faculty would need to be involved. But as I was quoted saying in an internal university publication, not every faculty member wanted to advise students and not all were good at advising. But, for the moment, I needed to set aside this concern and concentrate on what I could and had to achieve first. My first task was to demonstrate to ten or so women who worked in the office that I valued and respected their work and that I would do everything in my power to make their jobs easier and to convince others, particularly the faculty, that what they did was essential. When I noticed that they were comfortable with me at the helm, I implemented a change that, in my analysis, was necessary, namely, that each one of them had particular knowledge and expertise that made them more suitable for some tasks rather than others. It was not only division of labor but labor that would pay higher returns.

Enrollment in CAS&L had not been growing as much as in other colleges. Without consulting with the dean, I took it upon myself to strategize on how this trend could be reversed. I enlisted the help of a few professors known for their enthusiasm and commitment to join me in going to the high schools in the area to make presentations about the value of a liberal arts education. For this I was armed with a good weapon. In my contact with the higher-ups at Ford, for instance, they had confided in me that those who climbed the corporate ladder within the company were not necessarily those with degrees only in engineering or business but those who were steeped also in the humanities and the social sciences. I convinced the faculty that joined me to emphasize this concept as much as possible. I believed in what we preached, and we were gratified to see that our strategy was showing some success. Our enrollments began to grow slowly but consistently.

In the Fall of 1985, I made my first foray into what I would describe as a wholesale change. What I planned as my next move, in my second year of tenure as an associate dean, was going to seriously test my ability to convince, cajole, and charm. I was quite cognizant that what I was about to try would meet probably with derision on the part of some, incredulity on the part of others, and resistance on the part of many, including the staff in the office of advising. For it, too, I needed not only the approval of the dean but financial support as well. I wanted direct and effective advising on the part of the faculty. I had no power to dictate what all faculty ought to do, but I could, with the help and permission of the Dean, select a group of respected professors, have them trained appropriately by professionals, and involve them directly in the art of advising, counseling, and directing the largest possible number of students while they were under the auspices of our college while preparing to move to whatever college their interests would lead them. I did not want to have to beg for participation in the process. I wanted them to either be paid for their work in this area or to be released from some teaching.

With this goal in mind, I created what was called CAS&L's Board of General Academic Advisors.

program aids CASL students by Steve Wasko

a lot of
chan-
nhanced
e factor
86 en-

l Letters.
rts is
t itself.
77 and
ad been
dvising.
s than
iL asso-
ently
t efforts.
vising
g Dean
ority
l CASL
o give
, and
nuch

CASL Pre-business advisor Katy Crapo joins Associate Dean Manuel Esteban and Board of General Academic Advisors member Gerald Moran in formulating advising strategy for UM-D's largest academic unit.

This was an important step to indicate to those directly involved and all those other skeptics that student advising was a worthwhile effort and one that carried recognition and plaudits. I picked two professors from the social sciences, two from behavioral sciences, one from humanities and one from the natural sciences. They were not expected to duplicate the efforts of the staff but to supplement them with more specific information, something I made clear to both the professors and the staff. I did not want in any way to undermine the excellent work the professional staff was discharging. This experiment worked relatively well. It was not perfect by any stretch of the imagination, but it was a good move forward. Advising was now on the radar of all professors. It became an accepted reality. Some departments began to provide advising sessions at the beginning of each semester and annual evaluations at the end of each academic year. By the end of academic year 1985-1986, *The University of Michigan, Dearborn Reporter*, ran a lengthy article entitled *New Advising Program Aids CAS&L Students* in which they heaped enormous praise on the new project. It also quoted Vice Chancellor Arden, the person responsible for all academic programs in the university, who claimed that "all these things taken together work to create an atmosphere where students feel a much bigger part of the institution, and where they are treated with more respect". He also credited us for "getting closer to the point where advising is seen as an extension of teaching, as it should be". Furthermore, the article continued, "advising had some positive effect on retaining a larger number of students". The dean called me into his office and, though not one to shower people with compliments, applauded my vision and efforts and the initiative I had demonstrated in elevating a function that had been considered only as the realm of a few female employees into an integral part of the responsibilities of most if not all professors.

In the fall of 1986, the dean announced that he had accepted the position of Vice Chancellor for Academic Affairs at U of M, Flint. There was no time to mount a national search to find a replacement. Our own Vice Chancellor appointed a search committee to select an acting dean for the 1986-87 academic year. I considered whether to throw my hat in the ring or continue in my current position, uncertain as to what the future would hold with first an interim dean and later a full-time one who could be the same person or a different one. This was an opportunity for reflection. I asked myself a simple question: What had I learned in the past two years? I had been able to identify areas of weakness, analyze the situation, come up with new structures and strategies, gain the support of the staff, seek allies to implement new approaches, persuade respected professors to join in a project that had never been conceived before, and ultimately show that I was capable of leadership. Probably even more telling, I admitted to myself that I had actually enjoyed the challenge and that administration in and of itself was not so bad. Only bad administrators made it suspect. Without realizing it I had made a decision.

A number of very senior professors who considered themselves the *sine qua non* of the College declared themselves postulants. They could barely hide their disdain for me when they learned of my intentions to apply also. How could I even pretend to be in the same league as them? In all honesty, I did not hold out much hope, but I wanted it known that I had the chops to stand next to them. It was not the first time I had faced bad odds. I was becoming accustomed to being the David against Goliaths. Since there were several candidates, a process was created permitting each one of us to present our credentials and to make our case. At the end of the process the search committee made its recommendation to the Vice Chancellor, and he called to congratulate me. I was to be the interim dean.

The 1986-87 academic year went by in a blur. It was obvious that I would not have much of an opportunity to leave a big imprint on the College. All I was able to do was to continue the work that Dean Wong has started. I introduced with success a few minor changes in the manner we conducted administrative functions, but they were all basically cosmetic and without great consequence. Any effort on my part to make substantive changes was met with tacit opposition. Department chairs and faculty representatives to the Executive Committee of the College had fallen into a wait and see attitude. They did not want to undertake any serious project without knowing who would be heading the College the following year. I could understand their hesitation, but I had wanted to move more aggressively in the areas I had identified as in need of improvement. In the meantime, a search committee had been established. One could predict that there would be internal candidates, probably some of the same who had vied for the interim position. What made the situation dicey for internal candidates was the Chancellor's expressed preference for external candidates. As he said, he wanted new blood. Most of us did not consider his attitude to mean that he was absolute in his decision. We thought he had expressed a preference, not an absolute prohibition.

Since I saw changes that urgently needed to be made in a number of areas, particularly in general education, I submitted my application for consideration. I was, of course, hoping against hope to emerge victorious once again. But I took seriously the warning from Chancellor Jenkins that he had a strong preference for a person external to the campus. I was not too certain that I would be satisfied and fulfilled going back to being a regular member of the faculty. I owed it to myself, I thought, to cast a wide net and see whether I was marketable as a prospective dean. I had good credentials both as a professor and as an administrator with years of demonstrable service in various roles and functions.

I identified about eight vacancies in other institutions that offered some appeal and sent my application to them. Of those, I received several positive responses. Some colleges moved more quickly than others. The University of Wisconsin, Stevens Point, and California State University, Bakersfield (CSUB) were way ahead of the others. They wanted to be in a position to make offers before their competing institutions were ready to do so. I got invitations to visit both campuses. I was received very well at both and was impressed by the respective administrators and faculty. While the other three colleges that wanted to invite me for interviews were still trying to find a suitable schedule, I received offers from both Stevens Point and Bakersfield. In the meantime, I had also jumped all the hoops that Dearborn created. I thought I had acquitted myself rather well. My fate was, of course, out of my hands. The search committee submitted three names to the Vice Chancellor and the Chancellor. I was one of the three. I was pressured by both Stevens Point and Bakersfield to make a decision. I went to Vice Chancellor Arden to inform him of the two firm offers I had. He made clear that his choice would have been me. The Chancellor, however, preferred one of the other two. I was devastated. I had gone from regretting having come to Dearborn to loving it. The Vice Chancellor advised me to accept the CSU, Bakersfield position. He knew that I was hurt and disappointed but promised me that, one day, I would remember his advice and would recognize that it was the one to follow. Of course, I doubted his sincerity at that moment, but time would prove him right.

That evening I let Gloria know that we would have to leave Ann Arbor and all of our very dear friends. It was up to her and Jacqueline to help me choose between the two pending offers. Of course, I could always wait to visit the other colleges. There was however the possibility that if I waited too long the two offers would be rescinded. When I told Gloria and Jacqueline that Stevens Point was described to me as a winter paradise, they immediately said: *California, here we come!* I called President Arciniega, at CSUB, to inform him that I would be joining his administrative team. My next move was to call U of W, Stevens Point to express my gratitude for their trust in me and to decline the offer. I also wrote to the other three institutions to let them know that I was no longer in the running.

In 1987 I was promoted to full professor. It did not remove the painful sting of being rejected on my first try at promotion to associate professor and tenure, but it did put me in a stronger position to request full professorship at CSU, Bakersfield, a request that was granted, but without tenure. Administrative positions were not protected. Tenure was. But whether or not to grant tenure fell to the jurisdiction of faculty committees. Tenure was to be recommended by the faculty and only then approved by administration. I was not worried, however. I was confident that I would succeed both as an administrator and as a professor.

There were reasons for us to be excited. We would be going to California, even though Bakersfield was not comparable in the least to Santa Barbara, to warmer weather. I was about to begin a new adventure, this time in higher administration. New challenges and opportunities were bound to keep me on my toes and engaged in a way that would leave little time for regrets. But this move was also painful in a number of ways. We were about to leave behind our neighbors and closest friends, Chris and Ruth, Dick and Susan, Ron and Paul. Even more traumatic was leaving behind our daughter. Jacqueline, who had just graduated from U of M with a major in political science and two minors, one in Spanish and one in French, had decided that she would not be coming with us. Despite having been born in Canada, and having lived in Medicine Hat, Calgary, and Santa Barbara, she considered Ann Arbor home. Besides, she had a good job, a boyfriend, and many intimate friends. She wasn't ready to leave all of this behind. Half in jest, she accused us of abandoning her. Normally, she said, it is children who fly the coop. Ironically, we were the ones flying the coop and leaving her behind. Gloria and I shared Jackie's feelings. We came to the same conclusion. Despite our earlier qualms about our move to Michigan, the deep and enduring ties we had forged with our friends turned the fourteen years we had spent there, without a smidgen of doubt, into the most fulfilling, gratifying, and memorable period of our lives.

There was something Gloria was not about to miss, however, her job at the bank. She had been assigned to a bank branch not too far from our home. She liked the people she worked with but being a teller was tedious and tiring. Boring, however, it had turned out not to be. She was held up twice at gunpoint in a short period of time. The first time, even though she had been trained to react in a certain manner, in the "unlikely" event, the trainers had said, of a hold up, she froze. She came home all shaken up. The second time it was quite different. She put to practice all her training. She pushed the alarm button, gave the robber a stack of bills that contained an ink dispositive that would explode. She did it so well that the thief was caught, and Gloria was given a reward. She was relieved, however, when she was transferred to a desk job at the main branch.

A few months before we left for Bakersfield, after realizing and accepting the reality that it was unlikely that we would get back to Canada, Jacqueline, Gloria, and I undertook the requisite steps to become US citizens. With all the paperwork and interviews complete the only thing left for us to do was wait until we were called in for the swearing ceremony. All we needed to do, then, was put our house on the market. We did and it sold in one day. Once again, we were ready to embark on still another segment of our incredible journey.

CHAPTER VI

CSU, Bakersfield, 1987–1990

▲ ▲ ▲

OUR OFFICIAL WELCOME UPON ARRIVING at CSUB was unbelievable. Gloria and I were incredibly affected by all the attention. You could almost touch the excitement exuded by the faculty, staff, administrators and community members who were present to make us feel wanted and consequential. Gloria, who had always avoided being turned into a public figure, seemed to enjoy the spotlight and became a more outgoing person, undergoing a sort of metamorphosis right in front of my eyes. In fact, she announced that same evening that she would welcome the role of first lady of the School of Arts and Sciences and in order to discharge her new responsibilities responsibly and effectively she would not be seeking employment outside the home.

We moved into a brand-new home on one of the hottest days of the summer. It was 117 degrees inside the garage. We had wanted warmer weather, but this was ridiculous. We were too busy to worry about the heat, though. Besides, the house was brand new and, compared to the one we had left behind in Ann Arbor, modern, sunny, cozy, and without any need for repairs or enhancements. I very much appreciated this since I was tired of the constant repairs that our old home had necessitated. It had two bedrooms and a sort of study/den which we turned into a TV room with a comfortable sofa bed. We did not expect a lot of visitors. Those who knew its location had told us that Bakersfield was one of the ugliest cities in southern California. It turned out, however, that a good number of guests came to visit us there. All of them loved our location, near the University, and found that the city itself was not as ugly as they had thought.

We were introduced to many important city dignitaries in an attempt to make us feel welcome and for me to understand who the powerbrokers in our new community were. One of these powerbrokers was the local congressman. Months later we would seek his help with a serious problem. Somehow, Immigration had either misplaced or lost our naturalization paperwork. It had no record of us. The congressman promised that he would do everything in his power to investigate what had happened. Weeks later he informed us that his efforts had been successful. We would soon be called upon to participate in the swearing in ceremony. We asked him whether he was in a position to request that our applications be transferred to the appropriate court in our county. He smiled benevolently but indicated that given the unreliability of the Immigration agency, he would advise us not to take this risk. We should just jump on a plane, go to Detroit and finalize the process there. And this is what we did. We became US citizens in 1988. We were relieved and happy. After eighteen years of living in the States, we would finally be able to vote in the next elections. We were elated.

It was shortly after this momentous event that our daughter called us to say that, if we did not mind, she would come to live with us for a period of time. She and her boyfriend had decided that they should take some time to ponder about their future. How could we possibly have any objection? We welcomed her with open arms. She ended up spending two years with us. Gloria and I were happy and settled but her arrival and time with us made those two years brighter and filled with joy. While there, she was admitted to the Business School and completed the MBA program in Management. But I am getting ahead of myself.

As I had started to do as soon as I became Associate Dean in Ann Arbor, I attempted to hit the ground running in Bakersfield by having a series of systematic meetings with all the various constituencies. There were two constituencies that were new to me. Both faculty and staff were unionized. It was, therefore, not sufficient to speak to faculty groups to get a feel for what faculty and staff thought. I would also need to meet with union representatives to gauge their perspectives. In any event, my goal was to listen and learn. I wanted to get a feel for the institution and a sense for what would be the issues that required immediate attention and those that could wait. It did not take long to ascertain that the School faced a substantial number of challenges and needs. Rather than be intimidated by them I judged them as great opportunities to face them head-on and make a difference.

One thing became obvious from the outset. Everyone wanted and expected me to be different from my predecessor who had been at the job since the inception of the School. He was depicted as a benevolent autocrat. He did not manage through consultation. He ruled with a strong grip, to put it mildly. I immediately allayed whatever concerns they might have had concerning my administrative style. It was obvious that I would be consultative since I was right then and there consulting them and listening to their views, concerns, aspirations, and objectives.

There was a lot to learn. The California State University functioned quite differently in almost every respect from the University of Michigan. Even though there was much to learn I needed to take charge without delay. How much was expected of me became crystal clear when I was handed the Performance Appraisal Summary that I would need to submit to the VP for Academic Affairs on an annual basis. It delineated the areas under which I would be evaluated and thus what my duties and responsibilities were going to be. As an associate dean and later as acting dean at U of M, Dearborn I was never formally evaluated. In my new role, it would be quite different. The process was comprehensive and exhaustive. I was going to be reviewed in no fewer than eight different areas. How I would manage:

1) human resources,
2) financial and material resources,
3) systems and operations,
4) information/communication,
5) opportunities for affirmative action/equal employment. There were three additional areas:
6) demonstrate ability to produce work that was of quality and quantity,
7) show ability in problem solving, and

8) an all-encompassing self-evaluation comprising growth as an administrator, and commitment to identified goals and projects.

As I started to understand the complexity of my job, I concluded that I would need an associate dean. I hired Edwin Sasaki, a professor of psychology. Time would demonstrate that I had made an excellent choice. We worked very well together. We made an excellent team. With his intimate knowledge of the School and with his counsel I was able to identify several necessary changes. He was also willing to assume some of the most difficult and onerous tasks we faced. At one point I asked him to become the interim chair of the Department of Biology. It was a great department, probably one of the best in the School but some of the faculty were reactionary and obdurate. They opposed any effort to diversify the faculty. They held the belief that diversification was tantamount to lowering standards. They made Ed's brief interim chairmanship a living hell, to the point that I feared for Ed's health. In time, and as Ed and I instituted some of the changes we felt were essential for the better functioning of the School, they relented somewhat. Our relationship with some of the senior members of this particular department, however, was never a smooth one; thorny would best describe it.

The innovations I proposed were meant to improve the actual administration of the School, enhance recruitment, advising and program development, modernize equipment and facilities, encourage long term planning, diversify the faculty, foment, and increase participation in research, grants and contracts, introduce a better, more transparent and equitable system of resource allocation, and seek a better relationship with the local newspaper and the community as a whole. It was a very daring, ambitious and multi-targeted plan but one that, if successful, could prove to be a good model to follow. Before anything else, however, I sensed that without understanding the methodology undergirding the allocation of resources from the State to the California State University system and from there to the twenty campuses and then within each campus, and in particular, CSUB, it would be almost impossible to achieve many of the objectives I had set for the School of Arts and Sciences. I must admit that notwithstanding my efforts, even after a few years, I continued to view budgeting in the CSU as a byzantine and labyrinthian process offensive to my acute need for clarity and transparency. Since I was in no position to effect any change at the system level, I was committed to introduce clarity and transparency at my level. In my first year I directed my attention to correct past inequities. My plan was met with overwhelming approval. Henceforth, my job became easier as I had gained the trust of most of the faculty. A lesson I had already learned as acting dean is that one cannot order faculty; one has to show and convince them that the direction in which one wants to head is the one that makes sense for all concerned.

As I was informed, there was a basic allocation that took into account the basic, general cost of running the campus. On top of that, resources were allocated on what was referred to as FTES (full-time equivalent students), and FTEF (full-time equivalent faculty). FTEF followed from the generation of FTES. There were other considerations. Additional monies were allocated according to the mission and specialty of each campus. Cal Poly San Luis Obispo, for instance, always received more generous funding because of the very nature and costs of its technical programs. This type of funding, particularly as it affected the least unique campuses, led to what I judged to be unhealthy games played by the various departments to secure more funds. Since dollars and faculty positions followed FTES, it stood to reason that the more students a department could attract the more resources it would receive. The greatest number of students were found in the first two years, in general education. This meant that each department maneuvered to have as many of their courses as possible included in the general education requirements, not always in concert with what would best respond to the needs of students. I identified this issue as one to be tackled once I secured the trust of the faculty.

One way or another, however, funding in California was always one of feast or famine with famine being far more frequent. In times of plenty, it was relatively easy to administer resources. In times of scarcity, we were forced into retrenchment, cuts, and even elimination of programs. Invariably, this pitted administration against faculty and staff, college against college, department against department. In the sixteen years I worked in the

CSU I lived through feast and famine and can say in all honesty that the latter ages one rather prematurely.

When I attended UCSB as a graduate student I never understood why there was tuition and then fees on top of it. Shortly after I started at CSUB I understood why. Between the resources allocated through the State and the tuition, we were able to offer students basic instruction. Fees, however, allowed different departments, depending on the nature and expense of their particular programs, to secure additional resources that could be directly applied to enhancing their curriculum and offerings. Fees soon became as essential as tuition. Unlike tuition, fees were subject to different rules and regulations but above all provided greater flexibility to departments. In case I had not quickly comprehended those resources were scarce, and that every possible means to enhance our budgets not only would be welcome but expected, Vice President Dorer made clear to me that he expected me and the School's other administrators and faculty "to attract external grant and contract work, particularly grants and contracts which include reasonable coverage of direct and indirect costs." All of this was unknown territory and language for me. I realized, however, that given the paucity of resources, this was an activity that required quick and aggressive action.

Another possible source of revenue was fund raising. When I arrived at the CSU, few if any top administrators were expected to devote much time to this activity. As funds from the State dried up, fund-raising became one of the main responsibilities of Presidents and Deans. There were always donors willing to help, of course. Unfortunately, much of their generosity was directly mostly to athletics. At CSUB, for instance, a group of well-heeled donors raised enough funds to erect a beautiful building, to provide a spectacular venue for our basketball team.

The relationship between my predecessor and the Vice President for Academic Affairs had not been a collaborative one. In fact, the relationship between my predecessor and the other deans, according to lore, had been one of confrontation and animosity. I made it one of my goals to display and seek collegiality, collaboration, and mutual respect. I did not behave this way because I wanted to gain their trust. I did it out of a firm belief that cooperation is more productive than rivalry and antagonism. In no time I developed excellent partnerships and friendships with the other deans and demonstrated to the Vice President that I could be trusted to do what was right for the School and to follow his general directives.

University News

California State University, Bakersfield - Fall 1988

Deans share hopes, aspirations for campus

by Patricia Jing

Meet the deans of the Schools of Arts and Sciences, Business and Public Administration, and Education.

On a bright, hot morning in August, typical of the long dog days of summer in Bakersfield, the three deans joined in a wide-ranging conversation with University News. They spoke about their insights and experiences, their hopes for CSUB. All three spoke of the unique opportunity their arrival means for Cal State Bakersfield, filled with promise and challenges, an occasion for self-evaluation and renewal. They agreed that the 'smallness' of the campus community attracted them, as well as its reputation for caring and quality.

Michael Carrell came to take the helm at the School of Business and Public Administration from the University of Louisville, his alma mater, where he served as chair of the management department. Carrell said his decision was confirmed by the enthusiasm which students expressed and the collegiality of the faculty. On his way to interviews at other schools, his wife convinced him he 'wouldn't find a better place than CSUB.'

Adria Klein already knew many of the faculty in the School of Education, where she recently took over as dean. That was a 'big factor' in her decision to leave CSU San Bernardino, where she was associate dean of the education school. She spoke of the quality of the faculty and programs in the CSUB School of Education.

Manuel Esteban and Mike Carrell share a light moment as they take a break from duties.

Cal State Bakersfield! Everyone had transferred from another school. Those who were at San Diego State and UC Irvine didn't like the lack of intimacy, the lack of contact, the 200-person classes — and they really liked the quality of teaching here.

Klein: I also got to talk with students. All of them said what you were saying, Mike, about the small [...] teaching in particular, I went to

rules and regulations before you really can find that there is flexibility.

University News: This is a unique position to be in, to have three new academic deans. What do you think about it?

Esteban: It is an ideal situation. Adria and Mike are going to bring their own personal styles. What you're

Adria Klein settles into her new quarters as the school year begins.

VP Dorer was a good mentor to me and little by little not only did he begin to offer me greater latitude to make long-lasting decisions for the School but encouraged me to continue the same path by praising in his evaluations of my work the goals, projects, and plans I had espoused, developed, and turned into reality.

When I was associate dean, I assumed that I could learn from those more experienced than myself. In 1984 I participated in a three-day Management Development Seminar sponsored by the National Association of Academic Affairs. It was a valuable learning experience. I decided to follow a similar strategy in early 1989. This time it was a two-day seminar for deans, which focused on the "Changing Role of the Dean." It was during these two days that I fortified my idea that as a dean I needed trustworthy and influential collaborators and motivators to buy into what I perceived as essential and necessary changes.

One of the advantages of a large system, such as the CSU, is that it often brings together administrators with similar responsibilities. Deans of social and natural sciences, humanities, arts, music, etc., met at least biannually. At times these reunions were scheduled in the ample offices of the central administration in Long Beach. More often than not, however, they were held either on-site at some of the individual campuses or off-site, in some attractive location. Spouses were often invited. Gloria loved these gatherings as they not only gave us a chance to visit different parts of California but brought us together with people who shared common interests and faced similar challenges. As dean of the School of Arts and Sciences, I attended each and every one of these meetings thus coming into close contact with the deans of sciences, humanities, etc. As was almost always the case in such situations, I came to the conclusion that they were all more intelligent than me, that they were in possession of the keys that revealed all the mysteries surrounding the budgeting process, that they were so steeped in the intricacies of administration that I might learn from them. And, perhaps, I did.

One of the most interesting of these recurring meetings took place in a swanky restaurant in San Francisco. It was hosted by the Dean of Creative Arts at CSU, San Francisco. His name was August Floyd Coppola. His brother was none other than Francis Ford Coppola and his sister Talia Shire. August's son is Nicolas Cage. At this dinner organized by August, all his relatives were there. Gloria and I had a chance to talk to the whole family. One of the meals served was paella. August called us over to his table. He introduced us to his relatives and asked what we thought of the paella. Gloria and I were somewhat awe struck and all we could utter was appreciation for the invitation, the ability to meet and talk to his august family, and, by the way, we were able to inject, the paella had nothing to envy the best found in Spain. August was clearly pleased with himself. We found Talia Shire to be extremely shy, Francis Coppola aloof, but Nicolas, outgoing, engaging, and entertaining. August, too, was entertaining. In fact, he was a showman. He often arrived late at meetings. He loved grand entrances. I recall one particularly tardy entrance when he opened the door and came in dressed from top to bottom in white but covered with a red cape. A difficult image to erase.

At the same time, I was working hard on important issues at CSUB, I was also involved in education at the national and international level. In early 1989, for instance, I was elected to a three-year term on the Board of Directors of the Council of Colleges of Arts and Sciences (CCAS), an association with over 350 universities nationwide. Founded in 1965, its main objective was to promote liberal arts and sciences in American higher education. Each year CCAS developed a specific agenda. For 1989-1990 its goal was to develop strategies to recruit students, emphasizing minorities and women. This was a goal that I embraced wholeheartedly and with enthusiasm.

The Lilly Endowment Team,
from left to right, Manuel A. Esteban, Joyce Kohl, Jacqueline Kegley, and Charles Bisak
June 1989

By the middle of the summer of 1989, we submitted a seventeen-page, detailed five-year plan, the first ever developed for the School. It was a collaborative effort that grew out of the two comprehensive and detailed projects that three professors and I developed during our participation in the 1989 Workshop on the Liberal Arts sponsored by the Lilly Endowment, at Colorado College, between 17 June and 01 July.

I had recruited Professors Jacqueline A. Kegley, from the Department of Philosophy and Religious Studies, Joyce Kohl, from the Department of Fine Arts, and Charles J. Bisak, from the Department of Biology. Together, the four of us drafted a meticulous proposal which we submitted to the Lilly Endowment. We knew that this was a very competitive field but hoped that our objectives were worthy of funding. We were elated when we learned that our project was funded fully. We were about to spend two incredibly productive weeks on a professional level. Those two weeks were deterministic for the future of the School but, as I was to find out later, also on a very personal level. The four of us worked assiduously on two distinct projects. One was on "Recruitment and Retention." The second one was on the "Internationalization of the Curriculum." They were both very specific proposals that, if accepted by the administration and, above all, by the faculty, would systematically change the focus and the implementation not just of two major pillars of the mission of the School but affect every department and most activities. Upon rereading these two documents in preparation for this memoir, I am amazed at how precisely we were able to identify existing flaws in how we operated at most levels, what were the assumptions that led us to our conclusions, how detailed were our recommendations for implementation, and how prescient were our objectives.

In the two years I had spent at CSUB, I had come to the conclusion that there was nothing structurally wrong with the University as a whole or the School of Arts and Sciences in particular. The campus was still suffering from growing pains. CSUB had its origins in 1965, as Kern State College. It became California State College, Bakersfield in 1968. Not until 1982 did it officially become California State University, Bakersfield, a mere five years before I arrived in 1987. In many ways it was a campus searching for its unique and singular place within a large, bureaucratic system. What I and the three professors were attempting to do was to help the School establish itself as a perfectly good destination not only for good, qualified students and excellent new faculty, but also propose a series of strategic steps that would ultimately improve our academic programs in a way that retention of good students and faculty would become a non-issue.

With these objectives in mind, we identified problems associated with the recruitment of students, particularly "merit" students.

1) CSUB did not project a clear and well-defined image either to the community at large or to our potential student body,
2) our academic departments in the School did not "advertise" the specific nature and distinctive features of their programs,
3) not enough attention was given to the Personalized Honors Program in existence,
4) CSUB did not make potential students sufficiently aware that the School of Arts and Sciences was in a position to grant a significant number of merit scholarships.

We proposed no fewer than seven goals and objectives to correct the problems we had identified, ranging from enhanced and expanded articulation with high schools and community colleges in our service area, to increasing the role of the faculty in outreach efforts, expanding the curriculum, particularly courses and programs having cross-cultural, interdisciplinary, and/or international perspectives, increasing the number and amount of merit scholarships, graduate fellowships, and assistantships, internships, and cooperative education opportunities, and designing and developing brochures for each academic department and program highlighting strengths and unique features of each program, such as low student/faculty ratio, personal contact with full time faculty. We also provided a detailed list of possible solutions to both the retention of students, particularly to those who left after completing their general education, and of faculty who at times felt that there did not exist enough support to continue the evolution of their professional career.

Given the part of California where the campus was located and the inhabitants of the region, we recommended the internationalization of the curriculum. Some of our recommendations included: giving students a multi-cultural, global, and international perspective appropriate to their respective discipline(s), including an awareness of the interconnectedness of the world in which we lived; assisting the faculty to develop and expand their knowledge base in order to allow them to add dimensions of global and international perspectives to their courses; and developing a program that would systematically enlist the skills, expertise, and support of the Bakersfield business and industrial communities, e.g., petroleum and agriculture, which by their very nature are international in their perspectives.

Just as we saw a desperate need to improve recruitment and retention of excellent students, we also recognized that we were about to enter a period of fierce competition for limited human resources. We needed to have a clear understanding about how to recruit highly qualified and talented faculty and, above all, how to retain them and not lose them to other universities or, worse still, see them move into the private business/industrial sector. We estimated that in the next five years, as the campus grew, we would need to recruit no fewer than 50 new faculty. We outlined a series of steps, from better training to forming alliances with the business/industrial sector to lure and keep good prospects, to making offers that contained release time in their first year to establish a program of research or creative activity, and equally important, provide start-up funds where appropriate. Something that is now taken for granted, we also proposed the purchase of more computers with supporting hardware and software. Beyond concerns about students and faculty, we also touched on the need for better facilities both in the arts and in the sciences. Given the stingy method of allocation from the System, it was patently clear that a major push had to take place to dramatically augment the money from the State with monies from, for instance, the National Science Foundation, the Foundation for the Humanities, and from grants and contracts. None of the problems we identified nor the solutions we proposed were in any way revolutionary. They were basic, traditional and commonsensical. But what was usual and common at other institutions of higher learning was scarce or lacking at this young, growing university.

My three colleagues and I left the issue of facilities and resources for last. We knew that our analysis of the need in these two areas would require aggressive action and an infusion of funds that, we were quite aware, could not possibly come quickly enough or in sufficiently large amounts to address the desperate needs in some specific areas. The University and the School would need to find ways to raise at least five million dollars from external sources, a considerable amount of money, heavy lifting for a campus that did not even have a full-time development officer. The Fine Arts Department was in desperate need of more space, not just somewhere that had been expropriated from some unsuitable location. The Music Department was small, but its director was incredibly creative and had a tremendous following. Although we had a nice theater it was used for too many events, large classes and other functions totally unrelated to Music. We hosted a very successful Pacific Rim Film Festival in cooperation with the East West Center of Hawaii that required additional flexible seating capacity. A recording studio for the Department was also an unmet necessity. We outlined at least four or five other areas where renovations and new facilities were essential if we were going to grow and provide excellence in our academic offerings. And then there were serious deficiencies in the Sciences, particularly in terms of adequate laboratory space and specialized scientific equipment. The Biology Department was probably the one whose needs were the most pressing. Chemistry also suffered but we had just hired Dr. Michael Mikita, who became amazingly successful in securing funds for very sophisticated equipment. We were quite aware that everyone did exceptionally well despite the many physical and financial limitations. For the first time, however, we had pinpointed specific needs and a plan of action that, if followed, could place CSUB in a better position within the system and make it far more attractive to students and faculty.

VP Dorer was impressed by the plan, threw his weight behind it and hoped for a successful implementation. In his evaluation of my work for the academic year 1988-89, he wrote some very encouraging words that, coming from him, meant a great deal to me and pushed me to make an even more sustained effort to turn into reality the goals we had identified and set for ourselves. Here are some of the points he made in his judgement of my accomplishments: "I believe he is providing strong leadership to the School of Arts and Sciences. Certainly, his approach to hiring faculty has been exemplary. He is imaginative and creative in using resources. He has an excellent attitude toward engaging department chairs and staff in more meaningful roles and responsibilities. His sense of a dean's role... is excellent." He continued: "Dean Esteban is articulate, straightforward, and thoughtful in his presentation of issues that demand attention ... I very much appreciate his sense of responsibility and his tact and tenacity in addressing difficult situations. His sense of humor is a great help." Encouraged by his words, by the support I received from faculty and staff, and by the success of the five-year plan, I forged ahead, convinced that we were on the right track.

I was pleased to receive a letter from the president of Mercy Hospital, a major employer in the region and a very successful hospital. In it he informed me that Dr. Dorer had shared our proposed Five-Year Plan. He confirmed that he and VP Dorer had agreed to each appoint members to a task force "for the purpose of following through on many of the ideas we shared at our recent meeting." He believed that "there are opportunities for us to assist you in achieving some of your goals." Help for our Nursing program and our sciences departments was on its way. All we needed to seek now was similar support and buy-in from the many petroleum and agricultural industries in the area. I could not be happier with the results of all the work many of us had devoted to this plan. The future shone brighter. I should perhaps add that in my second year in Bakersfield I was recruited to join the Board of Directors of Mercy Hospital, a position I found both interesting and one that opened a lot of doors into the upper levels of society in the region.

While we were involved in attempting to implement at least those recommendations that were not opposed by anyone or did not require resources we still did not have, something happened that caught us by surprise. Out of the blue, the University was visited by a group from Barcelona. They ran a private college that wished to work with our School of Business to create a joint MBA program that would be accredited by AACSB. I should not have been involved in this venture, but since I spoke Castilian Spanish, Catalan, and, of course, English, I was asked by both the Dean of the School of Business and VP Dorer, with the President's

El Periódico de Catalunya
6 abril 1989

MANUEL A. ESTEBAN, deán en California

El deán norteamericano equivale al decano de universidad española. Manuel Esteban nació en el barrio de Sants y ostenta tal cargo y honor en la facultad de Artes y Ciencias de Bakersfield. En Catalunya fue un chico de recados y vidriero de oficio que no podía entrar en la Universidad de Barcelona. Pero él estudió en Francia, Canadá y Estados Unidos. De haberse quedado aquí, no sería nada.

"Es imposible dejar de ser catalán"

C) JUAN VALGAÑÓN

Un catalán, en la 'corte del saber' norteamericano.

■ Manuel A. Esteban Beltrán manda en una universidad californiana. Tiene un sugestivo historial de publicaciones sobre literatura francesa, española y catalana. Preside la representación americana del comité de desarrollo de proyectos entre Catalunya y California. También asesora en relaciones entre universidad y empresa al Management & Bussines Institute de Barcelona, una de las aspirantes a universidad privada de Catalunya.

–¿Cuándo marchó de Barcelona?

–Tenía 15 años. Trabajaba de meritorio en una gestoría y mi padre me enseñaba el oficio de vidriero. Una empresa francesa contrató a 25 vidrieros de Barcelona y marchamos a un pueblo de Francia donde sólo había la fábrica de vidrio. Aprendí francés y vendía ropa. Luego contrataron a mi padre en Canadá y allí también trabajé de vidriero.

–¿Cuándo empezó a estudiar?

–Siempre había estudiado por correspondencia. A los 20 años pude examinarme del equivalente de COU en Canadá. Mi hermano, que ahora es profesor de matemáticas en Canadá, me enseñaba inglés. Luego obtuve becas de mucho prestigio y la vez graduado, la carrera académica me fue un paseo triunfal.

–¿Vivía de las becas?

–Sí, y bien, aunque los veranos trabajaba de vidriero y de pintor de brocha gorda.

–¿Y cuando escribía tantos estudios sobre literatura?

–Pasa que allí, si no apruebas en seis años, ya no puedes ascender en la carrera académica. Tuve que escribir en tres años todo lo que exigen en seis.

–¿Por qué se doctoró en francés?

–Porque pese a que tenía las dos licenciaturas, parecía que doctorarse en castellano no tenía mérito para un español, pese a que en casa no lo hablábamos. Y a los americanos le parece más difícil la cultura francesa.

–Usted ha escrito sobre Ionesco, Zola, romanticismo, modernismo catalán, Rodoreda, Baudelaire, Cervantes, Miró, y hasta de cocina catalana.

–Sí, y se me criticaría en una universidad que primase la alta especialización. Tuve suerte de que la mía era de Humanidades, y no estaba mal visto ser disperso. Era ideal; hacia lo que quería y me interesan muchas cosas.

–Entre ellas, la decadencia.

–Sí. Me interesan mucho Zola y los decadentistas franceses a los que llamaba parásitos. Él también era decadentista en sus temas y la influencia de Zola en Catalunya fue muy grande. Es curioso, porque Rusiñol y los modernistas catalanes admiraban a Mallarmé, Baudelaire y a Zola, que les atacaba por no comprometerse con la sociedad. La razón es que el Modernismo catalán también quería renovar y regenerar el país y, como Zola, daba mucho valor al trabajo, el estudio y la ciencia. Por ello aquí gustaba el Zola más mesiánico.

–¿Quién le enseñó el valor del estudio?

–Mi padre. Nos decía que estudiásemos porque nos enviaran donde nos enviaran, el saber es lo único que nos podríamos llevar y no nos podrían quitar.

–¿Cuánta gente depende de usted en California?

–Es una facultad de ciencias, artes, letras y negocios. Son 17 departamentos con más de 150 profesores.

–¿Quién le enseñó a administrar una institución así?

–Mis compañeros me presentaron a elecciones y aprendí sobre la marcha. Parece que no lo hago mal porque ya son cuatro años.

–¿Es buen vendedor?

–El buen vendedor debe ser íntegro. La integridad es vital. Es una de las cosas más valorada.

–Los especialistas en literatura no tienen fama de valer para los negocios.

–No tengo nada que ver con los negocios, pero doy cursos en Barcelona y presido el Comité California–Catalunya como excusa para estudiar más catalán y para volver a Barcelona siempre que puedo. Añoro Barcelona.

–Usted tiene nacionalidad americana, y los americanos tienen fama de ser primero americanos y luego otra cosa.

–No es mi caso. Tengo la nacionalidad americana, pero también la canadiense. No tengo la española pero soy catalán. Canadá y Estados Unidos me han dado todas las facilidades para estudiar y trabajar, y les estoy sumamente agradecido. Son países que dan grandes posibilidades a la persona.

–¿Cómo fusiona tres culturas?

–Bien, porque siempre he sido el español y ver una cultura desde otra cultura da una perspectiva que creo más objetiva. Mi hija dice ser una catalana nacida en Canadá y desea trabajar en Barcelona. La obligué a estudiar castellano, pero en casa hablamos catalán y pienso en catalán. Es imposible dejar de ser catalán.

–¿Qué habría sido de usted de haberse quedado en Catalunya?

–Cuando era chico de recados y pasaba por la plaza Universitat, miraba aquel edificio y me parecía una casa misteriosa. Sabía que no me dejarían entrar en ella. De haberme quedado, o no sería nada o sería un don nadie.

blessing, to steer this project. As the project began to take shape, I was sent to Barcelona to evaluate their facilities and the quality of their educational programs. They had wanted this visit to make a splash in the news. And it did. Even though all those responsible in Barcelona were Catalan, I insisted that the presentation I was to make, in front of TV cameras and journalists, be in Castilian Spanish. I wanted President Arciniega to have a copy of what I said because whatever agreement was proposed had to meet with his approval. My family saw me on TV and were very proud. I was interviewed by *El Periódico*, a major newspaper in Barcelona. They were interested in knowing how I had ended up in the US and had achieved such a high-level position.

I told them about my humble origins and the opportunities that both Canada and the US had afforded me. This type of confession was not typical. Benedicto, for one, told me in no uncertain terms that, in Spain, one exaggerates one's credentials and creates a persona that may or may not have any parallel with the real one. It is essential, he proffered, that one be admired, and to do this, one has to be willing to confabulate. But I had spent too much time in North America. I could not and would not betray my origins nor would I create a persona that wasn't me.

While working with these Catalans, I wondered how informed they were about the American university structure and system. I found it difficult to fathom how they had come across our business school. After all, though an excellent fully and deservedly accredited program, ours was not ranked among the top in the nation. I always suspected that they had mistaken us for UC Berkeley. CSU, Bakersfield and UC Berkeley shared similar abbreviations. But, could they have really been so ignorant? I could not bring myself to believe it. I also wondered whether in some context or another they had become aware that I had been appointed by the CSU Chancellor "to serve as the CSU representative to the California Catalonia Sister State Legislative Task Force" According to the Chancellor my "record of scholarship on issues related to Catalonia and [my] fluency in Catalan made [me] an ideal member of this Task Force." The relationship between California and Catalonia had deep roots. Gaspar de Portolà, a Catalan, had been the first Governor of California, both Alta California and Baja California.

In any event, regardless of how and why they had chosen CSUB's Business School, all the work that both sides of the Atlantic had devoted to developing a possible partnership came to naught. When we informed the Office of the Chancellor of this project, we were told to cease and desist. We could not risk the possibility of losing accreditation. There was nothing we could do at the campus level. The partnership died in its infancy. Nonetheless, they still wished to have some of our instructors offer business courses at their specialized academy. They needed, however, someone who was at least bilingual. As we did not have such a person, they asked our daughter, Jacqueline, who was about to complete her MBA, to offer a couple of courses. She was more than happy to agree to their request. How could she possibly pass up still another chance to spend time in her cherished Barcelona and reconnect with family and friends?

Since Bakersfield was not too far from Santa Barbara, we tried to visit our friends Bill and Gaye as often as possible, particularly in the summer. Bakersfield was exceedingly hot for the three or four months of the summer. Santa Barbara provided a nice respite. On one of these visits, Gloria, Bill and I went hiking in Sequoia National Park. It was wonderful. The scenery was awesome. Even though we were not too far from civilization we had the sensation of being far away. Tranquility and peacefulness reigned supreme. The Twin Lakes Trail, however, was a bit difficult. Gloria ended up with blisters. The following day she could not put her boots on. Bill decided to take a long hike while Gloria soaked her feet in a creek. The water was so cold that the blisters shrank. When we returned to camp, we saw a bear trying to get into the metal box where we had left our food and anything else that could have attracted bears. The ranger explained to us that, if this happened, we should make lots of noise to scare the bear away. We did. It did not work. He also suggested throwing stones but making sure we did not hit the bear. I wasn't so sure that I could miss it on purpose. The bear continued to ignore us. He was so strong that he pushed the huge metal container as if it had been made out of straw. Ultimately, he got tired and left. We were incredibly relieved. When Bill returned, we told him about this experience. He proceeded to report that while he was on the trail, he had come face to face with a bear as well. He was petrified, but the bear must have been surprised as well, as he rolled down the hill to avoid him. We had a good nervous laugh. We celebrated our close call by drinking wine that we had carted up the hill in our backpacks. The following day, Bill and I went swimming in the lake. The water was placid and extremely cold. But we both loved it and felt rejuvenated when we came out and dried out on the rocks in the sun. We had such a great experience that we did it a couple of times more, once again with Bill and another time with our friends from Eureka, Karen and Rex.

That same summer, Gloria, our daughter Jacqueline and I took an unusual short vacation. Almost as soon as I had arrived in Bakersfield, a local attorney had called to arrange a meeting with me. It turned out that he spoke French exceptionally well and wanted a person with whom he could practice. He and his wife Anne, a Chinese woman from Hong Kong, quickly became friends of ours. They were both quite charming and interesting conversationalists. In addition to his law practice, Dennis had a radio program. He talked about travel, tourism, and restaurants. He was given a contract to evaluate Hilton Hotel facilities in three countries. He and his wife invited us to join them on their trip. He had managed a special rate for our stay at the Hilton in Hong Kong, Kuala Lumpur and Bangkok. Since Anne was from Hong Kong, we not only got a royal tour but got entry into the private life of locals as we were invited to various meals and festivities. One of Anne's aunts was a famous local movie star. We got to rub elbows with her. At the Hilton in Hong Kong, I saw that there was a tailor shop that offered made-to-measure clothing for men in two days, at a very reasonable cost. I took advantage of this opportunity and had them make a classy suit, two shirts, and two safari summer suits. I looked like a million-dollar man when we got back to Bakersfield. We loved the whole trip. Malaysia and Singapore were fascinating. The highlight of the trip, however, was Bangkok. It is an incredibly vibrant city, and its cuisine is among the best. We had some of the most memorable meals we have ever tasted. After this incredible hiatus, we returned to our daily life in Bakersfield, not as glamorous or exciting but very enjoyable and rewarding.

I have noted that the two-week Lilly Endowment workshop was deterministic on a personal level. It really was. On the very first day of the two-week stay, we were asked not to sit around with our own team but to mingle and benefit from the knowledge and richness of the other teams and situations that brought them to participate in the workshop. I happened to join a group of four men from Humboldt State University, a sister CSU campus. The team was made up of an Associate Vice President for Academic Affairs, the Dean of the College of Arts and Humanities, the Chair of a department, and, if I remember correctly, the campus president of the faculty union. After a few pleasantries, they proceeded to delve into what seemed to obsess them, namely, their desire to get rid of a Vice President for Academic Affairs whom they considered noxious. When they inquired about the team I had assembled for this visit, they were surprised and impressed, I believe, that I had put so much faith in the faculty, given that almost all of them were administrators. Over the two-week stay in Colorado College, we met occasionally, and they inquired as to what my team expected to accomplish. At the end of the period, I was able to explain what we had done and how I expected to push for implementation once back in Bakersfield. We said our goodbyes and that was the end of our conversations. At least this is what I thought. Almost a year later I was to receive a surprising invitation from Humboldt State.

It turned out that all the opposition faced by the Vice President for Academic at Humboldt State University had either resulted in his resignation or his firing. Once the position became vacant those who had attended the Lilly Endowment workshop nominated me for the job. When I was asked to consider being a candidate, I found myself in a quandary. Of course, there was no guarantee that allowing my candidacy to go forward would result in a job offer. But, I thought, what would happen if it did? My work at CSUB was not complete. The five-year plan was a blueprint. It needed someone intimately involved in its development to guide it through. Some of the goals were being implemented but others remained because they depended on securing substantial funding that would probably only come from external sources. It was up to me to explore all options. Besides, Gloria and I were quite happy. We had become friends with Fred and Marylin Dorer and the other deans and their spouses. I did not want to betray their trust in me. We had also started opening our home to various groups. We entertained a fair amount, as part of my efforts to bring together many of the constituencies associated with the university. We hosted faculty groups at times, and community-leaders other times. We were going to need the help of the latter group if our ambitious project was to be realized. One thing we would not need to worry about was to leave Jacqueline behind this time. She was to get married in July of 1990 and would be leaving us to go back to Ann Arbor after the wedding.

The possibility of being a vice president at Humboldt State University (HSU) was alluring. I had always wanted to be part of a residential campus. And HSU is a residential campus almost by necessity. It is located in the middle of nowhere. The local community could not provide more than a few students. Practically all students live on campus. The University depended on aggressive recruitment, something that is relatively easy to do as it enjoys a great reputation. It offers some incredibly unique programs.

At that time its forestry department had no equal, the arts attracted exceptional guest artists each summer, the natural sciences offered esoteric specialties, in addition to the typical programs. Those who loved city living needed not apply. HSU was far from any small, medium, or large city. It had a privileged location. Nestled against the side of a mountain, within seconds of a redwood forest, with spectacular views of Humboldt Bay, it offered an almost paradisiacal environment.

I talked to Fred Dorer to seek his advice. He told me that regardless of my decision he would support me. When I mentioned the fact that there was still a great deal to be done on the implementation of the five-year plan, he opined that the foundation for a successful implementation had been laid. Our proposed five-year plan was very meticulous and clearly set the milestones to achieve. Others could take it from there. He admitted that he would be very sorry to see me leave, because he had enjoyed our productive partnership and our many racquetball games but agreed that HSU was a great destination. With my conscience somewhat relieved, I submitted my credentials to the search committee.

In the early months of 1990, I was invited as one of the five finalists to a campus visit and to undergo a series of interviews from a large number of groups with different agendas. The two-day visit was crowned by a dinner with President McCrone and his wife at a very elegant but quaint restaurant in Eureka, the historic Eureka Inn. I knew that President McCrone was a Canadian from Regina, Saskatchewan. We spoke at length about Canada, hockey, and Gloria's and my time in Alberta. The evening flew by quickly. I don't recall what we ate but know that it was very good. Both our hosts were charming, elegant, and engaging. But at the end of the evening, as Gloria and I retired to our hotel room, I wondered how he would evaluate me. He never asked a single question about my philosophy of administration or my preparation or even why I felt qualified to move to such a responsible position after only three years as a dean. He did not ask why I was interested in the position. He did not explain what he expected for his second in command. It was a bewildering experience. I did not know what to expect. He must have found me compatible and been satisfied with what I could contribute to HSU because when he appointed me as his Provost and Vice President he said the following to the local paper, *Times-Standard*: "Dr. Esteban is an innovative and charismatic leader who will make positive contributions to Humboldt's academic program. His considerable experience as an administrator, professor and scholar will make him an asset to the university and the community."

Back at CSUB, I resumed the painstaking implementation of our long-range plan as if I was to remain there for years to come. The secret was out, however. Everyone, from faculty to staff to custodian, to administrators, was contacted to find out what kind of a person I was and what were my qualities and flaws. I pretended not to be aware of all the gossip. Gloria and I also had some other type of planning to do at home. Jacqueline, who had been apart from her boyfriend for two years, went back to Ann Arbor to participate in the wedding of a school friend of hers. While there, she reconnected with her boyfriend who had not stopped sending her love letters and romantic poems. He asked her to marry him. She accepted but indicated that the wedding had to take place in Medicine Hat, where she was born and where her four grandparents lived. The wedding was to take place July 7th, the very same day Gloria and I had married 28 years earlier, and the day my mother was to celebrate her seventy-first birthday. We arranged as much as could be done long distance. Our relatives were placed in charge of everything else. Jackie understood that she was leaving a lot of important details to others, but she was undeterred about where the wedding was to take place.

In late Spring of 1990, I received the official offer from HSU. After I accepted it, Gloria and I made a quick trip to visit the campus again and to look for a house. There were few on the market, but we found one equidistant from the campus in Arcata and the neighboring town of Eureka. It was situated a bit removed from any major road, not that there were that many major roads around, on the side of a hill with huge pine trees that hid from view gigantic and magnificent redwood trees. To access the house, we had to drive up a steep driveway that made a circle around a type of rotunda. The house itself was not fantastic but it had a high-ceilinged living room with a stone covered fireplace that gave it a rustic but majestic air. We bought it immediately. As difficult as it was to access Humboldt, we immediately knew that we were going to host a good number of visitors. Gloria loved the area so much that, when we finally moved there, she would insist on driving me to work using the backroads so she could imbue herself with the misty air, the mysterious atmosphere that was projected by the many redwood trees and the general beauty of the area.

I had feared the reaction of faculty, staff, and administrators with whom I had collaborated so closely at CSUB once they learned that I was to leave after only three years. They not only took it with equanimity but set up a series of send-offs that left Gloria and me with tears in our eyes. The farewell parties ranged from the solemn to the ridiculous. We liked both. Both were meant to show the affection everyone felt for us and the pride they took in my "promotion." I remember in particular one of the ridiculous ones. I was presented with gifts that I would need in Eureka/Arcata: galoshes, moss remover, goggles to see through the heavy mist typical of the area, a slicker for the heavy rains. There was another gift that touched me in particular. Earlier in our time at CSUB, Gloria and I bid on a number of items, including for a parakeet which I made very clear we certainly did not need or want. We failed on every bid but, as luck would have it, we ended up with the damned bird. This was a source of mirth for many people. Well, in the ridiculous farewell, we were presented with yet another parakeet to keep the first company.

I was particularly touched by the poem Jeffry B. Spencer, Chair of the English and Communications department, wrote wishing me farewell. Given that she was a rather reserved woman, the warmth that emanated from her words touched me profoundly. Here is the poem"

There once was a dean named Manuel
Who suited Cal State very well,
But raiders from Arcata
Made him say "See you later,
Adios, au revoir, and farewell."

So, we mourn as we murmur goodbye,
With a sob and a groan and a sigh,
Hoping sooner or later
He'll come back from Arcata
Rejecting the damp for the dry.

Gloria and I enjoyed the bonhomie of the situation, but all the sincere good wishes made departure more painful. In a way, I felt a bit guilty. On the one hand, I would have wanted to stay and attempt to steer the School onto a more solid footing. On the other hand, I was attracted to the challenges of a new job and the reality of being in a residential campus, something I had always wanted and had missed. Regardless of feelings, we were on still another leg of my academic and life journey.

CHAPTER VII

Humboldt State University, 1990–1993

▲ ▲ ▲

BEFORE TAKING OVER THE VICE Presidency in Academic Affairs at HSU, Gloria, Jackie and I had very personal and important matters to take care of. In two different cars, ours and the one we had bought for Jackie as a present for her MBA, we took off from Bakersfield, first to Eureka. Gloria and I left our belongings there, including the two parakeets who had almost gone crazy on our drive north, and continued north to Medicine Hat.

When we got there, we had very few days to make all the arrangements that my mother had not been able to make. Jackie's friends from the States and one from Calgary came to be bridesmaids and to help her convert a rather insipid area in the local Moose Lodge (how Canadian could you get!) into a festive "restaurant" and "dance hall." They were magical. By the time they were done, it had been transformed from dull to adorable.

Medicine Hat is not easy to access. To get there one needs to fly into Calgary, rent a car, and drive three hours east. Despite all the obstacles and inconveniences, the wedding was attended by a lot of family and friends. Jackie's soon-to-be husband Rafael's parents and two brothers came from Puerto Rico. Many of our Michigan friends were there as well. They had known Jackie since she was nine and they loved her dearly. They were not about to miss the chance to see her get married in such a quaint and out of the way place. Dick and Susan with their two kids, Matt and Sarah, Ron Morash, Neil Flax, Helene Neu, a fellow graduate student at UCSB and now an instructor at U of M, Alan and Lonna Baum, all came from Ann Arbor and Livonia. Harvey and Robbie and their daughter, Monica, came from Bozeman, Serge and Nelly, and our dear friends Angela and Vicenç came from Calgary. There were also our friends Bert and Erika and their daughter Tammi, Jackie's oldest friend. Of course, we had Julio, Nory, and one of their two boys, David. The other boy, Jason, was in Europe. Needless to say, Jackie's four grandparents were there, as was my grandmother, her great grandmother. There were also a bunch of uncles, aunts, and cousins. We had three incredibly joyful days all together going from one party at my parents' house to another at Gloria's and at the Moose Lodge. We had a disc jockey, and everyone danced for hours, including Neil who confessed that he had never danced in his life. Gloria and I were overjoyed to be reunited with such dear friends and family. Jackie's grandparents could not be prouder of their granddaughter who had done the impossible to celebrate the wedding where she was born and where they lived. All in all, everyone who attended agreed that it had been one of the most fun weddings they had ever attended. A great success by all accounts.

After honeymooning in Banff, Jackie and Rafael went back to Ann Arbor. Gloria and I spent a few more days with family and friends in Medicine Hat and Calgary and then drove down to our new home.

HSU was named after the famous German scientist Alexander Von Humboldt. It started as a teacher's college in 1913 and after a few changes in its designation became part of the CSU in 1974. HSU is the northernmost campus in the CSU, situated on a hillside at the edge of a coastal redwood forest. It has commanding views overlooking Arcata, much of Humboldt Bay, and the Pacific Ocean. Because of the campus location, squeezed between the ocean and the forest, it has no room for expansion. This geographic limitation has made it possible to limit enrollment, and thus maintain its sense of intimacy. When I got there the number of students was probably around 5,500. It is not much larger today. By last count, it has around 6,500. The student-faculty ratio has always been low, around 18 or 19 to 1. Students have always had a close relationship with their professors. Student satisfaction was high, and I believe that this continues to this day. In 1982 a national publication listed HSU among the top 31 "lesser known but of higher quality institutions in the U.S." In 1990,1991, and 1992, despite the forced budget cuts that I will detail below, a *US News and World Report* study ranked HSU among the best universities in the West. This was based on five criteria: 1) quality of the student body, 2) quality of the faculty, 3) reputation for academic excellence, 4) financial resources, and 5) ability to recruit and retain graduate students. To say the least, I was impressed, delighted, and a bit intimidated by what my jurisdiction comprised.

HSU welcomes Esteban

Times-Standard   May 9-1990

New academic affairs official heads for 'treasure' campus

MANUEL A. ESTEBAN
"Innovative leader"

ARCATA — Manuel A. Esteban, dean of the School of Arts and Sciences at California State University, Bakersfield, has been named vice president for Academic Affairs at Humboldt State University.

He will assume his position in mid-July.

Esteban has been dean and professor of French and Spanish at Bakersfield since 1987. He earned a bachelor's degree in French in 1969 and a master's degree in romance studies in 1970 from the University of Calgary, Canada. He was awarded a doctorate in French in 1976 from the University of California, Santa Barbara.

In making the appointment, President Alistair W. McCrone said, "Dr. Esteban is an innovative and charismatic leader who will make positive contributions to Humboldt's academic program. His considerable experience as an administrator, professor and scholar will make him an asset to the university and the community."

One of Esteban's immediate goals is to talk with as many constituencies as possible before the academic year begins.

"I'm a firm believer in collegiality and consultation," he said. "I need to know what are the perceived strengths and weaknesses so that I can reinforce the strong points and take whatever steps are necessary to turn any weakness into strength.

"Humboldt," he said, "has a very good reputation. Recently U.S. News and World Report listed Humboldt as a real treasure campus. My interview visit to campus reinforced my positive impressions."

Esteban rose from instructor to professor of French and Spanish at the University of Michigan-Dearborn from 1973 to 1987. During that time, he served as acting chair of the Humanities Department, in addition to being associate dean from 1984 to 1986 and interim dean from 1986 to 1987 of the College of Arts and Sciences.

He is a member of the Council of Colleges of Arts and Sciences, the North American Catalan Society, the National Academic Advising Association, the National Association of Academic Administrators and Modern Languages Association of America. The California State University Trustees appointed him to the California/Catalonia Sister State Task Force in 1988.

The author of a book, numerous articles, book reviews and other publications, Esteban has been editor of the North American Catalan society quarterly publication since 1986. He has made a number of presentations throughout the United States.

Esteban, who will hold the academic rank of professor of French and Spanish at Humboldt, has been on the board of directors for the American Cancer Society in Kern County and Bakersfield Mercy Hospitals. He and his wife, Gloria, have a daughter, Jacqueline.

The first few weeks at HSU were very pleasant. I made the rounds throughout the campus and met one-on-one with the Vice President for Student Affairs, Buzz Webb, Vice President for Business and Finance,

Edward Del Biaggio, Vice President for University Development, Don Christensen, the dean of Graduate Studies, Susan Bicknell, who had been chair of the forestry department, the Dean of Undergraduate Studies, Whitney Buck, who had been a member of the team from HSU I had met at the Lilly Endowment workshop, the Deans of the College of Behavioral and Social Sciences, Lee Bowker, the College of Health, Education, and Professional Studies, Bette Lowery, of the College of Humanities, Ron Young (who had also been part of the Lilly Endowment group), of the College of Business and Industrial Technology, Lee Badgett, of the College of Science, James Smith, of the College Visual and Performing Arts, Robert Everding, of the College of Natural Resources, Richard Ridenhour, the Dean of Admissions, and Bob Hannigan, a very able person, whom I valued so immensely that I eventually stole him away from HSU. I also met with, among many other important administrators, the director of Special Programs, Enrollment Managers, the director of Student Advising, the union leader, department chairs, academic senate leaders and all the other people I believed I needed to know and felt that they, in turn, had to know me. My main goal was to demonstrate instantly that I was willing to listen and learn.

It took no time at all for me to recognize that HSU was different. All concerned knew consciously or unconsciously that theirs was a unique place, a place of privilege. Every effort was made to distance itself from the connection with the CSU, hence, the insistence on being Humboldt State University, not CSU, Humboldt. The latter appeared nowhere in any official documents that I can recall. President McCrone was also unique in many ways. As a Canadian of Scot ancestry, he often dressed, on almost all official functions, celebrations, and graduations, in a Scottish kilt and had a Scottish bagpiper preceding or following him. This added a touch of distinction and elegance to any official function. He never explained why he did it nor did he seem to care what anyone thought of the spectacle provided. Nobody questioned him and everyone respected and admired him. This was his campus, and his personality was felt throughout, even though he seldom seemed to meddle in what the VPs were engaged in. He was not one to provide the VPs with clear and concise directives nor was he one to offer overt criticism. But not one of us wanted to place him in a situation where he would need to do what was clearly uncomfortable for him. He gave us latitude and freedom to act as we felt appropriate, but we created our own guardrails based on what we inferred he wanted.

Whereas at CSUB there was a great deal that needed to be done to bring maturity to a young campus, I failed to see any major issues that would necessitate my immediate attention here. The campus was well established. It had seven colleges when I arrived. It had an excellent reputation because it was fully focused on the success of its students. The faculty were for the most part excellent and devoted to their students and the institution as a whole. Along with the typical academic programs found in most universities, HSU, probably because of its geographical location, offered programs not found elsewhere. Its engineering department was not interested in just the typical accreditation. They knew what they wanted to accomplish, and their graduates found good jobs easily. Engineering concentrated primarily on Environmental Resources and Environmental Science Management. There were also programs in Rangeland Resources Science, Fisheries Biology, Geology, and a very large and encompassing Department of Forestry. Marine Biology had its own ship to conduct deep sea research. I actually spent a whole day on it. Other than getting pretty sick and being bored, it was a learning experience. The university also offered a well-respected degree in Native American Studies. In fact, everything I encountered and discovered left me thoroughly impressed. It became obvious that I had a lot to learn since I had never had to deal with such a rich variety of programs with incredible complexities and physical and technical needs. The campus had not been resting on its laurels. Well before I arrived, President McCrone had established a Commission on the Future Directions and Mission of HSU and had submitted its far-reaching recommendations to the Academic Senate for a response. The Academic Senate received the document but counseled against a rapid implementation as its recommendations implied serious fiscal and programmatic changes that required deeper analysis.

On 22 August 1990, I delivered, as was traditional, the Provost and Vice President's annual address to the faculty as a whole. This custom of having the provost deliver the annual address to the faculty was not done either at CSU, Bakersfield or at CSU, Chico. There it was the president, not once a year but every semester. I detailed the reasons I had vied for the position I was to assume and provided my vision for the near and long-range future. I wanted to begin, however, with some levity. With this in mind, I expressed my deep pleasure of finally having made it to HSU. I reminded everyone that back in 1973 I had applied for a teaching position in the Foreign Languages Department. I didn't even get a reply. The reason I was telling this now was not for the sake of recrimination but to show them how persistent and patient I could be. It had taken me 17 years, but finally, there I was.

I was looking forward to a rather peaceful period, with plenty of leisure time to explore the natural wonders offered by the topography, and the exuberant flora and fauna. And, in fact, we did manage to become quite familiar with all the natural beauty that surrounded us. But insofar as peacefulness in the job, I was soon confronted by challenges for which I was somewhat unprepared. Nothing of what I experienced and accomplished both at UM, Dearborn or at CSUB prepared me for the situation I was about to encounter. I was forced to change gears quickly.

What had I learned about myself that had made me successful in the past and that I could count on at this juncture? Willingness to listen. Ability to analyze situations. Readiness to work cooperatively with all relevant constituencies. Ability to submit plans of action, only after they were clear in my own mind. Seeking buy-in from those who were bound to be the most directly affected. Communicate readily, be willing to entertain alternatives, be patient and avoid precipitous decisions. And, above all, consult, consult, consult.

In his excellent and detailed book, *A View from the Hill. A History of Humboldt State University*, published in 1993, William R. Tanner writes: "Manuel Esteban became new provost and Vice President for academic affairs in 1990. Upon assuming the position, he said 'I want HSU to be the premier CSU campus.' And I sincerely believed that because of its unique nature and richness of programs, this was an achievable objective." Tanner continued, "he arrived, however, just in time to cope with serious budget questions facing the university." To underscore this point he added: "in 1990, for example, the University found its budget reduced by $2 million … in 1991 HSU's budget was cut by another $7 million. Cuts over the next two years would go even deeper (p.121)" This was the unprecedented abyss the campus was facing.

Even without spending an inordinate amount of time analyzing the situation, it was obvious to me that a number of steps would have to be taken in academic affairs. It was untenable to continue with seven colleges with their concomitant administrative positions. Administrative streamlining at all levels had to be achieved. We would not be able to fill any type of vacancies. A significant number of classes would have to be eliminated. Enrollment would need to be reduced. Student tuition and fees would be increased for several years in a row. These steps would be the first to be contemplated. Upon further analysis, other even more painful ones would have to be considered. What made such draconian measures somewhat acceptable, at least in principle, was that everyone was cognizant that this was not a made-up crisis. It was patently obvious. As I stated above, in the section on CSUB, California's funding of education was one that could best be described as feast and famine. We were now deep in the midst of famine. Thus, everyone understood that there was no alternative but to effect deep and serious cuts. The devil, however, was going to be found in the details.

There was a standing committee within academic affairs that dealt with budgetary issues. Given the extreme nature of what we were about to undertake, I immediately sought to expand it to include greater representation. By the end of Fall 1990, I submitted to the Academic Senate for consideration three different alternatives with specific recommendations to deal with the 1991-92 shortfall and additional ones to face those we knew were coming for subsequent years. Among the former was the recommendation that we reduce the number of colleges from seven to four. The Academic Senate accepted, in principle, the move from seven to four but urged that it be done finding the "means to maintain the unique identity and special characteristic of the Natural Resources program." It further asked that I "establish the details for implementation of a new college structure."

As I said, the devil is in the details. How to restructure academic affairs from seven to four colleges? How to redistribute the departments within the new structure? How to determine who would be the three deans to lose their jobs? What process should be followed to make these determinations? Before determining the new name and the departments that would constitute each of the four colleges, I started a series of systematic meetings with each department to get a sense of the most natural niche for each one of them. Of course, I also met with each of the seven deans. Although I suspected which deans would survive and which would not, I did not wish to make this decision unilaterally. I left the decision up to the faculty who chose to vote on this issue. All of this, easily stated, required almost Solomonic dexterity on my part. It also took weeks of consultation. Ultimately, and after a lot of cajoling, persuasion, hand holding, and appeals to reason and logic, we came down to the naming and the departments which would comprise each college. The four colleges were: Behavioral and Social Sciences, under Dean Lee Bowker; Professional Studies, under Dean Bette Lowery; Arts and Humanities, under Dean Ron Young; and Natural Resources and Sciences, under Dean Jim Smith. Deans Lee Badgett, Robert Everding, and Richard Ridenhour lost their deanships not because of lack of competence, but as the cruel and direct consequence of streamlining and restructuring.

Academic years 1991-1992 and 1992-1993 were not going to be any easier or less hurtful. In a way, reducing administrative costs had been relatively easy, though painful. Faculty and staff were supportive of these cuts. But though necessary they were not sufficient. More sacrifices were in store. While engaging in these first cuts, I became aware that Academic Affairs had no real control of its own budget. The system that had been in place heretofore made the Vice President for Administration the final arbiter. For instance, when faculty took leaves of absence for a number of legitimate reasons, Academic Affairs received only part of the professor's salary to find a part time instructor to back-fill his/her departure. The rest of the money went back into a pool controlled by the VP for Administration. Further, the CSU scooped up any money left unspent at the end of each fiscal year. So, to avoid such rapacious practice, campuses would spend all possible leftover money to pre-purchase needed materials for the following year. Whatever money was squirreled away by this practice would also end up in the same pool controlled by the same person. This meant, in our particular case, that VP Del Biaggio often got to play the role of a generous Santa Claus. For instance, he often told President Mc-Crone, who used to drive a rather old university car, that he should allow Del Biaggio to buy him a new one.

Such generosity rankled me because it was clear that a good percentage of the money controlled by VP Ed Del Biaggio should have been under the control of Academic Affairs. I liked Ed a lot. He was charming, gregarious, fun to be with, and quite engaging. But I was not about to let my affection for him affect what I considered a matter of equity and fairness. I talked to him and tried to find out exactly how much was owed to us. All I got was an offer to help. I did not want help. I wanted what was rightfully due to Academic Affairs. Faced with resistance I decided to express my frustration to the President. I explained to him that I could not possibly make informed decisions on what more should be reduced, cut, or eliminated to meet our budgetary shortfall unless I knew exactly what Academic Affairs' true budget was. The President understood my predicament and informed VP Del Biaggio to "lay all the cards on the table" so to speak. This was done but it did not sit well with Del Biaggio. Some of the leverage and power that had made him such a kingmaker had been diminished considerably. I don't know what part this played in his decision, but he left for a position at CSU, Sacramento at the end of 1992. President McCrone did not replace him. Instead, he asked Don Christensen to assume some of Del Biaggio's responsibilities and named him VP for Development and Administrative Affairs. A significant savings had been achieved by this consolidation. President McCrone led by example.

With full knowledge of Academic Affairs' true budget, I directed the expanded standing budget committee to consider other cuts. After a lot of analysis and discussion and with the unique mission of HSU uppermost in the collective mind of members of the committee we recommended that Home Economics, Industrial Technology, Range Management, and Speech and Hearing Sciences undergraduate programs be discontinued, as well as the MA Program in Education. The Academic Senate accepted only the recommendation to discontinue Home Economics and the MA in Education, but not the others. In another resolution, however, the Senate modified its initial decision and recommended to the president that the Industrial Technology, Range Management, and Speech and Hearing programs be put on a one-year probation. If at the end of this period they were not found to be resource neutral, they would be terminated. The academic year 1993-94 was to necessitate something we had managed to avoid for three years. A virtual moratorium on all tenure track faculty hiring proved to be insufficient. This was followed by the laying off of some faculty. Dark years indeed.

Not everything was dismal. HSU continued to function well despite the many disruptions and cuts. Faculty continued to devote themselves heart and soul to their students and were faithful to their long-standing commitment to social and environmental responsibilities, students continued to come to HSU. As some had expressed, they believed that it was a place for those with a spirit of adventure and a passion for making a difference in the world. And in the midst of this upheaval, we still managed to shore up various important offices, such as the Academic Information and Referral Center, the Testing Center, and Academic Computing. In 1992-93 we also saw the need to create a Center for Faculty Resources and Development, with adequate financial support, because we all believed that faculty development was essential. Of course, we had to admit that to fund it properly we would have to wait until the budgetary crisis was behind us.

If ever there was a time when external resources were desperately needed, these years of budgetary famine were it. Fortunately, some of the academic and athletic programs had been and were very adept at raising funds. In 1987, as an example, Madonna, who had visited and performed at HSU, contributed $700,000 worth of equipment to theater arts. Between 1988 and 1995, the campus hosted the Humboldt Summer Arts Festival. This festival brought a lot of notoriety to the north state, additional resources, and a considerable number of very high-profile professional performers to campus. I can recall two of these: Richard Earl Thomas, the John Boy of the successful TV show *The Waltons*, Florence Henderson, of the *Brady Bunch*, and the famous movie director Herbert Ross. The National Endowment for the Arts called this "a model program for the West." Athletic Directors Frank Cheek and Chuck Lindemenn raised a great deal of money by organizing sports banquets that attracted a lot of patrons who wanted to see and hear from the likes of Joe Kapp, Jim Plunkett, Steve Young, Bill Walsh, and George Blanda, to mention a few sport celebrities. President McCrone for his part continued to be very engaged in the Humboldt community. His faith in the inherent value of HSU was so contagious that he was quite successful in fundraising. This faith was further manifested in 2009, seven years after his retirement, when he and his wife made a very substantial and highly celebrated donation to the university.

I would not want to create the impression that our three years at HSU were in any way memorable only because of the effects of budget cuts. In fact, there were very happy and enjoyable years. Our daughter and son-in-law came from Ann Arbor to spend our first Christmas with us. They enjoyed visiting the region and we loved having them with us. Gloria's parents came each year for six to eight weeks. They loved the area so much that they considered moving there. All three of them often drove me to work and then went to Ramone's, a bakery that served the best scones we have ever had. Gloria adored the surroundings and was particularly happy to be able to share this natural richness with them. We also had a rewarding social life. We became friends with three people with whom we met often for social activities and dinners. Rafa Cornejo was a professor of Spanish, who, coincidentally, had been at UCSB at the same time as Gloria and me. But we did not know Rafa then. He was now married to an Argentinian woman, called Celina Echagüe, who worked at HSU as well. There was another member of the Spanish Department, Andrés Diez, who joined all four of us often. They were all a lot of fun to be with and we got together as often as possible.

VP Buzz Web and his wife Judy invited Gloria and me to join a very exclusive group of friends who enjoyed great meals, good wine, and engaging conversation. We did not know at the time, but the first invitation was a sort of trial. I guess we passed because we became regular participants. The group was rather eclectic, made up of university people, both administrators and faculty, and a local doctor and his wife. The one overarching rule was not to discuss university matters, something Gloria and I appreciated immensely.

Although I always gave greater preference to my campus duties, I continued to be active at the national level as well as within CSU. In 1991, for instance, I was asked to serve on the Advisory Board of the Institute for Teaching and Learning (ITL). The mission of the ITL was to assist faculty in teaching their disciplines to students through intercampus collaboration on research, development, and dissemination. It was a very successful program that encouraged cross disciplinary research projects involving both faculty and students.

There were at least two other activities that brought a lot of joy to me. Every noon a group of faculty and administrators, led by Buzz Webb, met at the Redwood Bowl and went for a five-to-six-mile run. We always headed to the neighborhood known as Foggy Bottoms, a flat area. On the way back to the stadium, however, we had a very steep hill to get to the gym. I was not the best runner in the group, but I was good at running uphill, as long as the hill was not too long. I derived great satisfaction from beating my fellow runners up the hill. We were all great believers in Juvenal's dictum of *mens sana in corpore sano*. I also took advantage of the ping pong table we had bought. I challenged everyone who came to visit. The only one who represented a true challenge was my son-in-law. He was so aggressive that the paddle slipped out of his hand and went through the window out into our backyard. While Jackie and Gloria were shopping, he and I went to have the glass in the window replaced so that Gloria could not see what we had done. It was also while at HSU that I was initiated into golf. I bought the right equipment and the appropriate clothing. I took lessons. I looked the part in everything except in the results. I was rather capable in many sports, but golf was not and is not natural to me.

I have always loved woodworking. When I found out that the Department of Industrial Technology included advanced courses in sophisticated cabinet making I enrolled in two different classes. The instructors were excellent. The machinery and tools were somewhat antiquated, but they kept them working perfectly and what was missing in technology was more than made up in ingenuity and inventiveness. To this day, almost thirty years later, I still possess most of the pieces I built. The most precious are a headboard for one of our beds and a matching night table, built piece by piece and assembled without a single nail, and a parsons' table made from two types of wood, walnut and birds-eye maple with carved spindle legs.

Gloria and I took advantage of the many opportunities to delight in the natural beauty that surrounded us. I remember one of our outings in particular. A professor of geology, Hal Jackson, invited Buzz, Judy, Gloria and me to join him on a field trip to Lassen National Forest. It was early Spring. When we arrived at the campground, we saw it was closed. The ground was still covered with patches of snow. We decided to stay there anyway. Buzz and Judy lent us their pop tent and they chose to sleep in the open air. When we got up in the morning the ground was covered with snow. It was also rather cold. Gloria and I were fine, but the sleeping bags wrapped around Buzz and Judy were totally white as were their faces. Gloria and I felt sorry for them but, deep down, happy that we had slept inside the pop tent. That day we climbed Mount Lassen. We also went to the Subway Cave, the underground lava tubes. Professor Jackson was a fount of information. The whole trip was exhilarating and inspiring.

While living in Humboldt County, we also experienced the force of nature in all its impressive plenitude. It was in 1992. Gloria and I were having breakfast at our favorite restaurant in Arcata when all of a sudden everything began to shake ferociously. In a second, everyone at the restaurant got up and went out into the street. We all seemed to be drunk. The ground was shaking and moving. We were in the midst of an earthquake, one that hit 35 miles south of Eureka at a magnitude of 7.2. When things settled down a bit we went back home. That night we experienced a series of tremendous aftershocks, two of which registered at 6.5 and 6.7. Gloria and I stationed ourselves under the door frames, as recommended. We hardly slept that night. Our house suffered minor damages as did the campus. However, when we went to Ferndale, a quaint Victorian village with dozens of well-preserved Victorian storefronts and homes, we witnessed the destructive effects of the earthquakes: shattered storefront glasses, brick façades collapsed, about 30 to 40 homes knocked off their foundations. It was estimated that the damage caused to this small town of about 1,300 inhabitants, amounted to over $10 million.

While we lived in Humboldt County we were overtaken by our own personal earthquake. My brother called me in January of 1991 to inform Gloria and me that my mother had suffered a massive stroke that had left her totally paralyzed on the right side and unable to speak or move. She was totally incapacitated. Gloria and I flew to Calgary and Julio drove us to Medicine Hat to see her. It was a traumatic experience. I have never felt as useless as I did, seeing her in the hospital bed. I suppose she was under sedation because she barely reacted to our presence. Although with time she improved slightly, she was never again able to speak or move. She could not even operate her wheelchair. My father, then 80 years old, was incapable of taking care of her. She had to be placed in a specialized nursing home. While my dad was still alive, my brother went at least twice a month to help them. When our father died in December of 1993, my brother moved my mother from Medicine Hat to Calgary into a very nice facility not far from where Julio and his family lived. I was relieved to have my brother and sister-in-law looking after my mother. Julio is a born caregiver. I knew that my mother could not be in better hands. This gave Gloria and me peace of mind.

1993 was a year filled with surprises. Early in that year I received a phone call from the chair of the Vice Chancellor Selection Committee at UM-Dearborn. She was a professor in the English Department whom I knew very well. She wanted to know if I would allow my name to be put forth as a candidate for the position. Apparently, a number of people from within the institution had nominated me. I thanked her and those who placed their faith in me but expressed my puzzlement at the surprising and totally unexpected solicitation. How could I possibly be qualified for the Vice Chancellor's position when I had not been deemed sufficiently qualified for the deanship of CAS&L, I asked her? She explained that a lot had changed since I had left. I said that a lot had changed for me as well. I was extremely happy at HSU. I thanked her again but said that I had no intention of leaving the CSU. I don't think that this shines a good light on me, but I must confess that I derived a fair amount of satisfaction turning the offer down.

A few months after the phone call from UM-Dearborn I received a letter from CSU, Chico. I had been nominated as a candidate to replace the retiring president, Robin Wilson. Gloria and I were so happy at HSU, and I had been so busy that I never considered even remotely the possibility of leaving. What I liked most about HSU was its residential nature. Few CSU campuses could be considered residential, with the exception of Cal Poly San Luis Obispo and Chico State. If I was going to be a university president, HSU would have been my choice. I knew, however, that President McCrone had no intention of leaving. In fact, he served 28 years, retiring in 2002. What made the presidency at Chico State appealing was precisely its residential nature and the location of the campus, right in the middle of downtown. CSU, Chico is a true college town.

Although distinct from HSU, whose location and academic programs made it distinctive, Chico State also offered many unique characteristics. Founded in 1887, it was the second oldest CSU campus and the sixth oldest public college in California. I was well aware also that *Playboy* magazine had just ranked it the number-one party school. This is something that, in my eyes, diminished its well-deserved academic reputation.

Gloria was not too enthused with the possibility of still another move. She liked it where she was. She enjoyed the setting, our house, our friends, our social life. In short, we had a good life. I managed to convince her that being nominated and being chosen for the job were not the same. Still, should I let the chance to preside over a residential campus with a solid academic reputation slip by? Would I regret not allowing my candidacy to move forward? Again, as she was prone to do, she left the decision in my hands. Before I made a final decision, I went to speak to President McCrone. He told me he was not surprised that I had been nominated. He had known, he said, that sooner or later I would move up to a presidency. He stated that he would be sad to see me go but that he thought Chico State would be a good choice. He volunteered to be the first to write a letter or recommendation. He was and is a true gentleman, almost from a different era.

There were a lot of candidates. Five made it to the final stage, four white males and one African American female. Paul Weller, President of Framingham College in Massachusetts, was the first to visit the campus and undergo the grueling series of interviews. He was followed by Yolanda

Moses, Vice president for Academic Affairs at CSU-Dominguez Hills. The next candidate was Melvyn Schiavelli, Provost at William and Mary. Dennis Heffner, who had been CSU, Chico's Vice Provost and a member of the faculty for eighteen years and was at that time Vice President for Academic Affairs at CSU, San Bernardino, was next. I was the last candidate. I found it interesting that Larry Mitchell, staff writer for the local newspaper, *Chico Enterprise-Record*, started his article about my preparation and credentials with the following: "No one in Manuel Esteban's high school graduating class ever predicted he'd be in the running to become a university president. That's because Esteban had no graduating class. He never attended high school."

For those of us in the CSU, particularly those who had occupied positions at more than one sister campus, there were no secrets. Any and all individuals and constituencies could contact their counterparts and get the skinny on any of us. This familiarity afforded both an advantage and a disadvantage over candidates from outside the CSU. The positive side was that if we had performed well, this was a plus. The disadvantage was that, unlike those from the outside, we could hide very little. We were an open book. The book must have interpreted positively for I was invited for a two-day campus visit. Spouses were expected to accompany the candidates, so Gloria came with me. It was clear that we both would be inspected and evaluated.

The visit was quite a revelation. We had never been to Chico and were pleasantly surprised to see that this city, just shy of 100,000 people, was quite beautiful and offered a great variety of attractions. Top among them is the luscious Bidwell Park, the Sherwood Forest in the original 1938 Adventures of Robin Hood. Driving down to campus on the majestic Esplanade, a street/avenue that would make any city anywhere proud, was quite an experience. The campus itself, which a river runs through, was equally impressive, particularly when you see from the street the three most graceful brick buildings that welcome anyone accessing the campus: Trinity Hall, Kendall Hall, which houses the president's office, and the beautiful and imposing Laxson Auditorium, the site of the culminating series of interviews. Chico State has the look and feel of a private, residential college. The campus is right smack in the middle of downtown. For this reason, above all, malls have not drained away from it the vibrant atmosphere that hovers over the whole area. Students are either housed on campus or live within walking distance in private student apartment complexes. Restaurants, bars – many bars – unique boutiques and businesses of all sorts make this downtown a favorite destination for locals and visitors alike. Gloria and I were enchanted by what we saw.

The visit was also packed with interviews from morning to night, from breakfast to dinner. I met with the search committee, which was chaired by a CSU Trustee, as well as with a number of faculty, staff, union, student, and community groups. Gloria and I were invited to a dinner at the home of a lady who later became a close advisor and friend, the *grande dame* of Chico, Marilyn Warrens, who has just passed away at a very advanced age. There must have been at least twenty people. Gloria was seated at one end of the long table and I at the opposite end. Midway through the meal, we were asked to exchange seats. Everyone wanted a chance to see us up close and personal and to be able to ask questions. What could have been uncomfortable and stressful turned out to be a delightful evening. Gloria and I were impressed by the friendliness, congeniality, and strong sense of community displayed by all concerned. The *pièce de résistance* came at the end of the two-day visit. I was placed on stage at the campus theater. The theater was packed. It was a scheduled session open to anyone interested. I was told to expect questions from the audience. The session lasted over two hours. The questions covered every conceivable topic. I was very happy to be able to touch on so many important issues. I wanted to display my knowledge and understanding of the implications of the position I was to occupy. Of all the questions I remember one in particular. I thought it was a very appropriate one. I don't know who posed it but I would not be surprised if it came from a dean or some other experienced administrator. The question went something like this:

"As I look at your credentials, I see that you have a total of seven or eight years in administration with only six of them in the CSU. What in your six years at CSU makes you qualified to be a president and take the helm of as large, historic, and complex institution as Chico State?" To which I responded *grosso modo* as follows:

"It is true that I was a dean at CSUB for only three years and a Provost and Vice President at HSU for another three years. Under normal circumstances I would be the first to agree that this represents a very scant experience. But the nature of the jobs I held in both institutions and the myriad and often intractable challenges I was confronted with in both of them as well as the circumstances under which I had to operate tested all my abilities, knowledge, and determination. In a short six years I was forced to learn a lot, work closely with many different constituencies with often contradictory agendas, demonstrate flexibility and adaptability, communicate clearly, and act decisively." A woman in the audience asked how I had managed to move ahead so quickly. My response, quoted in the local paper was" "I don't waste a lot of time. I'm not very bright, frankly. I do have a work ethic. I work very hard. If there's something I need to learn, I learn it. I take the time." Asked whether, given the short stints at each of the last two positions I held, I could make a commitment to a longer tenure if I were offered the job, I responded that as long as I felt I was an effective president I would want to make this the capstone to my career. In fact, I added, regardless of how well I and others thought I discharged my responsibilities, I would not want to commit to more than eight or ten years. I indicated that, in my opinion, this should afford me sufficient time to make a positive contribution and leave a better campus for my successor.

That night I received the greatest compliment ever. And it came from someone I had known for over 35 years: Gloria. She said that she had always admired me for my dedication, persistence, discipline, and ambition. My performance at the theater, she said, left her in awe. She confessed that she had never imagined that I was so wise, articulate, patient, unflappable and, above all, so knowledgeable about so many topics, some of which, in her mind, were esoteric, arcane, abstract, and incredibly specific. I went to bed thinking that even though I might not be offered the presidency I had at least achieved one important goal, impressing the person I loved the most and the person without whose support and unflinching faith in me I would never have been able to be in the position of aspiring to the presidency of such a beautiful and respected institution. I kissed her and went to bed a very happy man.

On Friday, May 21, 1993, *Chico Enterprise-Record*, ran a front-page article announcing that I have been selected by the Trustees of the CSU to be Chico State President. There were some faculty, from what the article indicated, who had favored Yolanda Moses. They perceived her as more of a "change agent" with a stronger background. They speculated that I had been selected perhaps because VP Moses turned down the offer. When they contacted the chancellor's office, Colleen Bentley-Adler, a spokesperson for the Chancellor indicated that I had been the Trustee's first choice, that the presidency had been offered to no one but me. Of course, there were many who conveyed openly their support for me and expressed confidence that the right choice had been made. Nonetheless, upon reading this article I intuited that I would need to make every effort to demonstrate to these faculty and possibly others that I deserved the trust that the Trustees and Chancellor Munitz had placed in me.

Back at work at HSU, I was torn with mixed and conflicting emotions. I felt elation, happiness, and excitement. To have bested such an excellent group of candidates left me with a sense of pride and dread. I was quite cognizant that going to Chico meant leaving HSU and all the excellent colleagues with whom I had worked so closely and under stressful conditions for three years. Gloria in particular was loath to forsake a region she loved and the many people who had so generously befriended us. Just as they had done at CSUB, everyone wished us well in our new endeavors and credited us with much more than we deserved. Still, it felt good to leave on such good terms.

CHAPTER VIII
CSU, Chico, 1993–2003

▲▲▲

Life in a Fishbowl

BEFORE MOVING PERMANENTLY, GLORIA AND I went to Chico to get a better feel for the town that was to become our home. I made a courtesy call to President Wilson who graciously invited us to visit his home on campus, the Mansion as it was known. It was going to be our home beginning in August. From the outside it looked perfectly alright. Once inside, however, Gloria and I were quite taken aback. It turned out that the president and his wife were very private and had not permitted anyone to come into their home to make any necessary repairs in the 13 years that they had occupied the house. The kitchen countertops, for instance, made of formica laminate, had several of the corners held together with duct tape. As computers had become more common, they had wired the house to meet the necessary electrical demands. The wires were intrusively stapled to the walls. Our overall impression was of a run-down house in need of major repair. We did not know what the university was willing to do to bring it up to reasonable living standards, but we knew that this was going to be our home and were ready to accept living there regardless of its condition. Little did we know that our housing situation would become controversial and would somewhat derail one of my major objectives. In the meantime, however, Gloria and I left for Canada, to visit family, and then on to Barcelona for a couple of weeks. We needed to decompress a bit before we faced a very different lifestyle with new roles and demands.

As much as I admired President McCrone, I knew that I did not have the personality or the temperament to be the type of president he was. He was totally devoted to HSU and was seen all around campus. But he managed to always stay above the fray, leaving his vice presidents to deal with campus issues and became involved only when his seal of approval was necessary. He displayed an almost regal bearing. He embodied the institution but remained remarkably distant. Even if I had wanted to pattern myself after him, it would have been impossible. It was not in my nature. I had always been a hands-on administrator and, regardless of personal cost, I would continue to be personally engaged in any major project and enterprise that was bound to affect individuals and the institution as a whole. This was a worthy goal, but one that came at a high personal cost, at least in the first couple of years. The moment your administrative style is one of active participation you become the face of the project, you become the focus, the target of attention. You may get credit for the efforts and success whose merit belongs to others. But you also get blamed for events over which you may not have had any control. Now, place all of this into a fish-bowl environment and constant attention becomes all-consuming, difficult to live with, a constant source of anguish.

In his book *What Makes a Good leader?* Gary Wills makes a very wise observation: "leadership is always a struggle, often a feud. We have long lists of the leader's requisites—determination, focus, a clear goal, a sense of priorities, and so on. We easily forget the first and all-encompassing need – followers. Without them, the best ideas, the strongest will, the most wonderful smile, have no effect."

Being a leader in 1993 when I started at CSU, Chico, seemed to be more difficult than in the past. Everyone appeared to desire strong leadership. Yet, authority was often suspect and questioned. Most people expressed a preference for structure. Yet, we lived in an age of deconstruction. When asked, followers, to borrow from Gary Wills, indicated a desire for certainty. Yet, we lived in a period of great ambiguity and uncertainty about the future. They also hoped their leaders would provide a sense of security. Yet, we were in the midst of rapid change and instability. Similarly, most expected leaders to be agents of change, positive change, of course, at a time when many were uncomfortable with change, were quite adept at passive and at times even active resistance.

In my own mind, as a leader I would have to have a clear vision but could not be too far ahead of those I hoped to lead. Regardless of my preconceived conclusions, I had to show sufficient humility to demonstrate that I was willing and ready to listen carefully, learn, seek advice, be flexible, consult and convince. Chico State had a long history. I wasn't there to reinvent it but to try to improve it. As Simon Perez reiterated to me when he visited Chico State, "you cannot learn how to know if you don't first know how to learn." It is extremely important but not necessarily sufficient to be knowledgeable about the issues at hand. One has to detail them, place them into an understandable context, propose solutions and lead others to the same conclusions for the benefit of all. A leader must trust in order to demand loyalty. A leader should lead by example. This is what I understood as leadership and how I planned to proceed.

My predecessor, Robin Wilson, presided over Chico State from 1980 to 1993. From the articles I read and from what many volunteered, his tenure, particularly in the latter part of it, had been marked by controversy. Yet, as I read what caused so many to turn against his administration, I could find little that I could not support. He wanted to improve academic excellence, increase faculty research and publication, and change the university's party-school image. He angered students and Chico residents when he cancelled Pioneer Days in 1987 after the annual spring celebration by students, many of whom came from far away to partake in the famous festivities, erupted into rioting. It happened again in 1990 when local businesspeople, who benefited from this annual event, reorganized the celebration under a new name – Rancho Chico Days. He also eliminated ROTC. Where I would have disagreed with him was in his attempt to shut down the School of Agriculture. I found that, given the region rich in rice and cattle growing and the strong support it received from local farmers and ranchers, the School was an asset and had the potential of becoming an even greater asset and resource for the regional industry. What seemed to have hurt him the most, in addition to the elimination of Pioneer Days, was his overt elitism and disdain for the broader Chico community. It was made clear to me that one of my major responsibilities would be to bridge the chasm that had been created in the area of town and gown.

When I retired from the presidency in 2003, a Chico State alumna, Nancy McDougal Fox, a shining light in the community, who over time became very close to Gloria and me, put together a very creative and thorough album containing photographs and newspaper clippings that chronicled my ten years as president. Gloria and I will always cherish her effort and, as we refresh our memories by looking at her compilation, will relieve our wonderful moments and years in Chico. But, as much as I have always appreciated the hours upon hours that she must have devoted to recount and record Gloria's many contributions and the impact of my presidency, I have to admit that she produced a rather sanitized version of it, as my own recounting of those years will clearly reveal.

As I get ready to cover the ten years as president, I realize that I had suppressed quite successfully the most agonizing and painful experiences of the first eighteen months. Whereas I did not keep detailed documentation about my administrative years at either CSUB or HSU, I have an extensive one about Chico State. In re-reading the countless articles written in the two newspapers – the daily *Chico Enterprise-Record (E-R)*, and the weekly *Chico News and Review (CN&R)*, as well as the nationally recognized student weekly *The Orion* – that chronicled almost every one of my moves, words, and actions, plus the barrage of letters and messages I received from foes and supporters alike I have found myself reliving those ten years with a mixture of discomfort for the first eighteen months and generally great satisfaction for the remaining period.

I don't clearly know why I collected and kept for so many years the many examples of insults, slights, condemnations, and humiliations. There were far more people who praised me and my efforts, who defended me, who attacked my detractors than those who made it a point of attacking not only my policies but me personally. I did find solace in their private and open defense, but I found myself giving the critics greater weight. I was obsessed with it. What I have discovered now is that all those mixed feelings have resurfaced. I am in pain again, and again I obsess over the negative as much if not more than over the eight plus years where Gloria and I were the toast of the town and the university. As I contemplate my many successes and accomplishments and the manner in which the campus and the community as well as my presidential colleagues and fellow administrators bid us farewell, I should bask in a glorious tenure. The first eighteen months, however, created deep doubts in my abilities and left me somewhat tentative.

First, I want to explain the forces that converged to create the situational context I encountered. I will start with the consequences of budget cuts. Chico State, like every other CSU campus, had undergone devastating budget cuts. Unlike HSU, for instance, where all relevant constituencies had worked collectively and cooperatively to find acceptable solutions, Chico State had approached the cuts differently and the results were perceived by many to be inequitable. Rancor and recrimination were salient. Nerves were raw. Those who felt disenfranchised and negatively affected were desperately waiting for a new president to right the wrongs. One could easily observe and sense that the relationship between the faculty and staff was severely strained. The latter felt that they had not had sufficient input into decision-making. They also observed that the cuts had disproportionately fallen on their shoulders. Plant Operations, as an example, made up exclusively of staff, was disproportionately affected. In fact, in a conversation I had with President Wilson, he himself admitted this and encouraged me to address this problem.

The final budget decisions affected athletics unfairly as well. In fact, the athletics budget had been decimated. This was another very unhappy group of people who expected reparations and a more benevolent administration. I was determined to do as much as I could to help restore some of their resources but, above all, help them in fund-raising, since this was to be the future that awaited them.

There are a lot of aspects that make Chico State unique. One of them is the power that the student government exerts. For historical reasons, the bookstore and food services fall under its jurisdiction. This provides student organizations with powerful economic advantages that are completely outside the purview of the president of the university. Robin Wilson never liked this situation and when the time came to effect budgetary cuts, he saw an opportunity to wrest most of this power away from the students and find a way to mitigate the nefarious effect that the cuts were going to have on academic programs. Powerful alumni, however, banded together and pressured the government in Sacramento not only to prohibit President Wilson from raiding student auxiliary organizations but to enshrine forever their right to run these businesses without interference from the central administration. Wilson lost a battle but did not stop fighting. In fact, just before retiring, he wrote Chancellor Munitz a lengthy letter outlining the serious problem and begging for him and the Trustees to take some action.

This is how he perceived the gravity of the situation, as he described to Chancellor Munitz, on 7 June 1993: "The issue is the long festering relationship between the Chico State Associated Students Corporation and the Trustees. Since the 1988 legislation providing special recognition and protection for this group and affording them a virtual monopoly as a campus auxiliary, we have managed to get along with a cobbled-together agreement whose specificity resembles the airy nothingness of the British Constitution. Through the deft work of some of my staff, we have avoided most consequences other than wretched services performed at high prices, both of which are essentially beyond the control of either my administration or yours. Our attempts to change the status quo have been – and likely will be – frustrated by threats from Sacramento, where I am told "a disproportionate number of legislative staffers are alumni of the Chico Associated Students mafia." He expressed that "he feels concern for my successor and the racks and shoals that seem to me to be lying in wait for any new administration." Nothing was ever done about this issue. I had to deal with it as best as I could for the ten years of my tenure.

President Wilson also did something else to help me. He wrote me a confidential letter warning me of whom to trust and whom to keep an eye on. He was obviously very astute, as his evaluations of those under him were right on. He also recommended that I keep his assistant, Carol Berg. According to him she was a very able person whose talents were not sufficiently used. Based on his advice and my administrative experience I made two decisions that became fundamental for me. Until I arrived the President's Cabinet was composed of the president and the three vice presidents. I immediately expanded it. I upgraded Carol Berg's title to Executive Assistant and made her part of the Cabinet. Further, I called the chair of the Academic Senate to find out whether he would want to serve on my Cabinet and whether I could trust that whenever something confidential was discussed it would stay within the walls of my conference room. He agreed. I informed the vice presidents that henceforth the President's Cabinet would be formed by them, my Executive Assistant and the chair of the Academic Senate. If they were unhappy with my decision, they did not manifest it. To have the faculty on my side was essential. To have a person as capable as Carol to rely on in my office was not only a good strategy but a necessity. There were just too many concurrent battles to be fought not to surround myself with as many important and influential allies as possible.

There were at least two other sources of discord that resulted in bitter acrimony and an atmosphere of dread and imbalance. The Academic

Senate had discussed and approved a Sexual Harassment policy that sent some male faculty on the brink of apoplexy. When I arrived, this fighting was by no means settled. Another source of discord was the University's efforts in the area of affirmative action and diversification. Some timid steps had been taken to correct perceived inequities and discriminations. Despite the timidity of such small steps, there was a small but influential group of professors, all white males, who unashamedly equated the hiring of women and members of underrepresented groups with the lowering of standards. The poisonous claims of these individuals were aided and abetted not only by the local newspaper, through its editorials by both the opinion editor and the editor in chief in particular, but also by the California State Representative, Bernie Richter, who shared and spread their convictions.

Town-gown relations were at a low point, adversarial. This situation was exacerbated again by a local press that saw benefits in furthering the divide. Town and university people expected and wanted this chasm to be bridged as quickly as possible. It was made clear to me that this was of primordial importance. I was to do whatever possible to rebuild that bridge.

These, then, were some of the issues I encountered when I arrived. I was convinced that I could deal with them. They were perhaps a bit thornier than those I had encountered both at CSUB and HSU, but as I stated in one of my earlier interviews at the latter institution, "I believe my key contribution to HSU has been to develop and nurture an exceptionally open, collegial, consultative administrative style that permeates all interactions, decisions, and actions not only within academic affairs, but with all other university constituencies." My first impressions at Chico also led me to believe that my task at hand would not be as difficult as many predicted. Gloria and I were received by both campus and community in the most affectionate way. We were made to feel not only welcomed but desperately needed. For the first few weeks Gloria and I were constantly on the go, going to receptions held in our honor and meeting some of the most influential and prominent people in the community and university. I also met with then Governor Pete Wilson who came to neighboring Oroville to praise the partnership between the University and a very important laser company, Spectra-Physics.

The first few weeks were a whirlwind of positive, blissful energy and activity. As Robert Speer of *CN&R* put it: "For weeks Manuel Esteban, the new president of CSU, Chico, has been the toast of the town. He'd been feted by local bigwigs, given a fancy reception on campus by the faculty and staff, and been the subject of a string of laudatory media profiles. After the 13-year tenure of his temperamental and sometimes haughty predecessor, Robin Wilson, Esteban seemed down-to-earth and warmly expressive. Chico loved him" (9/23/93).

Then, I made a very stupid mistake. I had promised students that I would always be candid with them. When my salary was published, they saw that it was the lowest among the CSU presidents. They asked me about how I felt. I must admit that upon learning of my ranking I felt slighted. And I allowed this reaction to surface. Without really thinking that Butte County was among the poorest in California, I indicated to the students that I had been "flabbergasted" at how low my salary was going to be. I don't even know how I came up with such a ridiculous word. I had never used flabbergasted before nor, I believe, have I used it since. For good reason, of course. In any event, this one remark managed to destroy much of the good will I had built up in the previous two months. My remark was emblazoned on the front page of the *E-R*. What followed was an avalanche of angry letters gleefully published in the *E-R*. I had been totally ignorant of the resentment that existed locally toward bureaucrats and what they perceived as their bloated salaries, a resentment the *E-R* was only too eager to exploit.

But, as they say, ignorance is no excuse. I had stepped into a huge mess, and it would take a long time and a lot of work to undo the damage I had wrought. Unlike the *E-R*, which enjoyed creating controversy wherever it could, the *CN&R*, *at* times, was more objective and helpful. Robert Speer ended his commentary with the following paragraph:" The honeymoon is over, but the relationship remains. I'm impressed that President Esteban admits he made a mistake and regrets the problems it created. He's learned something valuable about Chico and Butte County. If he's the man I think he is, he'll be an even better president for it." I believe that Speer's balanced reporting and his less than veiled criticism of the manner in which the *E-R* plastered my insensitive comment on their front page prompted Jack Winning, the editor of *E-R*, to write an editorial in which, after saying that I had slipped up and put my foot in my mouth, he continued "but aside from that, he has been impressive." He finished his editorial by writing "It is a mark of Chico State's new president that he was on to other problems and other forums even as the criticism rolled in. There is nothing yet to suggest that the trustees did anything but make a good choice when they named Esteban to the post. His remark may have been ill-timed, but as Shannon Orozco, a member of the campus student government, noted, he was 'being open and honest. That is so rare in political life.' It was an apt comment" (9/26/1993).

I was very grateful to see how students reacted to the controversy and all the insults directed at me because of my inappropriate and insensitive comment. It was a great relief to see the opinion page of *The Orion*, the vaunted university weekly. It had a drawing of me at the bottom and over me boxes containing an overwhelming number of demands made on me by the many constituencies I represented. Next to this was an incredibly supportive editorial. Among the many points made, I remember the following: "As Esteban works twelve-hour days inside Kendall Hall, outside they are circling like vultures to make requests, ask for favors, and expecting him to solve the plagues that have descended on Chico State ... We should let Manuel Esteban be the right person for the job. He has already offered an energetic air and fresh outlook to the entire make-up of the campus. In simply becoming an accessible figurehead he has proven himself to be concerned and sensible." And the editorial concludes: "Manuel Esteban is starting a new job. Everyone new to a job makes mistakes. The worst counter mistake that the media, the community and the campus can make is to brand him a failure before he has a chance to fail." (9/27/1993) That this thoughtful evaluation of what I had done so far should come from a student filled me with admiration and hope. I knew then that as long as I kept working diligently and kept focused on the work at hand, I would succeed at CSU, Chico as I did at UM-Dearborn, CSUB, and HSU. It was just a matter of time.

As much as I brooded privately over the most negative comments and criticism, I was determined to demonstrate that nothing could distract me from my work to make Chico State what I said I hoped to accomplish, turning it into the jewel in the crown of CSU. In fact, while these articles and editorials were being written, on 24 September 1993, I was actively defending the CSU system as a whole in Sacramento. As the *E-R Sacramento* bureau chief, Michael Gardner wrote, "Maybe Chico State President Manuel Esteban should have been a lawyer. Esteban mounted a succinct but effective defense of the California State University System Thursday during a special Senate Education Committee hearing." I was responding to a report called *Beyond Business as Usual: A framework and options for improving quality and containing cost in California higher education.* I questioned findings in the report, particularly since much of the information was based on statistics dating back several years. I argued that there was no way the CSU of 1993 could or should be seen as the CSU of 1987. For many reasons but primarily because of successive years of budget cuts we were no longer conducting business as usual. I expressed the opinion that the report seemed to indicate that we had been sitting on our hands. Nothing, I said, could be further from the truth. Legislators argued that administrative costs were excessive. I countered that under Chancellor Munitz and the Trustees orders, the CSU was to reduce its administrative budgets by a total of 20%. I further argued that legislators ought to analyze the mandates that they imposed on higher education. A great deal of our bureaucracy was the direct result of legislative mandates, mandates, I further posited, seldom accompanied by the resulting cost of implementation. I also reminded them that it was some of the same legislators who threw up roadblocks. For example, local legislators helped beat back efforts by former Chico State President Robin Wilson to consolidate the College of Agriculture with another college, thus making administrative savings. I finished my remarks by indicating that at least at Chico State we were going to form a task force made up of students, faculty, staff, and community leaders to study possible efficiencies always with an eye toward safeguarding the integrity of academic programs.

A few days before my trip to the meeting in Sacramento, I had agreed to a joint appearance with Associated Students President Rick Callender in the Free Speech Area of the university. Students were encouraged to ask any question of either one of us on any topic whatsoever. Some of the questions revolved around the rising CSU fees for students while the Trustees were contemplating substantial salary raises for presidents. This was bad timing and difficult questions to answer without falling again into unsuspected traps. So, I was honest but guarded. Rick and I were there for a total of two hours. I am not sure we solved anything but both Rick and I demonstrated that we were available, caring, and willing to field even intractable questions. The event was covered by the press and we both received good grades for our accessibility and openness. We both agreed that we should be available to students more often. In December, we set up a table at the student union and fielded questions from students. We had planned for one hour but had so many questions that we were there for more than 90 minutes. Clearly these efforts were being well received at the very least by students, a constituency I highly respected. On 8 December 1993, the editorial in *The Orion* took balance of my first semester and came to the conclusion that, overall, it had been quite successful. "Much of his success stems from his accessibility and availability as a leader ... Esteban has become a prominent member of the community. He attends meetings, events and has made favorable impressions on community leaders." *Orion* contacted Tom Lando, the city manager, who said "our relations with the campus have improved greatly." Lando further indicated that "Esteban has gone out of his way to meet with him (Lando), the police chief and other community members."

Nevertheless, the misstep about my salary was totally and completely on my shoulders. I could not blame anyone for what it wrought. The decision on the part of the Trustees to discuss presidential salary increases at the same time that student fees were going up each year had little or nothing to do with me, but I still had to face uncomfortable questions about the inappropriate timing of the debates. And there was still another issue which, though nothing to do with me, was used against me by those same people who saw fit to crucify me for my insensitive comments about my low salary. This had to do with our housing. Since the end of World War II, every Chico State president has lived on campus in an ornate two-story, Italian-style stucco home with 12 rooms and two and a half baths, always referred to as the Mansion. Its claim to fame was that the house was designed by Julia Morgan, the most renowned female architect of the first half of the 20th century and also the designer of the San Simeon castle complex for publishing magnate William Randolph Hearst. How could anyone not be ecstatic about the possibility of living in a house designed by such a famous architect?

As I mentioned above, the house had not been properly maintained for all the 13 years that President Robin Wilson lived in it. As soon as we moved into Chico, we were told that as it was, the house was uninhabitable. A lot of work and maintenance would be necessary, and it would take time. Even the *E-R* had to admit that the Mansion was in desperate need of serious repairs: "After former president Robin Wilson moved out, it was found the residence had serious problems, including faulty heating and air conditioning systems, dry rot, crumbling concrete in the basement and asbestos that needed removing." What were we to do in the meantime? From the Chancellor's office we were told to find temporary housing until the house was rendered habitable again. The university recommended that we rent the house of a professor who was on sabbatical. Since it was fully furnished, we had to store all of our belongings. It was not an ideal situation, we would not be able to settle into a permanent lodging, but we accepted the reality of our situation. For this, the Office of the Chancellor offered us a $1,500/month housing allowance. Even though we had no control over this situation, we were immediately criticized. But this was just the beginning of the story. When workers from plant operations gave me an estimate of how much it would cost to do all the necessary repairs and upgrades to the Mansion, I was horrified. It was to be more than $250,000. There was no way that I would agree to this. How would I be able to convince people that, in the midst of severe budget cuts, we had to take such a large amount from our general fund? I immediately called Chancellor Munitz to see if he could help with the funding. He clearly did not believe that repairs would cost so much. He asked me if it would be alright if he sent an architect from Sacramento to determine what needed to be done and how much it would cost. Of course, I had no objection. I wanted to put a lot of distance between me and the ultimate decision that was really in the hands of the CSU Trustees and the Chancellor himself.

The assigned architect came from Sacramento and after realizing that he was inspecting a "national treasure" he concluded that this was not a project that could be left to the workers of the university. It had to be done by a master craftsman who would respect the integrity of the original design. To make a story short, when the estimate arrived even Chancellor Munitz was shocked. We were told that it would cost anywhere from $800,000 to one million. At that moment, the die had been cast. Neither Munitz nor I saw an easy way out. He asked me to see if I could find donors who would be willing to cover the enormous cost of restoration. I could not imagine any one person or group of people coming up with almost one million dollars in donations so that Gloria and I could live in the Julia Morgan home. In the meantime, however, we were to remain living in our temporary lodgings.

Eventually, Marilyn Warrens, always the first to offer help, agreed to make a huge donation and offered to help raise a lot more to make the necessary restorations. As the major donor, however, her generosity came with a condition. The house, once all the inside and outdoor work was completed, was not to be used as housing for us but for receptions and gatherings, something the university lacked woefully. I brought her proposal to the Chancellor and he to the Board of Trustees. After evaluating the situation and seeing no other alternative, they saw merit in what Mrs. Warrens proposed and directed Gloria and me to purchase our own home.

This move, however, became yet another *cause célèbre* that was purposely portrayed by the *E-R* as my sneaky way to "finagle" my way into receiving permanent housing allowances to supplement my salary. No matter how often the Chancellor's Office and the Vice President for Administration at CSU, Chico defended the decision as a clear attempt to save inordinate amounts of general fund money to repair the Julia Morgan house while at the same time end up with a classy and beautiful building where they could hold elegant receptions, something which the university lacked, a couple of professors of history and the *E-R* in particular made sure everyone knew that I was the first president since World War II not to accept living in the university-provided house. They did not fail to mention as well that I would be receiving a "substantial" housing allowance.

Gloria and I would have been happy in a number of the houses we were shown by our real estate agent. But we needed one that would be ideal for entertaining large groups of professors, staff, community leaders, etc. Eventually we settled on one that was quite nice inside, and also perfect for the many receptions we were expected to hold. It had a nice pool and around it a very extensive concrete area that could easily accommodate about 80-100 people for outdoor dinners. Of course, in the fishbowl in which we lived now the house was soon on the front page of the local newspaper. The front of the house was attractive but nothing out of the ordinary. I guess it did not look presidential or imposing enough. This was not going to allow the newspaper to make a big deal out of it. So, maliciously, it managed to manipulate the photo to make it appear much longer than it was. It was becoming more and more obvious to me that another one of my tasks was going to be to sooner rather than later meet one-on-one with the publisher and editor of the *E-R*. I put it on my to-do list.

With so many fronts to fight on, I made the decision that rather than battle against these accusations and conspiracies I would simply take time to meet as many professors and staff as humanly possible to give them a chance to know me, ask me whatever questions they might have, and allow me also the opportunity to present myself to them and provide explanations for everything. With this in mind, as soon as the academic year started, I had my executive assistant send invitations to a light breakfast around my conference table to eight faculty twice a week. A couple of months later I started to do the same with staff. I wanted to make absolutely clear to the staff that they too were valuable and that I welcomed their input. The only rule was that not two people at once come from the same department. I wanted to be exposed to as many points of view as possible. Only rarely did I have, particularly faculty, come ready for a fight. Most of the time these get-togethers were friendly, encouraging, and a great avenue for open dialogue and a better common understanding. It actually took years for me to meet with every faculty and staff member around the conference table. I was told that these invitations were eagerly awaited and greatly enjoyed. I had hit on the right note. In time, I won over the support of most faculty and staff. Patience, perseverance, openness, accessibility, willingness to listen, and a desire on my part to communicate openly and freely paid off handsomely.

In the meantime, however, in addition to the usual and regular running of the institution, there were many fires to be put out. There was nothing boring about this new job. One of them dealt with a racial harassment policy that had been adopted in 1991 by the Chico State Faculty Senate and signed off on by then President Wilson. It was meant to protect members of ethnic minority groups against racist remarks or actions that insulted or intimidated them. From the very moment of its implementation, it attracted the attention of a significant number of faculty in particular who viewed it as nothing more than an attempt to codify political correctness. The leader of the group against this policy was, Joseph Conlin, a professor of history. He had already tangled with President Wilson. He just continued his fight with me. He was to become my nemesis. Professor Geshekter, also a professor of history, a wanna-be-Conlin, but without his sharp wit and malicious humor, became his sidekick. Together they plotted to get me fired. They did not succeed, obviously, but they did manage to make my job a lot more difficult. Professor Conlin was not just against the policy. His comments and letters published in the *E-R* came across as sexist and racist.

As I studied the racial harassment policy that had been approved I could not but wonder how it had passed muster when analyzed by the Chancellor's legal counsel. It struck me as in conflict with First Amendment rights. I consulted with legal counsel again and this time they agreed that as written and applied, it violated First Amendment rights. Therefore, on 22 November 1993, I wrote a memorandum to the campus community explaining the legal reasoning for my decision to rescind the policy. This policy had been used only by various groups from various CSU campuses to file complaints against professor Conlin. I wrote to him that the university would not take any steps to punish him for violating the campus Racial Harassment Policy.

I did not want anyone to think that by rescinding the harassment policy I was siding with the likes of professor Conlin. Consequently, I issued a memorandum on 1 December 1993. In it I stated: "Those of us in the academic community are among the most sensitive, I believe, to the value of the First Amendment to the U.S. Constitution because of its importance not only to our political freedom but also to our commitment to the search for truth." I continued: "one of the university's professors continues to publish, privately and in local newspapers, letters and articles which many in the university community find deeply offensive ... Whatever his motives, his continuing commentary does not contribute to a positive learning environment and indeed is seen as intimidating and deeply offensive by many." I concluded by saying: "I urge the campus community to focus on their educational goals, to strive to make this a better place for all people, and not to be thrown off balance by his untoward writings. This is a very good university and a wonderful place. Let's work together to keep it that way."

Even though I never mentioned his name, Professor Conlin knew he was the target of my criticism and warning. He could not remain quiet, so he reacted in typical fashion. He hurled insults upon me. He resuscitated my gaffe regarding my salary. After which he repeatedly referred to me as *Mo Money Manny*. He accused me of having "finagled" not living in the university mansion to benefit from the housing allowance, and even brought up the price we had paid for the home we had bought, as if that were not paid with our own money. Professor Charles Geshekter, of course, also had to chime in, accusing me of not having the vaguest understanding of what the university was about. Asked by the press to comment on Conlin's remarks, I said that I respected his right to use ridicule, sarcasm, and parody to make fun of me, but I had more serious matters to tend to than to play along with his games.

I could not get a break. The memorandum I wrote indicating that Professor Conlin would not be punished was described by Robert Speer of *CN&R*, on 2 December 1993, as bureaucratic legalese. He expressed admiration instead for "Conlin's witty excesses." Long before I arrived, Conlin had already caused havoc and managed to insult almost everyone. But he had become the darling of the press, his excesses were fun, worth quoting, entertaining. The fact that they were also destructive did not seem to matter. As Speer explained: "It's not hard to understand why so many university folk are afraid of Conlin. He's smarter than they are, he's protected by tenure, he's absolutely fearless, and he's got a lot of weapons, including the kind of wicked humor most bureaucrats find threatening because they're so humorless themselves." The fact was, however, that there were countless professors and even a Catholic priest who showed no fear of Conlin and published letters of their own to criticize him for his willful destructiveness and lack of collegiality. As for me, I did not see much to praise in a person who hid behind the protection that tenure granted him, even though tenure was never created to protect from irresponsibility. I did not believe that being fearless in the creation of a toxic environment was an admirable trait. And I did not admire a person who used his "wicked humor" to insult, demean, and intimidate. If Conlin was so much smarter than the rest, why didn't he use this supposed intellectual superiority for the cause of good, rather than to divide and destroy? Nonetheless, encouraged by the love affair he had with the two local newspapers, Conlin continued to be an indiscriminate bomb thrower who would be ultimately shunned by students, colleagues and most reasonable people alike.

Not surprisingly, the likes of Conlin and Geshekter were also opposed to diversity. Interestingly, the very same *E-R*, that had a symbiotic relationship with them similar to the one, in recent memory, between President Trump and *Fox News*, and loved siding with these two professors, published an article that demonstrated beyond any doubt that Chico State lacked woefully in diversity. Most departments were overwhelmingly made up of white males. Female faculty were concentrated in just five departments: Nursing, Child development, Theater arts, Health and Community Service, and Foreign Languages. And racial and ethnic diversity was limited primarily to engineering, technology, business, and foreign languages. No surprises there. In 1992, Chico State's full-time faculty numbered 599. Whites totaled 537 and minorities 62, most of whom were in departments where, in general and traditionally, white males were seldom in the majority. When I arrived, there were two individuals who dealt with the two most controversial issues on campus: sexual harassment and affirmative action. I saw a need to consolidate both positions into one. Already in August I indicated that I would be conducting a nation-wide search for a campus affirmative action officer who would handle both issues.

Budget cuts had decimated a lot of programs. There was little hope on the horizon that would change the situation. In fact, the contrary was true. State support was in decline. The survival of many programs would soon depend on systematic fundraising. Gloria and I were committed to helping in this necessary effort. Less than two months into my tenure I demonstrated Gloria's and my commitment by participating in the 15th Annual Mozart Mile, a five-kilometer run to benefit the 88-year-old Chico Symphony Orchestra. According to the newspapers, our presence in the race attracted a much larger number of participants than ever before. This was just the beginning of our efforts to demonstrate that fundraising was to become a high priority not only for the president but for anyone in a position to help in this important endeavor. We could no longer be in the *plus ça change, plus c'est la même chose* mentality. Times were changing.

Three successive years of budget reductions had also shone a light on the university's administrative structure. In my first faculty convocation at the beginning of the academic year, I stressed the need to analyze every aspect of all the functions, including teaching, to ensure that we were as efficient and effective as possible. To demonstrate that administration was anything but off-limits, I indicated that four experts would be coming to campus November 15-17 to evaluate our administrative structures, conduct open sessions, seek advice and input, and finally determine what would be the best course of action, if one was necessary. I also mentioned that the financial situation was so dire that an unprecedented event had taken place: All members of the CSU Board of Trustees plus all its campus presidents, and all members of the University of California Board of Regents plus all campus chancellors met at the Capitol in Sacramento, in October, to discuss common strategies to deal with the budget crunch. The spirit of cooperation between the two systems, CSU and University of California, was encouraging, but it was obvious that it was rather symbolic and yet a direct message to the governor and legislators that the present situation was unsustainable.

Just as Gloria and I had participated in the fundraising effort to help the Symphony Orchestra, in October we also toured the university's off-campus farm to learn more about the School of Agriculture's program and community efforts to keep it alive. Though I did not promise that the School was saved from the cuts imposed by the CSU system and Legislature pressed on with cost-cutting and consolidation efforts, I did indicate that the future was in their own hands. Much would depend on the commitment of a community group called Superior Ag, formed to raise money not only to sustain but to expand the School's regional role. Unlike my predecessor, I was willing to fight for their existence if they helped me build a strong case for their uniqueness and ability to adapt to a new reality. Though farming was totally outside of my realm of experience, I was impressed by the quality and dedication of the faculty and the determination of the farming community to make a go of it. I don't know why but I formed a strong bond with all those involved in the project. I became a strong supporter. In turn, in my darkest days at the job, the School of Agriculture became an indefatigable ally.

Gloria and I capped 1993 with a huge reception at our home. Hundreds of people—faculty, staff, student leaders, administrators, community leaders, alumni, friends of the university—came to partake in the holiday spirit and, of course, to see the house we had bought and whose façades had so prominently been displayed in the *E-R*. It turned out to be a very festive event and one that gained us much needed appreciation and support. Guests learned that I was not a "humorless bureaucrat" as *CN&R*'s Robert Speer had said, but that in fact I was blessed by a relaxed and relaxing personality and was not devoid of wit, a sense of irony, self-deprecation, and even charming humor. They also found Gloria to be an incredibly charming and unpretentious hostess. They had fun and so did we. We were also quite happy to bid 1993 goodbye.

Not everything had been negative. In fact, Gloria and I received a lot of support from faculty, staff, students, and many community leaders. There was one person in particular who became a rescuer for me. At one of the many receptions we attended, I met a professor of sociology, Walt Schafer, who specialized in and published widely on wellness and stress. I spent a while talking to him. He told me that he detected that I was under a lot of stress. In his opinion, since I was a runner, I should make every effort to take advantage of any free time to get out of the office and simply run, and he offered to run with me. I said that I was prey to circumstance and that I felt I had little control over my own time. In fact, even when Gloria and I went to breakfast on the weekend, something we have always liked, people recognized me and came to our table to introduce themselves, ask questions, offer advice, and simply chat. We tried to avoid tables for four, which seemed to be an invitation for patrons to come sit down with us. But even when we were able to secure a table for two, in the most remote corner of the restaurant, they just huddled and hovered around us. I was basically telling Professor Schafer that I would find it extremely difficult to get away for my usual 5 or more mile-runs. But, nonetheless, I encouraged him to talk to my secretary to see if we could schedule some runs.

Walt went to my secretary and told her that I would be far more effective if I took some time off for exercise. My head would be clearer, I would be more relaxed, and my health, both physical and mental, would battle more effectively with the natural and unavoidable stress that came from the job. He urged my secretary to see if she could squeeze in time for daily runs whenever I was in town and not otherwise involved in luncheons. If this was not possible at noon, he was willing to get me to run at whatever time was possible. I don't know whether I found his attempt to help me meddlesome at the time. The reality is that I knew that I had always felt more energetic if I exercised. So, I took him up on his offer and started running with him whenever possible. We did this for almost ten years, from August of '93 until I developed some heart issues as I turned 63. In fact, Walt became a great sounding board for me. He never took advantage of our friendship for personal gain, and he provided solace in my darkest moments. He and his wife, Teresa, became our dear friends and this friendship is still strong almost 30 years later.

I thought I was made to suffer unfairly, and I did. But I did not realize how superficial this pain was until in December, I received a phone call from my brother Julio. He informed me that our father was dying. If I wanted to say goodbye to him, I should get a move on. We got to Medicine Hat as quickly as possible. It wasn't easy to get there. Unfortunately, we arrived hours late. My dad had passed away. He was just 82 years old. I had wanted so badly to have him partake in my inauguration. I knew that he would have been very proud, that he would have seen reflected in my success, his influence, his constant reminder to Julio and me that we should not permit life to dictate for us but for us to shape our life, to construct it, to give it meaning. I was not able to tell him for the last time how influential he had been in my life and how much I owed to his constant pushing me to be the best I could be. Gloria and I stayed in Medicine Hat until dad was buried. The days we were there were extremely cold but not as cold as my heart felt having lost a father who had been at times difficult and excessively demanding, but who had always demonstrated that he loved us and would have done anything to provide us with a better life. This is precisely what he did in moving the family from Spain to France and from France to Canada. He gave us the chance for a future that we could never have even dreamed of had we remained in Barcelona. After the funeral, we returned to Chico more determined than ever to show that I was not a quitter. The challenges ahead were daunting, but to honor the memory of my father I had to prove that I was up to the task.

The hectic pace that had characterized my first semester at Chico State did not abate all that much. But I was finding better footing and a sense that I was beginning to control the situation rather than being controlled by events. I was undeterred in my quest to succeed as president and move the institution forward. I was cognizant that I still had a lot more atoning to do for my gaffe, attracting a lot more support and gaining more trust if I was going to achieve my institutional goals and objectives. But I was armed with patience and determination. Looking for more controversial statements from me, *E-R* did not waste any time after the CSU Trustees had made their final decisions on presidential salaries. Larry Mitchell, the staff writer fully dedicated to covering Chico State and me, it seemed, asked what my reaction had been about remaining the lowest paid president in the System. I wasn't about to fall into the same trap twice. I simply responded that I had no comment. Actually, I did not know exactly why I had received the lowest increase, but I had a strong suspicion, which I was able to verify almost two years later. The Trustees and Chancellor Munitz had also been the subject of critical letters sent to them by Professor Conlin. In fact, he had urged Assemblyman Richter and Assemblywoman

Marguerite Archie-Hudson, Chair of the Assembly Higher Education Committee on which Assemblyman Richter sat, to investigate the CSU, teaching loads of faculty, release time, administrative machinations, etc. Chancellor Munitz was annoyed at me for not being able to control or marginalize Conlin. I must admit that I was at a loss on how to achieve this goal. After all, many of his own colleagues had rebelled against him. His own department has passed a censure motion. The man was incorrigible. He obviously enjoyed being the bull in the china shop. But I was not about to discuss this with Larry Mitchell.

Instead, I directed him to Chancellor Munitz. I did take this opportunity that Mitchell offered to indicate that administrative salaries in the CSU, despite what the Chico community might think, were below national levels. In fact, I informed Mitchell that one of my favorite candidates for Provost and Vice President for Academic Affairs, Fern Johnson, former provost of Clark University in Massachusetts, had dropped out of the running because the pay was less than she wanted and because of uncertainty about the CSU's finances. I also took the opportunity to respond to those, like Professor Conlin and his acolytes, who accused Chico State of having too many administrators, that the five-person team of consultants that had been sent by CSU Trustees to study our administrative structure had concluded that "by and large ... This is not a top-heavy administration". One more myth debunked.

Every effort to normalize and calm the waters abutted itself against Professors Conlin and Geshekter. Chico State had the tradition of selecting a student speaker for each commencement. In a letter to the *E-R*, 16 March 1994, Conlin managed to debase the tradition, insult those who selected the student, and indicate that the criteria used to choose the student had the same low standards as those that had been used by the Trustees to select me. As usual, even though he had clearly insulted me as much as he had the student, I ignored him and refused to enter into a public debate with him. He did not deserve any more notoriety than the one *CN&R* and *E-R* were only too happy to grant him. But it is worth mentioning that the student he so shamefully belittled publicly was a Native American who the previous year had filed a racial harassment grievance against him.

The Orion used its editorial page, a week later, 23 March 1993, to accuse Conlin of betraying students' trust, by using his power as a professor to have access to the student commencement speaker's grades and making them public. It describes him as a man "who lacks professional ethics and a humane moral compass." It further argued: "Do not confuse Conlin's letter to the *E-R* with an intelligent and reasoned work intended to add emphasis or momentum to any debate. Like most of his works before, it is a piece structured to buttress his self-image as a guy who 'mixes things up,' and is nothing but a vehicle to his own self-aggrandizement. But this letter, and the *E-R*'s shared guilt by running it, is different from what has come in the past. Where before Conlin was a grating and embarrassing feature of the university community, he has now shown his potential to be a vicious, sniping, small minded and corrupt abuser of official power." *The Orion* put *E-R* on the defensive. It defended its printing of the student's GPA by saying that "we had no knowledge of any kind of violation of any code." A lame excuse, but there was little I could do about their printing the student's GPA. Professor Conlin, on the other hand, had gone illegally into student records which contained confidential information, and made it public to demean the student. After a thorough legal review, and under the recommendation of university legal counsel, Professor Conlin was punished. His punishment? Temporary reduction in rank from full to associate professor, with commensurate reduction in salary. This punishment was not meant to quiet Professor Conlin's fierce attacks. They continued. But little by little his following began to dwindle.

While these diversions were going on, I concentrated mainly on creating greater openness and good will on the campus, involving faculty in creating a positive vision for the campus' next decade, and rebuilding bridges with the community. I spoke at the local and nearby Rotary Clubs, Lions Club, Soroptimist Club, and any and all other community organizations. I also reached out to the alumni. In April, through the good offices of Chico State alum and KHSL-TV Sportscaster Royal Courtain, I was joined by Courtain himself, Jim Considine, CSU Trustee representative for all CSU alumni, and Marla Forrest, Chico alumni president. The one-hour program, dubbed *The Great Alumni Linkup* connected us with alumni all over the U.S. It turned out to be an innovative and successful program that elevated the role of the alumni association.

Chico Enterprise-Record/Wednesday, March 16, 1994/3A

Esteban has adventure at White House

By Larry Mitchell
Staff Writer

When Chico State University President Manuel A. Esteban walked into Washington's Hilton Hotel alongside President Clinton, some visiting Californians were amazed — not the least of whom was CSU Chancellor Barry Munitz.

"How did Manuel manage that?" Munitz said he wondered as he related the story at a conference for CSU professors in Monterey recently.

The chancellor opened his talk at the conference with the story about Esteban and the president. He said he and some other CSU executives went to Washington on a lobbying mission and to attend a convention for educators last month.

Munitz said he'd hoped to meet the Clintons, and as he waited in a large crowd at the hotel where the president was to speak, he was flabbergasted when Esteban and Clinton walked in together.

Well, how did Manuel manage it?

In fact it was more illusion than reality, but it was fun even so, Esteban said.

The key was Kelly Craighead, a recent Chico State graduate, who is deputy director for travel and advance for Hillary Clinton.

Esteban, who had accompanied Munitz to Washington, left the CSU contingent to go visit Kelly at the White House.

"I was hoping to get an introduction to Bill and Hillary," Esteban said in an interview. Unfortunately, the president was working on a speech and didn't want to be disturbed, and his wife also was busy.

As a consolation, Kelly gave Esteban a tour of areas of the White House the public doesn't normally get to see.

After that, Esteban thought he'd return to the Hilton to hear Clinton address the educators' convention.

But there was a problem. For security reasons, the hotel's doors

are closed half an hour before the president speaks. There was no way Esteban would be able to get in.

"I mentioned it to Kelly, and she said she'd see what she could do," Esteban said. "She took me to the chief of security; they did a clearance check, gave me a special badge and told me to wait at the motorcade."

Esteban ended up riding to the Hilton in an official vehicle, two cars behind Clinton's. "I sat with a speech writer and a couple of other staffers," he said. "It was kind of exciting to see from the inside what the president sees."

Esteban said at each street the motorcade crossed, police had

blocked off the intersection.

The people he was riding with told him Clinton normally doesn't see a speech he's going to give until he gets into his limousine: he simply reads it over on the way. But in this case, because he felt it was important, the president spent an hour going over his talk after he'd received it from a speech writer.

When they arrived at the Hilton, everyone got out of the motorcade and went into the hotel as a group.

Esteban said he happened to be walking a couple of people away

from Clinton as they entered.

To Munitz, who was waiting with about 1,500 other people in the vast ballroom, such proximity between the head of state and the head of Chico State was impressive.

There was an empty seat at a table right at the front, so Esteban sat down to hear Clinton's talk.

"He gave a very good speech," Esteban said. And when he finished, Clinton "came straight at me, shook my hand and said, 'Hello, Manuel,' "

The president knew Esteban's name from the name tag he was wearing.

As the president left, reporters who had been sitting nearby approached Esteban, wanting to know who he was and why Clinton had spoken to him.

"I said, 'I'm just the president of Chico State University,' but I added, 'It's a very important campus — the deputy director for travel and advance for Hillary Clinton is a Chico State grad,' " Esteban said. "They took notes. It was actually very funny."

Esteban met Clinton twice that day. For some reason, he said, he'd been invited to attend Clinton's signing of an executive order on Hispanic education.

So that afternoon, he and Allen Sherwood, Chico State's director of alumni relations, attended that session at the White House with 30 or 40 Hispanic members of Congress.

"I shook (Clinton's) hand again, and he remembered me and said, 'Hello, Manuel,' " said Esteban. "He's very, very charming. When he's talking to you, he seems to have all his attention on you."

Esteban said he mentioned to Kelly it might be nice if Clinton or Hillary or Vice President Gore could stop by Chico State some time and give a speech.

Kelly said she wasn't sure it was possible, Esteban said, but she'd see what she could do.

Chico State University President Manuel A. Esteban poses with Kelly Craighead in the Green Room of the White House during a visit to Washington last month. Craighead, who is on Hillary Clinton's staff, graduated in 1989 from Chico State, where she was Associated Students executive vice president.

It was during this linkup, I believe, that I connected with a 1989 Chico State graduate, Kelly Craighead, who had been Associate Student Executive Vice President, and who was now on First Lady Hilary Clinton's staff, as deputy director for travel and advance. Kelly invited me to visit the White House whenever I was in Washington. As it happened, in March, the American Association of State Colleges and Universities (AASCU) held its annual meeting in Washington. President Clinton was to address the roughly 1,500 presidents and chancellors and other dignitaries that comprised this influential educational organization. Kelly secured an invitation to the White House for me. She indicated that she would do everything in her power to get me an audience with either President Clinton or Hillary Clinton, or perhaps even both. I was beside myself in anticipation.

When I arrived at the White House I was bedecked with all kinds of tags, pins, and other identifications to ensure that I had the right to walk around there. I still have some of them. The others I was forced to turn in. As it turned out, the First Lady was not in and the President was revising the speech that he would be delivering at the Hilton, where AASCU was meeting. Kelly still held hope that I might have a fleeting chance to meet with President Clinton, if he finished his revisions in time. In the meantime, she was kind enough to show me around the White House. It was an unforgettable experience. I had access to parts of the building that I think most mortals never have a chance to see. She took me to the room where the military keeps the "football," the suitcase with the nuclear codes. Wow, I thought! Kelly told me that she had some errands to run but that I could continue to carry on with the visit. She also offered me as much coffee as I wanted. I took her up on the offer. I managed to have a number of cups, a decision I later regretted.

As I was walking around through the corridors of power, I realized that I could not wait any longer. If I was going to make it to the Hilton Hotel in time to hear the President's speech I had better leave immediately. I saw Kelly and informed her that I was leaving. She indicated that I did not have enough time to make it. For security reasons the hotel's doors close half an hour before the president arrives. I was devastated. Kelly was very helpful, though. She asked me if I would mind going to the Hilton Hotel in the caravan of cars that would transport the President. Of course, I wouldn't! She took me to the chief of security, they did a clearance check, gave me a special badge and told me to wait at the motorcade. She told me to wait by the exit door she indicated and not to move because once the President is ready to leave, he doesn't wait for anyone. By this time the coffee was following its normal trajectory. I wasn't about to seek a bathroom for fear of missing the President. I figured that I could wait until I got to the Hotel.

The President walked by and went into the first limousine. I was placed in the one behind him, together with those young people who had written the speech for him. They paid no attention whatsoever to me. They were grumbling that President Clinton always changed what they wrote and wondered how much he had changed this time. In any event, we left the White House. I was by the window and felt like waving to the people who lined the streets as we went by. All traffic had been stopped. We sailed through the streets. When we got to the Hilton the caravan parked under the covered portico that had been built after President Reagan's attempted assassination. We then came into the dining hall where all the presidents were already sitting. I don't know how it happened, but I came in just ahead of President Clinton. When Chancellor Munitz and my CSU presidential colleagues saw me make an entrance followed by the president, they were aghast. Chancellor Munitz was heard exclaiming "How did Manuel manage that?"

As I looked around the huge dining hall I saw nowhere to sit. Every available seat was taken. Someone found a table by the dais and asked the people sitting there to make room for me, and we were ready to eat and listen to President Clinton. I thought that would be the right moment for me to squeeze in a much-needed bathroom break. I stealthily moved toward the closest door but was stopped by a member of the President's security detail. No one was allowed to leave or enter. The doors were to remain closed until the President left. I pleaded with the officer, to no avail. I sat back and prayed that President Clinton would be more parsimonious with his words than he usually was when delivering speeches. He wasn't.

I must admit that I don't recall a word about his speech. I was in too much physical pain. I was ready to explode. As soon as he was done speaking, I was ready to jump. But he was not done yet. He wanted to mingle with the crowd. As he came down from the dais, I was the very first person he encountered. He shook my hand and, even though I never saw him read my name tag, he called me by my name. The fact that I was the first person to be personally greeted by him also impressed my colleagues. Since I was the first, he addressed after coming down the dais, a number of journalists surrounded me wondering who I was. I told them that I was the President of Chico State University, a very important campus with famous graduates, such as the deputy director for travel and advancement for Hillary Clinton. They took notes. I read the papers the following day. Nothing I said had made it. When he was finally escorted out of the building, and they opened the doors I made a mad dash. I made it just in time.

Before I went to Washington, I had been invited by the White House to attend Clinton's signing of an executive order on Hispanic education. I had not planned on attending, but after not having had a chance to speak to Clinton in the morning, I decided to go. So, that afternoon, Allen Sherwood, Chico State's director of alumni relations and I went to the session at the White House with some Hispanic university presidents and a few Hispanic members of Congress. It was a far more intimate gathering than the one at AACSU. When he was done signing the document, he made the rounds, shaking everyone's hand. When he came to me, he obviously remembered that he had met me a few hours earlier. He shook my hand and said "Hello, Manuel. We meet again, for the second time today." I was astonished at his memory. I was also impressed how, for the few seconds he devotes to you, he seemed not to notice anything but you. A wonderful talent if you wish to make people feel listened to and consequential.

I thought I would push my luck and ask Kelly if it would be possible to convince either the president or the first lady to come to Chico State to give a speech. She thought that their schedules would probably prohibit such a visit but that she would see what she could do. They never made it. However, shortly after that, I received in the mail a framed photo of Hillary Clinton dedicated to me and a note apologizing for not having been able to meet with me. I thought that this was a very classy lady.

As the campus was preparing for the 1994 commencement ceremony, there was tremendous excitement in the air. Among the activities that were to take place in early May was my official inauguration. Planning for this event had begun in the fall with a committee of students, faculty, staff, and luminary representatives of the community. I did not play any role in the planning, nor did I attend any of the meetings. I didn't even know what was being planned. Inaugurations are relatively commonplace events in higher education, including in the CSU. In fact, four of the CSU campuses had recently celebrated presidential inaugurations, Cal Poly, Pomona, CSU, Northridge, Sonoma State, and CSU, Fullerton. However, what should have been just one more inauguration became once again a *cause célèbre* in Chico. The planning committee had decided that this would be a great opportunity to highlight the excellence of the institution and bring together in a spirit of unity and cooperation all the various constituencies that composed the university and make common cause with the larger Chico community. Under the theme "Celebrating Worlds of Opportunity," events would include an inaugural run and walk, faculty lectures, several ceremonies honoring achievements of faculty, staff, and students, concerts, Cinco de Mayo, a panel discussion by CSU Chancellor Barry Munitz, California community colleges Chancellor David Mertes, President Alistair McCrone of HSU and Tomás Arciniega, CSUB on the future of higher education, a reception and dinner honoring seven alumni who had distinguished careers, the University Farm barn dance and barbecue, the inauguration itself, and a reception and inaugural ball to cap the week.

Once the details of the inauguration were made public, Professor Conlin, although he was quite aware that presidential inaugurations were commonplace and expected traditional academic events, immediately called it a coronation. In the echo chamber that he and the local press had created, it took no time at all before *CN&R* on 28 April 1994, its front page, entitled "Royal Blues," with a colorful drawing of me, a paper doll, in my underwear, including shorts with the colors of the Spanish flag, and a change of clothes, a blue suit and a royal robe and crown of the same royal blue that could be cut out and used to dress the doll representation of me as appropriate. Of course, the weekly paper did not have the courage to claim its ownership. It gave the impression, by the inscription at the bottom of the page, that they were just representing what they claimed: "Why Critics Call Esteban's Inauguration A 'Coronation." If so, the paper failed to demonstrate that anyone other than Conlin and his sidekick expressed anything but interest in what promised to be a week of intellectual dialogue, a demonstration of the quality of the university's academic programs, the excellence of its faculty and alumni, and the desire to put behind some difficult times and move forward with confidence and high expectations.

News&Review

CHICO

Royal Blues

Why Critics Call Esteban's Inauguration A 'Coronation'

AN INDEPENDENT WEEKLY NEWSPAPER   VOLUME 17, NO. 39   APRIL 28, 1994

There were many who wrote letters to the *CN&R* not only in support of the inauguration itself but quite critical of the embarrassing manner in which the press was covering the event. Of all of them I was touched by the letter by a female faculty member of Religious Studies, Professor Peggy Beemer, whom I had never met, published 3 May 1994, in the middle of inauguration week: "The cover on last week's issue showing Manuel Esteban as a paper doll, and reference to the upcoming inaugural ceremonies as a 'coronation' do everyone in Chico a serious disservice. The inauguration is not designed to glorify Esteban, but to take the opportunity to celebrate this new beginning for the university and remind the community of its important role in university life. ... The work of the president of CSU, Chico is more important than ever in an economic environment where state resources are dwindling, and private funding sources are also drying up. Manuel Esteban has a crucial role to play in this city's future: he must run the organization which employs more people than any other in Chico. Rather than helping him do so intelligently and thoughtfully, he has been made a target of cheap shots which wrongly question his integrity, and which are designed to impede his ability to lead. There are plenty of legitimate and complex problems which face Chico and CSU Chico to which the public and press should be paying attention. Let's not be distracted by the name-calling theatrics of a few attention-grabbers and look instead to identifying problems which prevent town and university from working together toward their common goals and interests." I could not have said it better myself. I don't recall if I ever thanked her. If I didn't, I should have.

Although Jack Winning, the editor of *E-R*, criticized Chancellor Munitz's comments on the need to diversify the campus, and the speech made by President Arciniega, he did admit that the *E-R* itself bore some responsibility in making my first few months anything but blissful, that none of what they had done was "calculated to make a new president sleep more soundly." And, as if attempting to show some equanimity, he closed by writing: "But the president's a runner, and maybe he's close to getting his second wind. The reality of his existence ... is that he steers a big ship in a small pond ... and the crew members, if not outright mutinous, all seem to want to get their oars in. Most of what he's encountered was surely not in the job description." Indeed, it wasn't. Nonetheless, this is what I had inherited and, if I was to succeed, I was going to have to steer the ship better and manage to have all its crew members row in the same direction.

From a very personal perspective, inauguration week represented for me a culmination of all the work and sacrifices Gloria and I had made along the way to get to this point.

Manuel's Inauguration, 1994

The whole week was a whirlwind of activities and emotions. This is when Founders Week was created. It permitted us to honor the past and affirm our hope for the future. Of all the events and highlights, there are some moments that stand out for different reasons. One such moment was my meeting with seven CSU Chico graduates, one from each college, honored as distinguished alumni. They were incredibly talented, accomplished, and nationally and internationally renowned. I realized then that this was a very important event that needed greater visibility and recognition. In subsequent years, the distinguished alumni recognition became the main attraction of Founders Week, a major annual event highly covered by our local press as well as newspapers from the cities from which these outstanding people originated and/or lived. The dinner organized to honor these outstanding alumni was held at one of the gyms. It lacked the solemnity that should accompany such an important event. We needed to do better. The following year we held the event at one of the two golf course dining areas. The decorations were impeccable, the dress code became black tie, and the atmosphere that reigned was one of ceremonial dignity. It did not take long for this event to become one of the most anticipated and enjoyable yearly happenings.

The centerpiece of this particular Founders Week, however, was the inauguration ceremony itself, an event that included processional music, and a procession that marched from Butte Hall to to Laxson Auditorium, composed of almost three hundred faculty in caps and gowns led by honorary grand marshal Ted Meriam, a retired Chico businessman, one time mayor and former chair of the California State University Board of Trustees. When we all entered Laxson Auditorium we were received by eight hundred guests who were already there awaiting the beginning of a much-anticipated ceremony. Among the total number of attendees, 1,100, were some of the leading figures in California Higher education. I was presented with a bronze medallion designed by Professor Gregg Berryman, and cast by an art professor, Vernon Patrick, and a glass mace, made expressly for me, designed by Dave Smallhouse, and sculpted by Carol Boyd, a gift from master glassblower Smallhouse, from *Orient and Flume*, one of two exceptional Chico glass-making studios.

I was humbled to be on stage in the company of people I admired, like Presidents Tomás Arciniega, from CSU, Bakersfield, Alistair McCrone, president of Humboldt State University, and Norma Rees, president of Hayward University. There was also a very special person, Glenn Kendall, Chico State's president from 1950 to 1966, a gracious southerner who became my mentor and friend, as well as Betty Dean, president of neighboring Butte College, and a great colleague, Larry Vanderhoef, chancellor of the University of California at Davis, Rose Marie Ruiz (whose daughter was a CSU, Chico student), president of the National University of Costa Rica, Chico State's sister university, Chancellor Barry Munitz, Molly Broad, CSU Executive Vice Chancellor, Antony Vitti, chair of the California State University Board of Trustees, and Rick Callender, Associated Students president. And last but certainly not least, there was the incomparable Marilyn Warrens, president of the University's Advisory Board.

In front of the dais were seated some of the most important people in my life, beginning with Gloria, our daughter Jackie, and my brother/

teacher Julio. They were joined by our son-in-law Rafael, Bill and Gaye Ashby, our dear friends from Santa Barbara, Francesc, a friend I had met at the University of Michigan, who came for the occasion from Barcelona, and my intimate friend and former professor of Spanish, Serge Zaïtzeff. Last but certainly not least, a new addition to our family, Adriana, our four-week- old granddaughter.

Before the speeches began, university musicians and a choral group played "El cant dels ocells," The Carol of the Birds, a Catalan song that students learned to sing in Catalan, that has always been my favorite and never fails to lift my spirits and move me to tears. It did as well on this occasion for Gloria, Jackie, and Julio.

Don Heinz, Dean of the College of Humanities and Fine Arts, who served as master of ceremonies, began by citing the importance of rituals and ceremony. All the other dignitaries spoke briefly and expressed confidence in my ability to lead CSU, Chico to great things. I was humbled by their generosity and support. I was most touched by Marylin Warrens' short speech. She reaffirmed the University's Advisory Board's commitment to me by quoting Lauren Bacall, "you know how to whistle, don't you? Just pucker up your lips and blow. We'll be there for you." This drew the loudest outburst of laughter and brought some levity to a rather sumptuous atmosphere. With the exception of the manner in which Mrs. Warrens offered her unflinching support, I must confess that I was not totally happy with the implied criticisms of some of the esteemed guests and colleagues. I welcomed allies and supporters, of course, but I did not wish to be perceived as weak. I had faced many obstacles and challenges in our moves from Barcelona to Souvigny and from there to Calgary and Medicine Hat, and from there on a long and demanding journey of studies, scholarship, and administrative duties of all sorts to reach the presidency. I had stumbled in my first weeks in Chico, but I had not fallen, nor was I prepared to face such an eventuality. If anything, their veiled conviction that I might not be able to be the president that they imagined made me all the more determined to beat whatever odds might be stacked against me.

When all the guests of honor had spoken, it became my turn to address the people gathered at Laxson Theater. I started by expressing my deep gratitude for the opportunities that Canada and the U.S. had given me. I mentioned I was heartbroken that neither my father, who had died five months earlier, or my mother who was paralyzed from a severe stroke, were not in attendance. Needless to say, they were among the very first I called when I was offered the presidency. But I wondered what it meant to them, other than that it was important? How could my father, who had never gone to school, conceive of what such an achievement represented? How much had my mother, unable to speak and for whom it was difficult to confirm how much she understood, ever grasp completely the significance of this event? But Dean Heinz was totally correct when he spoke of the importance of rituals and ceremonies. Had my parents been present and been able to witness the solemnity and pageantry of the inauguration, they might not have understood what my responsibilities entailed, but they would certainly have been convinced that this was no ordinary job nor an unremarkable happening. They would have been impressed and incredibly proud. They would have seen in my success the reward for their many sacrifices over the years.

Fortunately, I had other people to thank who were present. First and foremost, there was Gloria, always at my side, always supportive, and Jacqueline, our beloved daughter, our pride and joy. Then there was my brother, Julio. While he was in grades eleven and twelve, he had helped me fill the enormous gaps that existed in my formal education and prepared me, with saintly patience, to pass the high school equivalency exams. It is education that opened worlds of opportunity for me. I asked whether we, as educators, were doing as well for our students today, whether we were opening for them the same doors of opportunity education had given me. This rhetorical question allowed me to move into what I believed we, at Chico State, needed to do to ensure that this did not just become one more rhetorical unanswered question. I wanted everyone in the audience to be aware of the task ahead for us as a community of scholars. Though faculty and staff were probably aware of this fact, I wanted everyone present to know that I had appointed a Task Force on the Future of CSU, Chico made up of community members, alumni, students, administrators, and faculty. The clear message here was that, to borrow from one of Hillary Clinton's campaign slogans, it takes a village. This was too important a goal to deal with intramurally only.

What was the charge to this Task Force? I expected the group to work on at least five major areas. Here is how I stated them at the time:

1) Identify the threats and opportunities that the current economic, political, technological, social, and cultural environment present for us as a regional, comprehensive university.
2) Take inventory of our recognized expertise and resources in the area of technology and determine the technologies which are likely to be of consequence in learning environments as we enter the 21st century.
3) Evaluate the role that CSU, Chico is already playing in the region we serve and identify ways in which we can better utilize the resources available ... to play a more intrusive and beneficial role in the ... development of our region.
4) Work toward what is being called a "seamless" education, one that brings into greater harmony and integration high schools, community colleges and the university.
5) Finally, imagine and implement the ways in which Chico can turn its residential situation into rich community building.

I concluded with the following statements: "Diversity cannot be excluded from worlds of opportunity. I am totally committed to the diversification of our students, faculty and staff. This is not a personal agenda. It is a national issue, and it is one of the key goals of the CSU." I further added: "We need to be driven by common goals, convinced that our individual well-being is inextricably intertwined with our collective effort, resolve, and purpose. Let us stand united. Let us work together for a better future. Let us continue creating worlds of opportunity." I was encouraged by the reception of my words. I received a standing ovation. Clearly, there were many who felt as I did and who viewed our common purpose and goals as appropriate and necessary. At the end of the ceremony, I became the 10th president of CSU, Chico, a dream come true.

Despite the overall impression that Jack Winning and others in the press may have had, it became patently clear to me that I was on the right track. I received an avalanche of letters, memos, postcards, and telephone calls from simple community members, from faculty, from student leaders, and most impactfully for me, from staff. Some departments unanimously signed letters of support and condemned the divisive tactics used by the local press. Whole departments signed letters of support. One letter in particular filled me with hope. It came from the secretary of the Department of Professional Studies in Education, Ms. Carlene Goodell, a person I don't believe I had ever met. It was a page long letter which I will not replicate here even though it deserves it. I do want, however, to reproduce some of her commentaries because she clearly understood and validated what I was trying to accomplish.

What a warm, wonderful inauguration. It was done with charm, style and simplicity. I have not talked to one person not touched by the genuineness of the event. ... I heard a spirit in your inaugural speech that could possibly be the cultural glue to pull us together and onto the same path. I heard the same sentiment expressed by others at the reception ... Your statements were filled with a sense of beginning and belief in the future. What a wonderful first step toward strengthening our University culture! Thank you for letting us all be a part of the inauguration. ... Thank you again for sharing your story of becoming and overcoming. It truly made you a person to us rather than "an office."

My goal to elevate the importance of members of the staff to ensure they saw themselves as an integral part not only of the university community but of our common vision and goals was paying off. The more I valued them and the more I listened and took their advice and input into consideration the more they became essential allies working toward a vision for a more productive and enhanced environment and mission. I needed them to help me move forward with all of our common goals. Faculty, too, were beginning to have faith in our future and stand up to bullies. On 17 May 1994, just over one week after the inauguration, the Faculty Academic Senate took aim at a perceived climate of hostility at Chico State. Senators unanimously passed a resolution praising "campus president Manuel A. Esteban for his constructiveness in promoting 'a spirit of collegiality' on campus." Jim Postma, chair of the Faculty Senate, said in an interview with the *E-R*, that the resolution was in part a response to what he called the negative tactics of some of Esteban's critics. "It's an attempt to make a statement that the senate and, I think, a large majority of the faculty like and want the kind of (open) communication Manuel says he wants, it is also a response to 'accusations by Conlin and others.'"

Even a Catholic priest felt a need to intervene. Father Michael Newman, Director of the Newman Catholic Center, could not let Professor Conlin's intemperate but repetitive attack on me pass. In a letter to the editor of the *E-R*, on 10 July 1994, he offered the following comments: "President Manuel Esteban does not have an easy job. He has taken on a task that is rather impossible, to put it mildly. He deserves respect. Referring to him as 'Manny' is disrespectful to him as a person – as would be to refer to Dr. Conlin as 'Joey' or me as 'Mikey'. I would project that whoever has the job of president will be the target of Dr. Conlin's anger. Why does Dr. Conlin have to keep explaining this to you people? Because the people are not in agreement, and his tactics are objectionable. Mother Teresa would be the first one to say that President Esteban is a good man. He may not do everything we would like him to do, but please give him credit for trying. And, as far as the church-going public is concerned, I would suggest that in this day and age character assassination is much worse than physical assassination. Doing unto others as you would have them to unto you is still the best way to live our lives."

Shortly after the inauguration I went to Barcelona. Because of the deserved reputation CSU, Chico had in the area of applied computer science and simulations, I had been invited as a guest speaker to the European Simulation Multiconference. I spoke about *Simulation Methodology and Applications*, one of the seven main themes of the conference. It wasn't a natural topic for me since it was so distant from anything I had studied, but, fortunately, the faculty in our program had prepared me adequately. I discharged my responsibility professionally, I believe. This was not the last time I would find myself giving speeches that fell far from my areas of expertise. I always found it fascinating and learned a lot along the way.

In August, before the beginning of a new academic year, Gloria and I made our annual pilgrimage to Canada to spend some time with Gloria's parents, my mother, Julio and family. Jackie and little Adriana joined us there. When we got to Medicine Hat, we received a gut punch. On 13 August, while we were on the last leg of our car trip, Gloria's father Cisco had gone shopping at Safeway in preparation for our arrival. He suffered a heart attack and died right in front of the fruit section. We were all distraught. He was only 83 and he was Gloria's mother caretaker.

Gloria was faced with a very unpleasant reality. One of the reasons we were in Medicine Hat was to help them move into a nursing home, a necessary decision given Vicenta's worsening condition resulting from her stroke a decade or so earlier, but one that had left Cisco destroyed. He loved his house, his garden, and his independence. Gloria adored her father. He was now gone. This in and of itself caused her tremendous hurt. On top of this, she now had to move her mother to a nursing home. We could not bring her to Chico because she would not have been covered by our medical insurance. How could Gloria possibly leave her mother there? Who would look after her? Since my brother had already found a very nice nursing home in Calgary for our mother, we promised Vicenta that we would do everything in our power to transfer her to where my mother now lived. It was a very desirable facility so we did not hold much hope that the move could be made any time soon. When we finally left Calgary for Chico, Gloria was racked with guilt. She promised her mother that she would come to visit her as often as possible. She kept her promise. Fortunately, my brother kept bugging the administrators at the nursing home in Calgary and within months Vicenta joined my mother. Not that the presence of my mother helped all that much. Her paralysis made it impossible for her to be much of a companion. Julio, on the other hand, was saintly. He went to visit my mother almost every day and often went to visit Vicenta as well and tended to her needs whenever necessary. Having Julio there gave Gloria some peace of mind. She had always loved Julio, whom she had known since he was 11. She now loved him more and was deeply indebted to him. She knew that had she had a brother he would not have been any more solicitous toward Vicenta than Julio was.

Back in Chico, as sad as we both were, I had little choice but to immerse myself in the job again. As we were beginning a new academic year, the public relations person at the university showed me a list of the many activities I had been involved in so far: he enumerated the number of speeches I had given, the press conferences I had participated in, the radio and TV interviews I had granted, the number and variety of meetings I had attended, the organization and clubs I had addressed. To this list needed to be added the monthly two-day trips to Long Beach to meet one month with the members of the Executive Council, made up of Chancellor Munitz and his staff and the other month to attend the Board of Trustees meetings, as well as the many other out of town trips to meet with political, educational, legislative, and alumni groups. I had also hosted many "faculty coffees" and "staff coffees" around my conference table, something I did until my very last year in office. The selection and appointment of a new Provost and Vice President for Academic Affairs, and the consolidation of two vice presidencies into one, thus reducing administrative costs, and the hiring of an Affirmative Action officer had also taken inordinate amounts of time out of my already overburdened schedule.

My calendar for the first six to eight months on the job indicates that I had been working at a frenetic pace. I then understood what had happened to me toward the end of my first semester. After one of these very hectic days, late in the evening I got into my car to head home. It dawned on me that I did not remember where home was. I sat in the car for a long while. Finally, I decided to leave campus in the hope that force of habit would take me home. For a while I just drove around. I still did not have any idea where we lived. I stopped, tried to relax, did some breathing exercises until I felt calm enough to once again let the car, in a way, direct me home. I ultimately made it. I did not realize it then but when it happened again a few months later in a much worse manifestation, such that Gloria took me to the hospital, I understood what had happened on that day. I was diagnosed with transient global amnesia. It isn't serious but it sure is frightening.

During an episode of transient global amnesia, your recall of recent events simply vanishes, so you can't remember where you are or how you got there. In addition, you may not remember anything about what's happening in the here and now. Consequently, you may keep repeating the same questions because you don't remember the answer you've been given. You may also draw a blank when asked to remember things that happened a day, a month, or even a year ago. This is exactly what happened to me. The most comical part of the second, more serious manifestation of this amnesic fit is the exchange I had with Gloria. She wanted to know what I had forgotten. My answer made a lot of sense to me: "how can I remember what I have forgotten if I don't remember?" Over the years I have suffered a few more such episodes. I always attributed it to stress and overwork. It is only in the last couple of years that a neurologist determined that these episodes were probably a precursor to a mild form of epilepsy that afflicts me now, though it is easily controlled with adequate medication.

Despite these episodes and the unrelenting attacks from the same guilty parties, I sensed that I was beginning to turn the corner at CSU, Chico. Not everything was peachy-keen, but there was clearly light at the end of the tunnel. It would still take another semester before I felt that I, the university, and the community at large were on the same path, but I now knew that this goal was achievable. I started the academic year 1994-1995 with renewed energy and a sense of purpose.

On 1 September 1994, I held my second Faculty Convocation. The theme of my presentation was *CSU, Chico, Campus of First Choice*. The faculty in Harlen Adams Theater was about 250 professors, "the largest in recent years," as the press indicated. Drawing upon the Task Force recommendations, I outlined a number of specific projects to be undertaken.

1) I asked the new provost, Scott McNall to create a "center for excellence in learning and teaching. This project would be funded with $100,000 gleaned from savings on administrative salaries.
2) Academic affairs had the responsibility to make the campus's general-education program more innovative, effective, and focused.
3) I gave the dean of regional and continuing education, Ralph Meuter, marching orders to come up with proposals to expand and augment distance learning, something for which Chico State was deservedly recognized.
4) I directed all three vice presidents to redesign the campus' budget process.

Overarching these specific goals, I asked the faculty to help "create a student culture that emphasizes intellectualism, service, and physical and mental health and well-being, and that de-emphasizes hedonism and immediate gratification." I told the audience that we were well on our way toward making Chico State's intellectual climate more vital. The presidential lecture series held during my inauguration would be revamped and continued each year. The theme for the 1994-1995 academic year would be "The Learning Community."

Tied to this theme, I intimated there was a very important consideration, and this was the nature of our general education program. This was a constant battle I waged at UM, Dearborn, CSUB, and now at CSU, Chico. I made the point to faculty that as it now stood, the general education (GE) curriculum was driven by the needs of departments to generate resources based on the number of courses offered, not the needs of students. The result of such a strategy was often a "smorgasbord" of some 300 courses, far too many to create the kind of GE or core curriculum they were meant to provide. In addition, too many of the courses were overly narrow and constrictive. As faculty, I explained, we often complain that students don't integrate knowledge, but we teach in a "little boxes" model. I expressed my preference for a more integrative and multi-disciplinary approach. First, we had to agree that GE requirements shouldn't be resource driven. What should drive GE, I added, "is a fundamental question: What do we want our students to learn in order to be good citizens and educated people?" I urged our new Provost to reevaluate GE and come up with recommendations to end up with a curriculum that would make CSU, Chico the university of first choice that we all aimed for. The following month, on 11 October 1994, I made a similar presentation to the Staff Council. I wanted to ensure that, since they had representatives on the Task Force, I kept staff well informed as well.

Exactly a month after my presentation, I received a copy of a letter Pat Gantt, Chair of the Staff Council, had sent to Richard West, CSU's Vice Chancellor for Business and Finance. In this letter Pat thanked Richard for making himself available to a group from the Staff Council. What fortified my belief in consultation was Pat's concluding paragraph: "Again, thank you for meeting with the Staff Council Executive Committee. We are privileged to work on a campus with an open administration, and a talented leader and individual as Manuel Esteban. He regularly sends a representative, or personally attends Staff Council meetings to respond to questions." A few days later I received a copy of a letter Pat Gantt had sent this time to Molly Corbett Broad, CSU's Executive Vice Chancellor. In a two-page letter meant to thank Ms. Broad for her willingness to meet with Pat and members of his Executive Committee, he devoted a couple of paragraphs to speak about me. "I wish to report on President Esteban's first year. He made an extraordinary effort to meet with every group within campus and the outside community. He was gracious, humorous, and listened carefully. Unfortunately, I feel, some administrators were somewhat reluctant to follow his leadership initially and tried his patience. They seemed reluctant to implement any changes. Add to that, the continual personal attacks from a malcontent history professor who offers no alternatives to solve problems. Manuel Esteban has a lot of patience. … His style is uniquely suited for Chico. Please convey this to Chancellor Munitz as well."

I also made an announcement that was well received by the faculty. The previous two years of budget cuts had been made basically across the board, an easy enough decision but one that had crippled considerable academic affairs. Since about 80% of the general budget is usually devoted to academic affairs, it took 80% of the cuts. This may have seemed equitable at the time but, in my opinion, it had missed its mark. I meant to demonstrate that cuts had to be made with this in mind. Consequently, I assigned greater cuts to advancement and student services. Academic affairs would be cut by one-fifth of a percent; business and administration by half a percent, and advancement and student services by 1.5 percent. This was meant to send a very clear message: the ultimate mission and primacy of a university is teaching. All else must function to further this mission. I was questioned about the importance that excellence in teaching would mean when faculty were considered for promotion and tenure. I explained that "no one should ever get tenured who is not a good teacher. That is a *sine qua non*. However, one cannot be a good teacher if one isn't currently in his or her field. Things change, and it's crucial to stay on top of them. So, currency is something that must be demonstrated in the Retention and Tenure process."

The Trustees and Chancellor Munitz gave some presidents a clear mandate: we had to increase student enrollment. The university had plenty of individuals who worked tirelessly in our recruitment efforts. I just did not want to leave it only up to them to work magic. I wanted to do all I could to achieve our assigned targets. I don't know whether it had been done before or not, although I assumed it hadn't, given the reaction I got when I proposed sending a personal letter to each prospective student along with a two-page, single-spaced copy of the article the *E-R* asked me to write to welcome the 1994-1995 incoming class, where I detailed why I had accepted the presidency at Chico State. It listed at least twenty reasons why Chico State should be a destination of choice for any students who wanted an excellent education. My letter and attachment went to over 5,700 students. I also sent a letter to the parents, offering help if they needed it for any reason. One mother in particular contacted my office (4 May 1994), and worked first with my secretary, Teresa Arnold, and later with me. I managed to resolve her daughter's problem and she was successfully admitted. The mother, Mrs. Carol Davis was so amazed and appreciative that I had taken the time to help her daughter that she wrote a very lengthy, hand-written letter to Chancellor Munitz. She concluded her long letter with these words: "President Esteban is most certainly an asset to the CSU system. Even in these extremely difficult times of budget cuts, etc. he has not lost sight of the individual. His sincerity and professionalism are truly admirable ... and we are most appreciative!" Chancellor Munitz was very diplomatic in his reply, dated 11 May 1994: "With so many students to bear in mind (15,000 at the Chico campus), President Esteban is certainly to be commended for his efforts on behalf of those few individuals who need his particular attention." I saw what I was trying to accomplish at CSU, Chico as building a durable structure. The positive reactions I received for my efforts were the necessary bricks to build such a structure.

Sending letters to prospective students and their parents was a necessary but insufficient part of my strategy. As a residential campus whose students came from all over California and out of state, the mandate to increase our enrollment was not easily fulfilled. Still, if we did not, we would experience a further budgetary cut. This was not a possibility that I would even contemplate. It was time for CSU, Chico to work more closely with the community colleges in our area. We needed more transfer students to come to us rather than go to other state colleges and universities. The relationship between Chico State and the colleges in our region had not been the friendliest in recent years. I saw it as my responsibility to mend fences, if that was what it would take. I started, of course, with Butte College. President Betty Dean and I had hit it off well and we were both willing and eager to work cooperatively. My second visit was to Shasta College in Redding, about 90 miles north of Chico. There I met with President Douglas Treadway. As the *Redding Record Searchlight* made clear on 19 May 1994, "Intent on mending relations with much of Northern California, Chico State University President spent Wednesday visiting with officials from Shasta College and Redding. The trip symbolizes a renewed commitment by the university to work more closely with educators throughout northeastern California, something his predecessor had ignored." Treadway and I explored the elimination of duplicate services, expanded needed course offerings and strengthened ties between both schools. We also talked about the possibility of offering some degrees through video tele-conferencing, something CSU, Chico was renowned for doing exceptionally well. Redding had wanted a Chico State satellite campus. I had to be honest and tell them that, given budget cuts, this was something that we needed to push into the future.

My next visit was to College of the Siskiyous, up in Weed. In late October I travelled up north to share with the College my vision for CSU, Chico but also for the role we could and should play in bringing together better regional relations and coordination. My address was tailored to a special group, the Northern Instructional Officers. I was convinced that my efforts would pay off not only in better relationships and cooperation but in attracting more of their transfer students to our campus. All the presidents of the community colleges and I agreed that it would be very productive if we were to meet once every semester.

Between such visits, speeches, letters to students and parents, presentations to faculty, staff, students, and community groups and organizations I did not fail to consider national issues that could redound to the benefit of our institution. In September, I heeded a call from Senator Barbara Boxer to attend her first Washington seminar to discuss ways in which universities could help spur the recovery of California's economy. The main goal was to identify means by which to assist California's businesses, stimulate job creation, and move California forward. It was a worthwhile trip as I made a lot of important contacts with Californians in sectors of the economy with which we could cooperate.

Something happened then that gave Gloria and me a sense that it was going to be difficult to relax and enjoy good experiences without having to worry about what terrible event could upend normalcy. In early October, Walt Schafer and his wife Teresa invited Gloria and me to join them on a hike up Mount Brokeoff. It was a somewhat strenuous hike but a beautiful one. At one point we stopped to marvel at the majestic views offered in front of us. The terrain was gravelly. As Gloria turned to begin our descent, she fell in such an unnatural way that we heard her leg bones crack. She went immediately into shock. While I stayed with her helping to prop up her leg to reduce her unbearable pain, Teresa ran down the mountain to seek help. Gloria had to be airlifted by helicopter to Enloe Hospital in Chico. Unfortunately, the helicopter could not land where she was. They found a clearing, but it was a distance from where she was. With the help of the helicopter pilot, Walt and I moved her to where the copter was. I expected to go with her but was told that the copter would not be able to lift off with an additional person. By the time the three of us got to the hospital Gloria had been treated. She had a broken ankle and a spiral break that went up her tibia. She was put in a cast that went all the way up to her hip. It would take a lot of time and several changes in the cast she was forced to wear before she was fully recovered. Instead of being the person who supported me, the tables were now turned. She needed my help for almost everything as she was practically forced into immobility, at least for a long while.

Ironically, at about the same time, an important event brought some sunshine to my life. I learned that I was going to be the 11th graduate to receive the Distinguished Alumni Award from the University of Calgary. I considered this an unexpected but much welcomed honor, as I indicated at the time of the ceremony, October 15, "one of the most important honors in my life. The University of Calgary is one of my favorite places. I had five great years there. In my prepared remarks I remarked that "the education I received at the University of Calgary changed my life radically ...

Although I have certainly benefited from it in economic terms, the greatest value to me has been personal, psychological, emotional, spiritual ... Ultimately the greatest resource a university has is its faculty, for they are the ones not only who instill in us a love for the pursuit of knowledge and self-expansion, but who also become our role models. I was fortunate to come into contact with professors who not only taught me the subject matter, but who instilled in me a sense of responsibility and commitment to the profession and to students."

I had offered not to go to the ceremony in Calgary, but Gloria insisted that I go. Besides, she said, you can come back with my mother who might be able to help us during my recovery. This is what I did. After the ceremony I went to get Vicenta, and she came to Chico to spend about two months with us. Unfortunately, by this time she was 83 and not too stable. The stroke she had suffered years earlier had, as she aged, weakened her leg. She was prone to fall, which she did one night as she got up to go to the bathroom. I had to rush her to the hospital. Then, instead of being a help to Gloria and me, I had to take care of two invalids. I was happy to help but domestic duties now cut into my ability to devote as much time to my official responsibilities.

Lest I forget, one area that could have given me heartburn became a success story. The School of Agriculture had proven resilient. With the help and support of major farm and cattle producers, it flourished. In 1994 it was selected as "Agribusiness of the Year." Tom Dickinson, Director of the School and Ray Watkins, Farm Manager were kind enough to grant me a lot of credit for this turnaround. Though thankful for their praise I told them that the merit was all theirs. They had accepted the challenge I put in front of them, namely, "sink or swim" and they had demonstrated that they were more than able to swim. Theirs was a true story of determination, vision, and adaptation. A success story.

By the Fall semester of 1994, I began to feel quite comfortable in my position. I was aware that there was still a lot I had to do to win over most sectors of the university, community, and especially the press, but I was imbued with a greater sense of security. If I was to succeed in my quest to turn Chico State as the university of first choice as I had promised, there were a lot of changes, some small and some more momentous that needed to be made. The changes I was contemplating would probably require more than just a desire to change but a sustained effort. With this in mind, I began to make changes that, I hoped, would change the culture of the university.

I was grateful for all the support many people of the community provided. But if we were going to have broader appeal and a more national reputation, we needed to expand many of the supporting organizations. I began by looking at the Alumni Association. Its board was made up basically of local individuals. I convinced the board that we would need to attract distinguished alumni from outside the city. We needed regional and national recognition. This is what we did. I did something similar with the Foundation Board. Even though its primary function was to help the development officer to manage all the resources that were not controlled by the state, there was no reason why the only people who served on it, as good as they were, should be limited to the local community. We expanded it to recruit businesspeople, mostly Chico State alumni, to serve. Such expansion gave the Board as a whole greater visibility and importance. By involving more influential participants we also enhanced annual giving.

The remaining group that needed my attention was the University Advisory Board. My predecessor had not placed much value on it. It all depended on what the role of this group was to be. It is true that it needed love and care. This took time. It could be argued that the time this required was best spent on other tasks. I saw this quite differently. In my opinion, an Advisory Board composed of influential members from across the state and possibly the country could function as a force for good, as each of its members could be incredibly influential in whatever sphere they functioned. The people I had in mind, though, would not be satisfied playing a minor role. Since they would be advising me, I would need to take the time to have formal meetings during which they would be brought up to date on everything that was going on in the university, I would need to seek their advice and listen to them, I would need to make sure they felt valued and engaged substantially. I was able to bring people on board who would have been the envy of many universities. In fact, to this point, it was the Foundation Board that had been the most desirable for community leaders to join. One day, when the University Advisory Board had been well established and had clearly become an influential voice for me and the university, some members of the Foundation Board came to me to express concern about their not having been considered for the University Advisory Board. At this point I realized that I had to be very sensitive and not give the impression that I valued one over the other. I did not move anyone from one to the other, but I did ask a couple of the Foundation members whether they would be willing to play dual roles and thus function as bridges between the two boards. This suggestion was well received and eliminated any possible type of friction.

There was another issue that needed immediate attention. We could not be the university of first choice for many because we were a party school. Being selected by *Playboy Magazine* as the number-one party school in the U.S. had not done Chico State any favors. I racked my brains to come up with ways to tackle this thorny issue. I knew how ingrained and attractive this appellation was to prospective students. Early on in my tenure I had driven in a Chico police car on a Thursday night monitoring the nature of party activities. Two major things struck me. The first one was parties going on all over, wherever students lived. But the police could not be everywhere simultaneously. As soon as the police closed one venue, because of excessive attendance that students, like ants in a parade, moved to the next one. What puzzled me most was why the students were partying so actively on a Thursday night? This puzzle in particular was solved when I was shown the schedule of classes for Friday. There weren't many. Why? The reply I got seemed logical but wrongheaded. Supposedly, given that students drank to excess Thursday night, they were in no condition to go to class the following morning. Thus, rather than teach classes to just a few serious students, it was considered best not to schedule classes on that day. My counter argument was that such a move only encouraged students to party and drink more. I suggested that we resume classes on Friday and ensure that perhaps exams or tests of some sort should be required on those Fridays to force students to realize that going to class on that day was essential.

I did not know whether my suggestion would bear fruit. I did know, however, that I needed to try something dramatic to enhance the academic and cultural visibility of the university. I came up with the idea of inviting famous people to campus who were bound to attract the interest of students as well as everyone else. This, I knew, was going to take resources that we did not have. I would need to secure donors and sponsors. Any one of these invited speakers would cost anywhere from $70,000 to $100,000. My goal was to invite Nobel Prize Winners. They would come, give a public speech, be present at a reception to which many attendees would be invited, and have a private dinner with those donors and sponsors that had made their visit possible. Each one of them would have the chance to have their photo taken with the honored guest. I broached this idea with prospective donors and sponsors, and I was very happy that they saw this as an opportunity not only to help the university but to put Chico on the map. So, with this vote of confidence, we moved quickly.

The first Nobel Prize Winner to come to Chico State was Elie Wiesel, Holocaust survivor, author, journalist, and the 1986 prize winner. It was a smashing success. Over the next few years, we had six more Nobel Prize Winners. One was José Manuel Ramos Horta (1996), a dissident who became President of East Timor in 2007. The others were far more famous: Lech Walesa (1983), the Polish dissident who became the first president of Poland ever elected in a popular vote; Desmond Tutu (1984), the South African Anglican cleric who was awarded the Nobel Prize for Peace for his role in the opposition to apartheid; Shimon Peres (1994) Foreign and Prime Minister and later President of Israel, who won primarily for his secret negotiations between Palestinians and Israelis and responsible for the Oslo Accords; Mikhail Sergeyevich Gorbachev (1990), president of the Soviet Union who won for his leading role in the peace process which today characterizes important parts of the international community; and then there was Oscar Arias (1987), President of Costa Rica, a very inspirational speaker and a generous person. With the Nobel Prize money, he established the Arias Foundation for Peace and Human Progress, whose mission is to promote just and peaceful societies with three programs: women's rights, the Center for Peace and Reconciliation, and the Center for Organized Participation. We tried several times to book former President Jimmy Carter, but his schedule never made it possible. Each of the Nobel Prize winners we were able to attract were spellbinding speakers. Their individual struggles and achievements were inspirational.

Shimon Peres in Chico
Nobel Peace Prize Winner

Manuel and Gloria with Nobel Prize Winner Desmond Tutu and his wife Leah Nomalizo Tutu

Manuel and Gloria with Nobel Peace Prize Winner,
Lech Walesa

Manuel and Gloria with Mikhail Gorbachev

José Ramos Horta, Nobel Peace Prize Winner, with Manuel and Gloria

They were not the only Nobel Prize winners to grace our wonderful Laxson Auditorium, Dr. Farid Murad, brother of our own professor of Anthropology Turhon Murad, won the prestigious prize in medicine for his research in nitric oxide. Nitric Oxide, according to Doctor Murad, protects the heart, stimulates brain cells, and kills bacteria. Chico State and the Chico community as a whole were enriched by the presence of so many Nobel Prize winners. Gloria and I, and those very fortunate guests who made up the exclusive dinners hosting them and had the great honor of being photographed with them, could not believe that we were actually in the presence of individuals who, by their beliefs and actions, had played such an important role in changing parts of the world. These were humbling experiences.

Other than Nobel Prize winners we also had other famous and consequential speakers join in our series. Robert Kennedy Jr. came to talk about the environment. James Carville and his spouse Mary Matelin, both celebrated political strategists and famous as well for finding love across the aisle, spoke eloquently and often disparagingly about the political process. Their talk, *All's Fair: Love, War, & Running for President* was introduced by

CSU, Chico's alumnus and Ronald Reagan's Campaign Manager Ed Rollins. A very special speaker was NPR's Nina Totenberg, celebrated commentator for *All Things Considered, Morning Edition* and *Weekend Edition*. In 1996 we were honored to have Cornel West, the Harvard professor, author, provocateur, and philosopher. He spoke on *Race Matters*, the title of his 1993 book. Donna Shalala, who at the time was serving as the 18th United States Secretary of Health and Human Services under President Clinton was another guest. We were also very fortunate to have Leon Panetta visit our campus on several occasions. Talk about a person who could fascinate audiences. He has held so many roles within several administrations that he could be considered a *passe-partout*. One gets tired just reading all the positions he has held among others, Secretary of Defense, Director of the CIA, White House Chief of Staff, Director of the Office of Management and Budget. Three other speakers worth mentioning were Carolyn Shoemaker, a Chico State Alumna and famous astronomer, astronaut Scott Carpenter, and Bill Wattenburg, another CSU, Chico alumnus, a scientist and inventor, always on call for the Pentagon, and talk show host in San Francisco. I was pleased to be a guest on his show a couple of times. I used those two occasions to sing the praises of Chico State.

In 1999 we were all aflutter because Maya Angelou was going to be spending two days with us. She was phenomenal. What a delight. At one point she told the audience "All of us have the possibility of being a rainbow in somebody's cloud … That's what I want to do, to lift us all up." She received a standing ovation.

We had also attempted to bring Nelson Mandela to speak but we were unsuccessful, unfortunately. We settled for Winnie Mandela. What a disappointment she turned out to be. She was arrogant, disrespectful, self-aggrandizing and self-absorbed. She was a celebrity, however, and her closeness to Nelson Mandela attracted many. The theater was full. What mattered most to me was that the community perception of the value of having Chico State in its midst was changing perceptibly. We were no longer dismissed by many as primarily a party school. Not only were we the largest employer that pumped more than $400 million into the economy of the region, but we were the center of intellectual and cultural activity.

There was one more thing I came up with to achieve a number of simultaneous objectives. I convinced some donors and the Foundation Board to help me raise funds for scholarships. This would be called the President's Scholar Program. These scholarships would provide sufficient funds to cover all educational costs for the student recipients. We would also grant scholarships worth considerably less to a few runners-up. At the beginning I was able to secure support for only two of these very special scholarships. I meant for them to be awarded only to freshmen. But unlike in any other situation, in order to be granted one of them, students would need to come to campus and participate in a day of special examinations to demonstrate that they were the type of students we wanted. I was cognizant that two scholarships were insufficient and that the type of student I aspired to attract would have many choices. But here was my hidden strategy. This was to be a recruitment tool. I expected that many students would be seriously interested in us, others might not, but if their friends came, so would they. They would visit the campus. They would like it. What was there not to like about a beautiful campus in a beautiful city, in an institution that was known for producing graduates who were considered well prepared academically but also socially and thus attractive to employers? This was meant to demonstrate that we were interested in academic excellence. We were all happily surprised and encouraged by the number of students and their parents who came to participate in this experiment.

While the students were involved in their exams, their parents were treated to the best Chico State had to offer. Most of the tours were conducted by our best students. It was a smashing success that was repeated as long as I presided over the university. The end result of this experiment, however, was that we attracted a good number of students who participated in this program, well beyond those who received the scholarship. To demonstrate the importance of this program we printed very smart brochures that detailed what the program consisted of, how the awards would be determined, who was eligible, how to participate, and the reception that would follow, hosted by the president. Once it became clear that this had been a successful effort, we were able to secure more funds and offer an increasing number of scholarships.

Creating a vase with the help of two master glassblowers

Above, with the famous ar...

In time I asked Steve Nettleton to be my co-chair for the President's Scholars Program fund-raising campaign. I had a target of $10 million. Before I left the presidency, we had raised over $16 million. This meant that we increased the number of these desirable and prestigious scholarships from a very humble 2 to 10 and from $5,000 each for two years to

$5,000/year for four consecutive years. We also increased the number of scholarships we granted to 20 runners-up from $500 to $1,000. The amazing thing is that the program became incredibly popular. The number of students who came to participate in the exams went from 111 in 1996 to over 220 in 2003, and the number of parents who accompanied these student participants grew to well over 400. At one point, when I was already well established in my position and had far more freedom to carve out time for experimentation, I surprised the students' parents. One of the stops in their visit was the glass studio, where they found me demonstrating the art of glassblowing, often assisted by Rick Satava, one of America's best glass artists.

In subsequent years, the annual holiday season card Gloria and I sent showed a beautiful photograph taken in front of Kendall Hall featuring all the presidential scholar students. The back of the card provided the name of each one of these exceptional students. Their parents were elated that their sons and daughters were so prominently honored.

During my second convocation I had detected that those in attendance seemed more alert and attentive when I spoke about the achievements of faculty, administrators, staff, and students. I made a note of it and in all subsequent years, after a brief presentation on issues related to budgets, committee recommendations, necessary changes, or matters of significant importance, I devoted most of my time to trumpeting the accomplishments of our colleagues and anyone related to the university community. My goal was twofold: to praise, of course, but also to demonstrate what was worthy of commendation. The message was clear. If you want to be highlighted for your accomplishments, this is what you need to be engaged in. I also ensured that my convocation presentations were widely disseminated, particularly with the press and with the parents of our students.

Another initiative I took to enhance the importance of scholarship, teaching, service, and community engagement was to create opportunities for faculty and staff to shine and be modestly monetarily rewarded. With this goal in mind, we began to have yearly events that recognized one Outstanding Professor, one Outstanding Teacher, an award for Outstanding Service, and one that honored an Outstanding Staff member. We also initiated a President's Leadership Program and later on the President's Visiting Scholars Program. There were receptions for each and every one of these honorees, and their accomplishments were amply covered in our internal publication *Inside Chico*. Soon after this I realized that given the often-antagonistic attitude of the local press I could not rely on it to express my views, goals, and ideas and those of the institution as a whole. Therefore, I started to publish regular communications through my *President's Newsletter*.

We bid 1994 farewell with a very well attended reception at our home. Gloria, the gracious hostess, was not able to mill around as freely as she did the previous year nor was, she able to stand around. She was in a wheelchair. Our guests came to her instead of her making the rounds. I don't think she was totally unhappy with the situation. She still managed to enjoy the evening.

I felt that 1995-1996 was bound to be a better year and in many respects it was. Some of the past problems lingered on but, by and large, my star was in ascendancy and the university was recovering slowly but surely. I continued my routine of giving talks to various constituencies, working with faculty, students, and staff, attending meetings, and traveling to Long Beach once a month. Several of my presidential colleagues were very involved in all sorts of activities that required them to travel to Long Beach often. I avoided such involvement as much as I could though. I did this for two main reasons. The first and most important was because I felt that I had a lot to accomplish at Chico State that required my presence on campus. The second was that I did not think that anyone in Chico would care how important my input in a system-wide issue might be. I knew that the press would have a field day if I spent lengthy periods of time working on issues that, in their collective minds, were of no direct consequence for Chico State.

My provost, Scott McNall, had been a tremendous addition to the University community. He and I saw eye to eye on most issues and coincided on how to approach most problems and challenges. He did not need much direction. He knew what needed to be done. This allowed me more latitude to carry out other tasks and be involved in projects beyond the routine business of running the university, particularly in the area of academic affairs. In February of 1995, I was able to sign an agreement with the Kokkola Polytechnic Institute of Finland. A couple of years later we signed a similar agreement with the Technological Institute of Monterrey, Mexico. Under the agreement, Chico State business and engineering students would be able to attend classes at Kokkola Polytechnic or in Monterey. In exchange, Chico State would host engineering and business students from the Finnish Institute and from Mexico.

On 11 February 1995, I served as moderator and speaker at the Mid-Valley Area Economic Conference. The main speaker was Tappan Monroe, chief economist at the Pacific Gas and Electric Company. He was, obviously, the main draw. But a lot of people were interested to hear what I had to say about Chico State's budget, enrollment, and the impact we would have on the region for 1995. Chico State's general fund over the past five years had declined by 17%, a loss that affected not only the university *per se* but had serious ripple effects throughout our service region. The office of the Chancellor had given Chico a target of precisely 12,854 full time equivalent students (FTE) and a budget based on this target. Every FTE below this target would result in a loss of $4,500. If all we did was match the 1994-1994 enrollment, which was 12,700, we would need to return a total of $693,000. In today's dollars (2021) this would amount to $1,100.000. I conveyed to those present that we had embarked on a very aggressive student recruitment campaign but could not predict whether it would be fully successful for 1995-1996 though I was confident that we could meet our targets for 1996-1997. No immediate comfort, of course, but lots of faith for the future.

That same month, following my commitment to work closely with the region's community colleges, I organized the first-ever meeting with President Stephen Epler of Yuba College, Betty Dean of Butte College, Martha Romero of College of the Siskiyous, Dennis Adams of Lassen College, and Douglas Treadway of Shasta College. The main purpose of the gathering was related to distance education. Each of the community colleges made a 10-minute presentation outlining their efforts and hopes for distance learning. Their ability in the area varied tremendously from college to college. This is where Chico State had the upper hand in the sense that for the last ten years our university had been at the forefront of this new technology. More than 300 different faculty at Chico state had taught in the distance learning effort, an achievement that no other institution in the entire world could claim in 1995. Our experts posited that Chico State was moving toward a new phase of technological development that would likely see the end of microwave transmission and the entry of satellite course delivery in the north state. We envisioned developing packages that could carry a student through two years of community college training and a culminating two years at Chico. We encouraged all presidents present to join us in this technological revolution that had already swept through the CSU and connected all of its campuses. They could partner with us if they wished and were willing to dedicate resources to this important endeavor. Our own efforts to make this association a reality, were greatly enhanced when the United States Department of Commerce gave life to our program with a grant for $400,000. Ralph Meuter, Dean of Regional and Continuing Education accepted my challenge to him to expand and improve our long-distance education. We were on our way.

In the midst of budgetary uncertainty, there was a bit of good news. The Pacific Gas and Electric North Valley Division Manager handed me a large rebate check of $672,900. We would use this to help pay off $5 million we had borrowed to build the Thermal Energy Storage Project, a project that in the long run would save the university millions of dollars.

As we ended the academic year 1994-1995, I began to visualize the campus, with all its many ongoing projects to truly make Chico State the campus of first choice, as a Kubrick cube. Little by little all the pieces were beginning to be lodged in their right place. I was quite optimistic for the future. In fact, I was eager and ready to begin the next stage. Before that, however, once again, we made our trip up to Canada. By this time Gloria's cast was gone and was free to travel. We spent time with our mothers and stayed at Julio and Nory's home. What a delight it was to be surrounded by people we loved and who loved us without reserve. The professional demands on me were such that I could not afford to spend more than ten days. But these ten days were regenerative.

If it meant helping our programs and/or bringing positive notoriety to the campus, I was willing and ready to do almost anything. For good or ill, I knew that it was not my presence but the presence of the president that drew more attendance to any event or occasion. I had never set foot on a baseball or softball field before. But when asked to go to bat, literally, to dedicate the new softball field that had been moved from a remote area of campus to a more central location, I was there. There is a photo of me about to hit the ball. I don't know enough about the sport to determine whether I looked good or bad. All I know is that I was amazed at how fast the ball came at me. I believe that I did not hit the ball well. To be totally candid and honest I must admit that I missed it. But it was fun to see well over 250 rabid fans, supporters, and sponsors watch me miss it. Even when I did things patently poorly the press seemed interested in having me on the front page of the paper.

Rose Marie Ruiz Bravo, who had attended my inauguration, had been chosen as the Rector of the Universidad Nacional of Costa Rica. She asked me to be part of the inauguration and to give a brief presentation. Since it was in the summer, when activity in Chico was less hectic, I decided to accept the invitation and take the opportunity to spend a few days by the sea. When we got to San José, not the most attractive city Gloria and I had seen in all of our travels, we expected to have someone waiting for us. Apparently, someone was assigned this task. But he or she was nowhere to be seen. Gloria and I had to find out exactly where in Heredia, where the University was located, we were to go. This was before cell phones. We dragged our suitcases around until we found a little store. I asked for permission to use their telephone. We had no local money, so it was a big favor we were asking. I think they saw how distressed we were and helped us not only locate Rector Ruiz Bravo but give directions to the person who was to take us to Heredia. The inauguration itself went well. Rose Marie had us meet with her parents, clearly members of the high society of Costa Rica. From there we decided to go spend a few days on the coast, at the resort called Flamingo Bay, not a very Spanish name. We had reserved an apartment which was advertised as well appointed, ideally located, and close to the water. None of this turned out to be true. It was sparsely furnished, far from everything, and not close at all to the water. We got there late and had no choice but to stay there. Early the following morning we went looking for a place that met all the requirements. We found it and spent a few wonderful days there. We met an Italian couple. She spoke very good English because she taught the language in Italy. He told me his name, which I understood to be Pepe, a common name in Spain. This is what I called him for the duration of our stay and all the activities we were engaged in together. Only after we were all back to our respective homes did we receive a letter from them. It was signed, Beppe, a typical Italian name, not Pepe. I felt really embarrassed.

As had become traditional, the *E-R* asked me to write once again a piece to welcome new and old students to Chico State for the start of another exciting academic year. As I had promised myself to do in all my convocations, I took this opportunity to highlight everything we were doing to improve the overall educational experience for our students, including creating a *Center for Excellence in Learning and Teaching*, part of whose goal was to initiate a system whereby outstanding teachers and scholars would be mentoring their colleagues, create clusters of 25 students who would move together through three common courses, and provide specific and intensive advising to hasten progress toward graduation with a new Four-Year Degree Program. Since I knew that my article was destined as much to parents as to students, I also outlined in great detail the economic benefits of a university education. Drawing from economic studies conducted by the U.S. Census Bureau in 1992, I showed what an individual with only a high school diploma would earn over a lifetime ($820,870), and I compared this to what could be earned with a two-year degree ($1,062,130), a four-year degree ($1,420.850), a master's degree ($1,619,970), a doctoral degree ($2,142,440), and a professional degree ($3,012,530). I thought it would be of particular interest to mention that our graduates, based on surveys done of employers in the West, remained among the most highly recruited and sought after. In fact, the recruitment of 1994-95 graduates had increased by 48% over the graduates of 1993-1994.

Despite concrete and evident progress on all fronts, there continued to be one individual in Chico who continued his unrelenting quest to create as much havoc as possible. In a speech he delivered in Sacramento to the Ivy League, professor Conlin railed against affirmative action, his colleagues, administrators in general and, of course, me. He intimated that the only reason I had been hired by the CSU was because my Hispanic name "looks very good on the stationary." Possibly one of the least insulting things he had said about me. He knew that I did not fall into the category of Latino or Hispanic. I was not and could not be an affirmative action hire. I counted as Caucasian as much as he did. But his malicious intent was to denigrate all those with Spanish names because in his mind they could not possibly be as qualified as white males like him. One might have come to the conclusion that he was a racist. His public statements give permission to others to express their own racism. At least, Conlin was open about it. Others were more cowardly. On August 24 I received an anonymous envelope addressed to me personally. There was no letter inside, only a photograph of me that had been published recently on the cover of the E-R. Written across my face was the following: "Is this what all assholes look like in Mexico?"

There were a lot of lighter and enjoyable moments that took the sting out of invectives like the one above. In early October, for instance, Dean Jim Jacob, of Behavioral and Social Sciences, Scott McNall and I, among several city dignitaries, such as Chico Chamber of Commerce President Scott Schofield who also happened to be the owner of North Valley Athletic Club, participated in a race. This was no ordinary race. It was a wheelchair race around campus to bring awareness about the difficulties and obstacles that handicapped people encountered. It did not take me long to realize that for both Scotts this was not going to be a leisurely executed race. They each meant to win. I made it patently clear that I was starting with a great disadvantage. I was nursing a sore back. No one took pity on me. As the gun went off, Schofield raced ahead. He should have been disqualified. He had no business as a very fit young man racing against older, softer academicians. For a while McNall and I were neck and neck. As we got close to the finish line McNall unceremoniously grabbed a wheel of my wheelchair and slowed me down enough for him to pass me. Schofield won. Mcnall was second, even though he did not dispute my allegation of interference. He showed no shame. I came in fourth position. Poor Dean Jacob came in last. Schofield proudly raised the trophy above his head. The big crowd gathered to watch the race applauded his feat. We were all happy. It was all for a good cause.

I was also happy and proud that, after a lot of work, the university was in a position to share with all constituencies the fruits of a long project. We finally published an elegant booklet entitled *The Strategic Plan for the Future*. It contained a letter from me, and an *Introduction* that read in part: "*Today Decides Tomorrow* reads the inscription above the doors of Kendall Hall at the CSU, Chico campus. It is the motto of a university that focuses on the future while carrying forward the best of its past" A chapter entitled *Our Vision, Our Mission*, and *Our Priorities*, with great specificity about the five major priorities, constituted the heart and soul of the document. The campus now had a clear blueprint for the next few years.

In 1995 the Western Association of State Colleges contacted me and asked me to serve as one of a five-member team to evaluate the progress the University of Guam had made in meeting most if not all the specific requirements for re-accreditation. Getting to Guam was not easy. We had to stop first in Hawaii. I had no objection. It did not represent any inconvenience at all. When we left Guam, we were quite severe in our judgment. The University hardly met the most minimal criteria. We gave them a deadline. WASC would be back in a couple of years.

December of 1995 ended up with what at first appeared to me like a small and easily brushed aside controversy. But, like a ball rolling down a snowy slope, speed picked up and what started as a minor point of irritation grew into a national issue. I could not believe how something that in almost any other university would have been no more than a blip or a minor irritation became, in the echo chamber that was the city of Chico, an issue that attracted national attention. Rush Limbaugh read the *E-R* article on the air and commented on it. George Will wrote about it and so did *The San Francisco Chronicle* and *The Chronicle of Higher Education*. The culprit of all the fuss? The word "dynamic." In an attempt to stress the campus' interest in strong teaching, Dean Heinz of the College of Humanities and Fine Arts\ encouraged departments who were advertising for new faculty positions to indicate that they were interested in "dynamic teachers." A rather innocuous description, according to many. But not for everyone. Members of the College's Affirmative Action Committee immediately objected to the term "dynamic," as, according to them. It could discourage applicants from certain ethnic groups and perhaps some women from applying. Some went even as far as describing the term as "Euro-centric" and "phallocentric."

Unfortunately, our affirmative action director, contacted those departments that had advertised positions using this term. According to some, she ordered them to eliminate the term and repost the ads. Others claimed that she just suggested that they reconsider the wording. As far as I was concerned, she had no authority to order departments one way or another. Either Provost McNall, Dean Heinz, or I could have easily dealt with the issue in-house, but we never had a chance. The exchange between her and department chairs was leaked to the press. The *E-R* was off to the races. I was angry at her, at those who were far too eager to go to the press, and at the *E-R* for exploiting something that was easily correctable. I felt that I needed to intervene and make the university's position clear. In a letter to the *E-R*, published 26 January 1996, I indicated that the word "dynamic" would continue to be used if departments saw value in it. I further stated that "I cannot accept, for instance, the premise that women and members of certain minority groups are less likely to be dynamic teachers than others. I believe that this argument would be offensive to women and members from under-represented groups." While I was at it, I took the chance to chastise the *E-R* for making a mountain out of a molehill but paying little attention to the *U.S. News and World Report* which had just rated CSU, Chico in the top tier of Western Colleges and Universities. Needless to say, the *E-R* used its editorial page to complain about my criticism of the newspaper's coverage of the university. I should have remembered that one doesn't get into contests with those who buy ink by the gallon.

All the controversy revealed a weakness in the manner in which the university handled issues of affirmative action. In March, after a very candid and uncomfortable conversation with her, I asked for her resignation. She refused. I terminated her. As I expected, she filed a lawsuit over her firing. Nothing came of it. The job of Affirmative Action director was a delicate position, one that should be handled diplomatically and with the clear awareness that not everyone viewed hiring practices from the same perspective. Sensitivity and diplomacy were essential. Neither of these two qualities had been displayed. In May we started a search for a replacement.

While all of this was going on, I was being evaluated. According to Trustee policy, presidents were to be reviewed every three years. Unlike those that took place every six years, this evaluation was limited to the opinions expressed by faculty, staff, students, and community representatives. I was rated in a number of areas: overall management of the university, relations on campus and within the CSU system, educational leadership, community relations, major achievements and personal characteristics. I had no idea what the end result of this process would be. After all, the last 30 months had been a sort of roller coaster for me. Although I could point to plenty of successes, I could also see that I had not pleased everyone with my decisions. I was therefore quite pleased when Chancellor Munitz released the outcome of the consultation with the various constituencies that had been asked to evaluate my performance. It was a very positive review. I was relieved to see that reviewers understood well the context for the early challenges I faced when I arrived. As Dr. Munitz summarized, I had faced "small town environment coupled with a newspaper hostile to the university and a few professors whose personal vendettas with the university were major distractions for the new president. He suffered many personal insults from these episodes which could have caused others to reconsider the job. In this context the achievements and accomplishments of the president and the university during the past three years are outstanding." He then outlined what he had asked me to pursue in the years to come:

1) Act swiftly to stabilize enrollment and reverse the enrollment decline, thereby strengthening further the fiscal context.
2) Selectively assert a more decisive style of leadership.
3) Continue to hold informal dialogue sessions with groups of faculty,

staff and students on a regular basis and continue to be visible around campus.

4) Continue the progress in university advancement.

5) Continue efforts to obtain media coverage about faculty, students, and staff achievements.

If there was a surprise in what he expected me to do going forward it was in #2, "assert a more decisive style of leadership." Most people did not understand what he meant by this. I did. Chancellor Munitz was very upset at the nuisance that Professor Conlin and Geshekter represented for him and some of the Trustees. He was also quite annoyed that Assemblyman Richter had turned him into a target of his attacks. Chancellor Munitz was probably upset at me for not having found a way to neutralize all three of them. This was also the reason, I thought, why my salary was among the lowest among the CSU presidents.

The *E-R* ran an article the following day reproducing almost *verbatim* what Chancellor Munitz wrote in his letter, including the indirect criticism he had made of the negative treatment the university and I received from the newspaper.

Overall, the Spring Semester of 1996 had started rather well. In February, Ralph Meuter, Dean of Regional and Continuing Education, and I, who had been working together for the last two years on expanding our offerings and modernizing our long- distance deliveries, made a presentation at the 1996 Industry Summit meeting held in Scottsdale, Arizona. Two of the presentations were selected for publication in the *ED Journal*, one of the two being ours. Our presentation was entitled *California State University, Chico: A Traditional University and Pioneering Leader in Distance Education*. Our purpose was to describe the background and experience of a traditional university campus as it developed into a pioneering leader in distance education. We enumerated the academic degrees we offered and how we had signed partnerships with some of the leading industries such as Alcoa Laboratories, AT&T, General Dynamics, General Electric, Hewlett-Packard, IBM, Lawrence Livermore National Laboratory, MCI, Pacific Bell, Texas Instruments, etc., with receiving sites in 17 states. Next,

we showed how between 1992-1996 we were driven by the desire to provide education on demand – anything, anytime, anywhere, available to everyone. The time was ripe for a major push in this direction. Technology
had already assumed center stage on the national agenda and the political environment required that we do anything but business as usual. The
arrival of a new Chancellor, Barry Munitz, a new Executive Chancellor,
Molly Broad, and a new Vice Chancellor, Richard West, who came to the
CSU from the University of California where he had been the leading
technology spokesperson, provided further impetus and financial support.
We followed this with the advances we had made at CSU, Chico and concluded with problems and opportunities for the future (*ED Journal*, Volume 10#2, J-4-7).

   After much controversy and a lot of going back and forth with the city
and having to convince students that more parking was necessary, I participated in the ribbon cutting ceremony to open the new and only parking structure in the university. It was a beautiful and desperately needed
building that looked far better than the surface parking lot on which it now
stood. We were also fortunate to have another ribbon cutting ceremony,
this time to herald new mediated high-tech classrooms. These came to be
because of a close relationship between the College of Business and the
private sector, represented by Bruce McDougal, a 1996 College of Business Outstanding Alumnus, the owner of a very successful business enterprise, and the husband of our supporter and friend, Nancy McDougal (who
added Fox to her name after her husband passed away suddenly and later
married our Alumni Director, Jack Fox). Such new facilities were meant to
equip Chico graduates with cutting-edge experience and know-how that
could only be achieved through successful public-private partnerships.

   Another momentous change was the reconstitution of the CSU, Chico
Advisory Board, made up of 22 members. They were chosen because they
combined a variety of specialties, businesses, backgrounds, talents, regions,
and above all a deep commitment to our institution. I could not have been
more impressed by the quality of these individuals and their desire to help
us achieve the goal that we had been seeking, to make CSU, Chico the
destination of choice for some of the best and brightest students.

Chico State's reputation was gaining international recognition. In June I was invited by the Ministry of Education to visit Taiwan and meet with a number of academic institutions to see what cooperation was possible. Gloria was invited as well. Our visit started in San Francisco where we were treated to a wonderful dinner hosted by the Taiwanese Ambassador. The next day we were on our way to Taipei. We knew this was going to be a classy invitation when we realized that we would be flying first class. It was the very first time for us. At the airport we were welcomed as if we were royalty. Gloria was given an impressive bouquet of flowers. The hotel where we stayed was incredibly luxurious. We had some free time and decided to take a stroll. We had to return rather quickly. The heat was suffocating and the noise from the traffic, mostly from motorcycles that carried whole families, was deafening. Nothing was spared to make us feel welcome and important. The meetings went well, but I could not see much that would form the basis of cooperation with them. From Taipei they flew us to Kaoshsiung, the largest city in Taiwan. If possible, they put us in a more luxurious hotel than in Taipei. Our suite even had a separate room with all sorts of athletic equipment. We were so high up on this high rise that we had a spectacular view of the city. At the end of our visit, they bid us goodbye with the same pomp and reverence that they had displayed at our arrival. I don't recall whether anything of consequence emerged from my talks with dignitaries and educational leaders. Gloria and I agreed that it was a voyage to remember. We had never been as pampered as we were on this trip.

In August, we celebrated another first. This time, in the area of sports. Chico State had a good baseball team but a rather dismal field on which to play. Our friends, Kathy and Steve Nettleton, who loved baseball with a passion, approached me with an offer I could not refuse. If they could partner with the University, they would invest heavily (roughly $2 million) in a state-of-the-art baseball complex. They had bought a professional team, to be called the Chico Heat. In exchange for their generous offer, they wished to use the park for their team. This was a perfect example of the public and private sector working together for mutual benefit. Kathy, Steve and I, in the presence of over 200 witnesses, broke ground. It was a very happy day for Chico, sports fans, and Don Batie, our athletic director.

With the Nettletons breaking ground for the new Baseball Stadium at the University.

Even though I was exceptionally busy discharging all my responsibilities and building all kinds of bridges, in September, I was asked to participate in the inauguration of my very good friend from Michigan, Chris Dahl. He was about to be inaugurated as president of SUNY College at Geneseo. He asked me to represent the U.S. Colleges and Universities and to say a few words. I chose to speak about leadership. I was very happy to see that Dick and Susan Nisbett, our dear friends, were also in attendance. Unlike my own inauguration that had caused a bit of a stir, Chris' was considered a totally normal ceremonial event and one for the whole College and community to celebrate. One could almost touch the peace and tranquility that reigned in Geneseo during the inauguration.

A month after my trip to New York, Gloria and I took a two-week vacation in France. We went to visit Michel Zaïtzeff, his wife Yolaine, and their daughter Nastassia in Lille. Both Michel and Yolaine taught violin at the Conservatoire de Musique. The first night at their home, Yolaine's parents joined us for a dinner worthy of the best chef in France. Michel is an exceptional chef and wine connoisseur. We then went on a trip through *la route des vins*, in Alsace. That part of France looks more German than French. Each town is a living postcard. We loved the sights and the fantastic meals we had along the way. We spent time in Lembach and stayed at the *Auberge du Cheval Blanc*. The auberge was almost medieval in appearance. The menu, which I still keep, was rich in choices. There were no prices next to each meal. This indicated that if you needed to know what the price was this was not the place for you. There we were introduced to *la tarte a l'oignon* always accompanied with *Crémant d'Alsace*. The wines of the area, mostly white, are superb. We also visited Wissembourg, went to the Chateau Fleckenstein, in the middle of a forest, the *Ligne Maginot*, which supposedly would keep German forces from entering France during WWII, Strasbourg, Cleebourg, Riquewihr, where we ate at a restaurant-winstub, *Au Tire-Bouchon*. From there we went to Colmar, known as the *petite Venise* and Eguisheim. Before we made it back to Lille, we went to Bruges.

The only problem with the trip was the return from Lille to Paris on the T.G.V, or *train grande vitesse*. We could have been killed. The high voltage electric cables broke unexplainably and ended up under the wheels of the train. Now and then, like a gigantic whip, one of them would hit the window where Gloria and I were sitting watching the splendid panorama. The train did not go off the rails, fortunately, but got stuck in the middle of nowhere. We had to grab our suitcases and walk along the rails for a long while until we got to an overpass. We made it up, with great difficulty, and had to wait for buses to come pick us up and take us to Paris. By then, we had missed our plane. All things considered this was probably one of the most memorable trips we have taken in France.

As soon as we got back from France, Gloria and I went to Atlanta for an AASCU meeting. We did not know much about the south and decided to make a quick jaunt to Savannah and Beauford, South Carolina. We discovered a new and wonderful world.

All the fun we had had for the last few weeks came crashing down when we got back to Chico. It seemed that tranquility was a word that could never be used to describe a campus atmosphere. I was informed that there was evidence that drugs were not only consumed but sold in one of our dorms. I was asked for permission to place an undercover agent there. I thought about it long and hard because I wasn't sure that this was the right thing to do. But those who were knowledgeable advised me that they had tried everything else, and it was time for a different strategy. I acquiesced. The unfortunate thing was that the young agent that was placed among students was not very professional. His behavior was exposed, and his spying was revealed. It made the university look as if it did not know what it was doing. I had anticipated that the student who would be caught dealing would feel betrayed and would be very angry. I did not anticipate, however, how many other students would feel violated. About 35 students out of a total enrollment of about 15,000 stormed into my office. I met with all of them, listened to their grievances and tried to reason with them. I apologized for a botched attempt to deal with a serious problem but tried to make them understand that the university had a responsibility to the students and the parents who did not want drug dealing to go on. I told students that, ultimately, the president is asked to make a final decision. As president you arm yourself with as much information and input as is available. Then, you must act. I did.

Before the end of 1996, there was one more serious battle to be fought. In November of 1996 California approved Proposition 209. Called the Affirmative Action Initiative, it basically amended the state constitution to prohibit state governmental institutions from considering race, sex, or ethnicity specifically in the areas of public employment. Pushed by professors Conlin and Geshekter, Assemblyman Bernie Richter who represented our district summoned several leaders of the CSU, including me, of course, to defend CSU's hiring policies. Though Richter kept me on "the witness chair", so to speak, for a long time, I had no difficulties repeating over and over again that Chico State did not engage in preferential treatments of any sort. If he had any evidence of it, I would be more than happy to see it and carry out an in-depth investigation. I continued that just because someone accuses Chico State of such nefarious actions doesn't prove any guilt. Words are cheap, I said. I would be more than happy to let any government investigators come to campus and make a determination. Hopefully, this would not only satisfy Assemblyman Richter but put an end to the ridiculous crusade that Conlin and Geshekter had embarked on. Other than plenty of local press, nothing came of the charade that we were exposed to in Sacramento. The Associated Students Government Affairs Committee passed a resolution supporting my appearance at the Sacramento hearing. It felt good to have students on my side.

In late October there was a debate between Professor Geshekter and Professor Carol Burr, Director of the campus Center for Multicultural and Gender Studies on Prop 209. The exchanges between the two professors got increasingly heated. At one point, one of the African American students got up to leave. A woman in the audience, who happened to be Mrs. Geshekter, and the student got into a verbal spat. Supposedly, Mrs. Geshekter said to Ms. Jackson, "I guess being rude is a Black thing, huh?" When Ms. Jackson asked Mrs. Geshekter to repeat what she had said, she said "Oh, now you're deaf. I guess deafness is a Black thing, too." Ms. Jackson took what was said as racial remarks and started to scream and point at Mrs. Geshekter with her finger. This prompted Professor Geshekter, speaking into the microphone, to scream at the student to stop or he would come down and "smack her in the face." The following day, students gathered to protest against the Professor. They then stormed my office asking for the professor's dismissal. I met with them, calmed them down, and promised to look into Professor Geshekter's behavior and threat. The event was investigated. The report to me indicated that:

1) There was every reason to believe that had Mrs. Geshekter not made offensive and racist remarks to Ms. Tiffany Jackson, the debate would have concluded without incident.

2) Although understandable given Mrs. Geshekter's provocative remarks. Ms. Jackson's use of obscenities and the uncontrolled nature of her outburst cannot be condoned, particularly in an academic setting.

3) In general, and with the exception of Ms. Jackson's outbursts, students on all sides of the issue behaved in a controlled manner during and subsequent to the incident.

4) Although Professor Geshekter has the right to express his thoughts and even use inflammatory and confrontational language, in doing so, particularly in the context of the emotionally charged debate of Proposition 209, he did not exercise sound judgment.

5) Professor Geshekter did threaten to punch Ms. Jackson.

6) Although one might accept his concern that he feared for his wife's safety, his conduct was inappropriate and unprofessional. Therefore, I asked that Ms. Jackson write a letter of apology to Mrs. Geshekter. How the University would deal with Professor Geshekter was a confidential matter to be determined.

Despite a few setbacks, we closed 1996 with optimism. In December I wrote a message to the campus community informing everyone that based on one of the recommendations that sprang out of the Strategic Plan for the Future, I had set aside a significant amount of money for a Staff Development Program. The idea was to foster the professional development of our staff. This was very well received not only by the staff, which was expected, of course, but by the university as a whole. It was one more example of my desire to see everyone engaged and my wish for the improvement of everything that might enhance the reputation of the campus and our ability to better serve our students.

The future looked brighter. Spring 1997 started as it had finished, with positive news. I was pleased to report that CSU, Chico had been re-accredited by the Commission of the Western Association of Schools and Colleges (WASC). WASC judged us primarily on our mission, vision, and strategic plan. According to the WASC team, our plan "is simple, yet powerful, and contains the core of ideas and issues that have been identified as critical, not only for survival but for encouraging CSU, Chico to flourish. The key to the future is the pursuit of the strategic plan." All of our efforts had been vindicated. We had known that we were on the right track, but WASC's conclusion confirmed it.

The quality of our students had improved, in large part because of our emphasis on merit scholarships, particularly the Presidential ones that attracted such interest on the part of students and parents. I knew that as much as we were doing to increase enrollment, we needed help in this area. I had been very impressed with Robert Hannigan, Dean of Student Enrollment, when he and I both coincided at HSU. I was determined to attract him to Chico State. We hired him away from HSU. He was given the title of Vice Provost for Enrollment Management. His charge was "to provide leadership in developing and implementing a variety of effective student recruitment and retention strategies, including increasing student quality while maintaining or increasing diversity." A tall order, but one he was more than prepared to discharge with tact and efficiency. I did not want him to feel that he would have to carry these responsibilities without help from the top. In fact, he and I teamed up often on the many trips made to recruitment sites. It took a while, but Hannigan delivered as promised. A lot of credit went to 22 faculty members who took personal time out of their schedules to contact 375 undecided students and promote the value of a Chico State degree. Everyone working toward a common goal meant that our enrollment not only met but surpassed our enrollment target.

Gloria was the honorary president of the Chico Symphony Guild. As such, she was involved in fund-raising activities. One of the ways to achieve this was to organize auctions. On February 8 there was one such auction.

Gloria and I decided to offer a traditional Catalan dinner for six. Gloria would be the cook and I would be both the sommelier and the server. Of course, we were expected to join the six guests at the dinner table. We did this on a number of occasions, always raising funds for a number of causes not always exclusive to the university. These events were always very popular and fetched considerable amounts of funds. Gloria and I enjoyed these dinners a lot and, through them, got to know much better some of the distinguished members of the Chico community. Of course, as was common when anything had to do with us, the dinner at our home made it to the *Lifestyle* section of the *E-R*.

No matter how well things seem to be going we could never sit on our laurels for long. The front page of the *E-R*, on February 6, ran a photo of Athletic Director Don Batie and me. The title of the article: *Chico State drops football*. The program that had begun in 1921 had come to an abrupt end. Title IX made it impossible for us to keep football. We just did not have the resources to keep football and meet all the Title IX requirements. It was not a capricious decision. But the timing could not have been worse. Coaches were caught off guard. The 18 students who had been recruited into the football program were suddenly without a team. Batie and I promised to do all we could to relocate these student athletes but their anger, well-justified, made Batie and me very sad. Because of changes in the Division II in which we played we were forced to join the California Collegiate Athletic Association (CCAA). Unfortunately, this Association did not include football. We were not the only CSU campus to be forced into this choice: Hayward State, San Francisco State, Sonoma State were forced into the same position. The decision was totally outside of our control. The lack of convenient opponents, growing costs and gender equity requirements were the main reasons for the necessity to drop football. The most interesting part was the reaction in the community. Gloria and I had been at a few games. They were always very poorly attended. Yet, given the reaction from the community one would have thought that the stadium was always overflowing with adoring fans. This had not been the case, sadly enough.

In early 1997, Professor Dan Toy, from the College of Business and I travelled to São Paulo, to hold a number of meetings with the Rector of the Lutheran University of Brazil (ULBRA) and other dignitaries. We signed a historic agreement that afforded our students one more new and exciting international educational opportunity. The consortium, known as Project Brazil, linked Chico State and approximately ten other U.S. and European universities to universities in Brazil. This provided exceptional opportunities for some of our more entrepreneurial students.

In April, as had become traditional, we honored once again seven distinguished alumni. They were all worthy of admiration. There was one, however, that drew my immediate attention because of his work and passion. He is a famous glass artist, William Morris. One can easily see his work by googling his name. When I found out about Morris' visit, I convinced him to give a demonstration in our studio and asked if he would please let me be his assistant. Which he did graciously. This was one of the happiest moments of the year for me. Together we made a beautiful piece which we auctioned very successfully to help the glass program. Lest Gloria think I have left out one of William Morris' personal gifts, I must add that he was about 6 feet one, had a spectacular physique, and to top it all was very handsome. He probably is still all of the above, despite the almost 25 years that have passed since that day.

On April 19, I presided over the dedication of our former Bohler Field as Nettleton Stadium. It had taken less than a year to refurbish the old stadium into the new, beautiful Nettleton Stadium. Steve and Kathy Nettleton were very happy with what had been accomplished with their very generous donation, the community welcomed with open arms the chance to have a professional baseball team in our city, our baseball student athletes and our coaches, proud winners of the national championship, could not be any happier with the new and very improved facilities, and I was enchanted to see how much could be achieved if the university partnered with the private sector. All in all, it was a dedication worth celebrating and one that injected much needed input from the community. There was so much excitement in the air that members of the Board of Directors of Century Clubs launched an aggressive scholarship drive to benefit not only baseball athletes but all sports at the university.

By June, one of our local papers branded Chico baseball the capital of the world. There were reasons for this type of exaggeration. The Chico Heat had their first game at Nettleton Stadium. Mayor Rick Keene gave a little speech. Once the stadium was full, the Enloe Hospital life flight helicopter, the very same one that had airlifted Gloria from Mount Brokeoff years before, flew over the stadium and landed in the middle of the field. As the ER article reported wrote: "My God, I thought, in all this excitement some poor guy has suffered a heart attack. No, that wasn't the case. Instead, climbing out of the helicopter in royal fashion and striding to the pitcher's mound was none other than CSU, Chico President Manuel Esteban. *El Presidente* then threw out the first ball, making that historic pitch while Rick Keene served as umpire. ... Then, less than 24 hours later, the Chico State Wildcats were on TV from Montgomery Ala., playing in the NCAA Division II national baseball championship. And who do we see sitting in the stands? President Esteban! What a fan!"

Not to be outdone, the City of Chico worked very closely with the university to complete a project that had been in the works for twelve and one-half years of discussion, planning, budgeting and reconstruction. In October, City council members, the vice mayor, the city manager, and a few people from the administration, including me, met to cut the ribbon that opened a bridge across the much-travelled Warner street. This bridge made Warner Street much safer for our students, but it also beautified a rather unappealing part of the campus. Not only were we trying to improve the educational experience of our students as well as the overall reputation of the institution, but we were in the process of considerably improving the appearance of the campus and its facilities.

It seemed that 1997 was going to be a year full of surprises. Allen Sherwood, an administrator at Chico who had been a prominent official in the U.S, Navy, was successful in getting Steve Nettleton, Ed Masterson, our Development Officer, and me to fly from the Navy base in San Diego to the USS Abraham Lincoln Carrier. Steve, who owned his own private plane, agreed to fly us to San Diego. From there, we boarded a U.S. Navy airplane, and we flew onto the Carrier. What an exciting adventure. To land on a carrier is nothing like landing on an airport. To land a plane, the pilot flies over the flight deck and attaches a hook on the plane to a steel wire on the ship, called the arresting wire. The arresting wire is attached to a hydraulic system that slows the plane down. It can stop the plane at a distance of 300 feet. No matter how well strapped you are to the seat, you are propelled forward so much that you feel you are going to be projected out of your seat.

We spent the afternoon witnessing planes land and take off. We ate in the mess, with the navy soldiers, we slept in racks, had breakfast in the mess the following day, spent time talking to the commanding officer, and finally took off. An aircraft carrier flight deck is one of the most exhilarating and dangerous work environments in the world, not to mention one of the loudest. The primary takeoff assistance comes from the carrier's four catapults, which get the planes up to high speeds in a very short distance. When the plane is ready to go, the catapult officer opens valves to fill the catapult cylinders with high-pressure steam from the ship's reactors. This steam provides the necessary force to propel the piston at high speed, slinging the plane forward to generate the necessary lift for takeoff. Just as landing felt like I was going to be slung forward, taking off glued me to the back of my rather uncomfortable seat. The only way to describe this great opportunity that is denied to millions upon millions of people is that not only was it exhilarating but it remains engraved in my mind. Wow!

Back on the ground, safely in Nettleton's very comfortable plane, and flying north to Chico, I marveled at the privileged life I was leading and how fortunate I was. Dreams did come true.

I made it back just in time to thank Floyd L. English, one of our distinguished alumni with a Ph.D. in Physics, who funded in his first year of contributions ten natural science students to the tune of $2,500/year for four years only to double the number the following year, an unprecedented one-year leap in gifts of this kind. July still held another revelation. Chancellor Barry Munitz announced that he was leaving the CSU to assume the directorship of the recently completed Getty Museum. Richard West, who along with Christine Helwick, Chief Legal Counsel for the CSU, had become great friends of ours, sent Gloria and me a short little handwritten note thanking us for hosting him at our home and thanking Gloria for the wonderful paella she had prepared for him. This little note held great news. In 1996-1997, in order to avoid faculty and staff lay-offs I had negotiated a loan for $600,000 from the Office of the Chancellor. I had no choice but to go to the same well again in 1997-98, this time for $1.8 million. So, CSU, Chico's debt was a total of $2.4 million. Upon leaving the CSU, Barry Munitz had made the decision to forgive the $1.8 loan. Then, Executive Vice Chancellor Broad informed me that the $600,000 loan was also forgiven. I could not have been more elated. One fewer major problem to worry about. I thought that I needed to thank Chancellor Munitz for his generosity. I gave him something that no other president could have offered him: I made a very special glass piece for him. In return, he invited me to the opening of the Getty Museum, an incredible event filled with famous people, including movie stars.

It will sound quite quaint in 2021 to think that among the promises I made in my annual Convocation speech in the Spring of 1997, was to reach the goal of putting a network computer on the desk of every faculty member and to install a new email system and a new automated degree auditing system for faculty and administrators. How times have changed!

Dean of Natural Sciences, Roger Lederer, Michael Abruzzo, chair of Biology, and I played a primary role in attracting Atlantic BioPharmaceuticals (ABI), Inc, a start-up company located at McGill University in Montreal, to relocate to Chico. They were going to conduct their research on a treatment for breast cancer and rheumatoid arthritis out of one of our buildings, Holt Hall, for two years before relocating permanently off campus. This was considered a great coup not only for the sciences at CSU, Chico – after all, biotech students would have a once-in-a-life opportunity to work directly for ABI – but as Mayor Rick Keen indicated in the press conference, a boon for the Chico community. In the same press conference, I lauded the venture for assisting the university in meeting priority #4 of the Strategic Plan, which was "to reaffirm our anchor position in the region." I also indicated that this venture was "an example of the wonderful results when the city, the community, and the University work together."

The Associated Students were discussing the possibility of building a new student union and greatly expanding the bookstore. You will recall that unlike most other universities in the country, these two functions, despite the battles fought by my predecessor, were controlled by students, not the university administration. Though they had a lot of money in their coffers, they did not have enough to carry out the costly project. I saw an opportunity to take advantage of the good relationship that I had always enjoyed with Associated Student presidents. With this idea of cooperation in mind, I directed our new Vice President for Business and Finance, Dennis Graham, to contact the student government and see what was possible. I had the feeling that something very positive could emerge if we found common ground. It took some time but ultimately, this cooperation bore fruit. We ended up with a beautiful building that met many of both our needs and those of the Associate Students.

From November 1 through the 6th, Gloria and I were invited to attend a conference of American and Mexican educators held at Guanajuato University. We happened to be there for the *Dia de los Muertos* as well as for the *Festival Internacional Cervantino*, a week dedicated to Miguel de Cervantes. The university is a masterpiece of new world architecture, elegant, imposing. Gloria and I were amazed that in the middle of Mexico we would be thrown into a truly Spanish environment, that of the *tunas*, a Spanish tradition from as far back as the 13th century involving groups of needy university students who sing accompanied by traditional instruments in order to earn money to pay for their studies. They are dressed in Spanish medieval apparel. Guanajuato is also famous for having a fully functioning subterranean city. Those responsible for the conference also organized a trip to San Miguel de Allende, a beautiful town with an impressive presence of American artists.

Between 16 and 18 November, I was in Washington to attend the annual AASCU meeting. I was asked to chair a session of AASCU Policies and Purposes along with James B. Appleberry, president of AASCU. In the same conference, a special effort had been made to guide new members. With this goal in mind, a workshop was organized to provide advice for those who were about to assume presidencies as well as to provide tips and guidance on the expected role for their spouses. I was asked to be a panelist covering how to learn about a new institutional culture, building an internal team and external relationships, and making the family transition. I was also to offer advice on how to avoid the pitfalls and potholes that often bar the road to a successful transition. The presentations went very well, and I was proud to have been selected from among hundreds of very qualified members of this important national organization. I was also happy to have had the opportunity to meet Edward James Olmos, the Emmy award-winning actor and outspoken activist for the Hispanic community and children's rights.

I was able to cap 1997 with a very delightful and inspiring farewell to two of our students. What was spectacular about these two young people, brother and sister, is that John McClintock was graduating in computer science at the tender age of 17, the youngest ever graduate in the history of Chico State. He already had a job waiting for him as a quality assurance engineer, designing tests for software, for Geoworks, in Alameda. Equally amazing, the second youngest graduate was his sister, Clare Hupp, at a much older age: 19. What made them even more endearing was their poise, charm, and humility. What a nice celebration. We bid 1997 farewell and welcomed 1998 in Calgary, with our family and friends.

Before we entered into a new year, Vice President Paul Moore and I evaluated where we were in terms of our alumni relations. We came to the conclusion that we needed help: we wanted a full-time alumni and parent relations director. We were successful in attracting a person with a good record, Jack Fox. He had been at UCSB as associate director for three years and then as its executive director from 1974 until 1981. He had also been at the University of Houston, where he worked under Barry Munitz. He had good credentials and he looked the part. Dapper, elegant, suave, charming, with a beautiful head of white hair. To fill out his team we also hired Sue Anderson as assistant director. The team was now in place. We expected great things from it, and we were not disappointed.

At the beginning of 1998 I made a series of announcements. First, we would initiate the President's Visiting Scholar Program. I spelled out in detail what this program was meant to accomplish, how it would be structured, what criteria were to be used to select the visiting scholars, how it fit into our strategic plan, and how it would benefit our students. This was followed days later with another announcement, the creation of an Undergraduate Awards Program for Research and Creativity. It was modeled after ones in place at such institutions as MIT, The University of Texas, and the University of Kentucky. The University Research Foundation had committed an initial investment of $25,000 each academic year with a promise to identify additional funds to expand the number of students who would participate in this student/faculty research project. Third on the list was a new Presidential Leadership Program. Up to five individuals would be selected to participate in a one-year internship program. It was designed to provide greater opportunities to our own faculty and staff to broaden their range of administrative experience and to increase the number of people able to implement change. Lastly, but just as important and precedent-setting was the announcement that, beginning immediately, we would grant two $5,000 awards annually to two departments, units, programs, or colleges which exemplified commitment to the first priority of the University's Strategic Plan, which "is to create and enhance innovative, high quality, and student-centered learning environments." Again, the money came from the University Research Foundation.

1998 had another auspicious beginning. SAP America, the world's fourth largest software supplier, through its University Alliance Award program, announced on January 29 that it had awarded $325,000 in Research Grants to four universities: Drexel, Georgia Tech, Purdue, and CSU, Chico. Our share of the award was $100,000. The four winning institutions had competed with Harvard University, University of Southern California, Central Michigan University, University of Florida and the University of Texas-Austin. In his presentation to Dean Rethans and me, the SAP representative indicated that "Chico State was our first partner in the University Alliance Program, and they have been on the leading-edge in implementing R/3 into the business curriculum."

Gifts and donations kept coming. CSU, Chico's College of Engineering, Computer Science, and Technology had received a number of million-dollar computer gifts over the past two years, but none bigger than the software package it received by Cadence Design System, Inc. It was a whopping total of $251.9 million. Chico State was one of only a handful of top universities that had the Cadence software. The others were MIT, UC, Berkeley, Georgia Tech, Carnegie Mellon, USC, and University of Maryland. We were in very good company indeed.

February was a very fulfilling month. On February 7, I was invited to attend a very important event at UCSB where I was granted that year's Distinguished Alumni Award. To have been recognized this way by the two institutions of higher learning I had attended made me feel honored and special. It is always something very special when your peers appreciate your accomplishments. As nice as the ceremonies both at the University of Calgary and at UCSB had been, I must say that they could not even remotely compare with the attendance, elegance, and exciting atmosphere that prevailed in CSU, Chico when we honored our distinguished alumni. Ours were gala events that made our honored alumni feel exceptional.

It was indeed quite a personal achievement to have been recognized at my *alma maters*, but I must confess that I valued in particular and especially honors that came from students and student organizations. The day I left for Santa Barbara I was informed that the CSU, Chico's Students in Free Enterprise (SIFE) Team had nominated me as *Best College President of the Year*. By the end of Spring semester, I learned that there had been a tie for the best College President. Chancellor Mickey Burnim, from Elizabeth City State University and I had been chosen as Best School Presidents.

I had no reason to doubt that 1998 was going to be a good year. In February I received a letter from the United States Information Agency, informing me that I had been awarded a U.S. Speaker and Specialist Grant to undertake a project in Argentina, from March 3-5, and in Chile, March 6. They did not specify why I had been selected nor what the criteria had been. The conference brought together ministers of education from various South American countries as well as representatives from Europe. My schedule was set up in great detail by the local American Embassy. I was in Buenos Aires for four full days. My meetings with different American officers were set for 30 minutes each. On my second day I was given a two-hour tour of the city. Then I met with Argentinian government officers and some academic ones. At 6 p.m. I gave a 45-minute presentation on *Financiamiento de la educación superior: el desafío de brindar calidad con un menor aporte estatal* (Financing of higher education: the challenge of providing quality with insufficient state resources) at the National Academy of Education, to an audience made up of members of the academy, university administrators and professors, and government education officials. On my third day, I met with more officers and made the same presentation to a different audience. The fourth day was devoted to a few more sessions on education in general and by seven in the evening I was taken to the airport to fly to Santiago. I don't know how much those I had addressed learned from me. What I can verify is that I learned a great deal about how different the two systems of higher education were, ours and theirs. *La Prensa*, Buenos Aires' most respected and most widely read newspaper published a two full-page summary of an interview it conducted of Professor Chester Finn and me. The questions sought to elucidate means by which Argentina could improve a serious problem, what *La Prensa* identified as *Los grandes problemas nacionales: la educación*, and it attempted to seek from Professor Chester Finn and me the manner in which American education dealt with declining resources. They were seeking *Modelos y sistemas educativos que nos pueden servir de ejemplo* (Models and Educational Systems that can serve as examples for us). Professor Finn concentrated in particular on the role of "Charter Schools." I limited myself to state-supported institutions of higher learning.

My stay in Santiago was limited to a day and a half. The purpose of my visit there was to participate in a seminar, held at the University of Chile, entitled *The relation between the university and the external world*. The audience was made up of presidents and representatives from all 25 state-supported universities and from a small group of selected private universities. I was instructed to assume two different roles. The first one was as a respondent to a lecture given by a representative from the University of Chile on *University-External World: The Mission of the University*. I was given 10 minutes to react to this presentation. After a brief coffee break, I made a presentation. This time, my topic was Universidad-Medio Externo y Alternativas de Financiamiento (roughly, University-External Sources and Financial Alternatives). This was followed by a session of questions and answers. Again, given the reaction to my presentation and responding to the lecture given by the University of Chile speaker I came away uncertain as to whether we were actually understanding each other despite speaking the same language.

Although the Chilean system of higher education seemed to me to be far more organized and disciplined than that of the Argentine model, they were both worlds apart from ours. In both countries I was interviewed by their most important newspapers. In both countries, as a perfect example of how universities could partner with the private sector to inject resources into their own institutions, I explained the California Educational Technology Initiative (CETI), the partnership proposal that could join the CSU with GTE, Fujitsu, Hughes Global and Microsoft. The partnership could bring the CSU $300 million for the campuses' computer and communications infrastructure, something that the CSU alone could not possibly do by itself. I also emphasized that as the government in California continued to reduce its financial support for higher education, we, in the CSU, were expected to raise non-state funds equal to about 10% of our annual state-funded budget. This meant that for Chico State, as an example, with a state allocation of about $80 million in 1998 we were to raise $8 million in indirect funds, gifts, bequests, and trusts. Several of the participants in both countries expressed an interest in coming to Chico to see how things worked close up. I told them that we would welcome them with open arms.

Upon my return to Chico, I was gratified to read a very extensive article written by Roger H. Aylworth, who now covered Chico State for the *E-R*. Roger had read the translations of my presentations and interviewed me at length. He did a wonderful job of summarizing the differences between the American system of higher education and those that prevailed both in Argentina and Chile. Perhaps I should not have been surprised by the positivity of the coverage. A few months earlier I had asked a powerful community leader and friend of the university to ask both Bob Peterson, opinion page writer, and Jack Winning, editor of the *E-R* to meet with me, either in a neutral environment or in the offices of the *E-R*. I did not want them to think that I was summoning them. They agreed. My only condition is that I be allowed to meet with each one of them individually. I wanted each one of them to know me, not through the articles that were written by their assigned journalist or by the missives they received by the likes of Professors Conlin and Geshekter, or the vitriol and diatribes that came from Assemblyman Richter, but by direct contact with me. I went to them as Manuel Esteban, not as President Esteban. I offered to be open, transparent, and willing to answer any question about any topic. I accepted and respected their responsibility to the public. All I wanted was a fair chance, to be treated objectively. I should be criticized when deserved, by all means, but I should be asked to provide a response to whatever accusations were levied against me or the university. I reminded them that there were always two sides to every issue. I just wanted them to be open to both views. The meetings went exceptionally well. The initial reservations and apprehensions they obviously had dissipated the longer we were able to talk candidly and the more they got to know and see me as a person, not as a symbol. From that moment on, my relationship with the *E-R* became franker and their treatment of me fairer.

I viewed these two meetings as essential and beneficial for the institution going forward. A patent example that my strategy with the *E-R* had worked was evident when in late 1998 the paper reported on the Trustees' decision to raise presidential salaries. I received a 12% increase. Whereas in past years this would have been a reason for criticism and much fuss, this time it was just reported not only as a matter of fact, but it even bemoaned my ranking as still being stuck in the bottom third for all 23 CSU presidents.

When it came to the issue of my new salary, *The Orion* seemed upset that I was the 17th lowest paid president out of 23 in the CSU. So, they dispatched a reporter to trail me for a full day to get a better idea of what I did. When Eva López, the reporter, called my office in mid-September, she was told that I wouldn't be available until 3 October. She could not wait this long. She came to my office and bugged my secretary Amy Boles until she got to see me. I agreed to have her follow me from 7 a.m. when I started until I was done for the day. After we were done, she thanked me and went about seeking the opinion of those who worked for me. She was quite impressed not only with everything I did during the day but with the variety of issues I had to deal with. On September 23 she wrote that "his job and his duties seem exhausting, but Esteban is a ball of energy and never seems particularly stressed." She further ascertained that "everyone who works closely with Esteban gave nothing but praise for the president, like Associated Students President Richard Elsom (who in 1993 had battled against me in opposition to the construction of a much-needed parking structure). Ms. López quoted Elsom as saying: 'he has a nice demeanor. I like him personally, and I think he's doing a really great job'." Nothing gave me more gratification than to know that students recognize that my number one responsibility was to our students.

After Barry Munitz had left the CSU, the Trustees chose Charles Reed as the new Chancellor on March 1, and he chose to visit our campus on April 21. We were of course very happy with his visit and wanted to make sure that he left our campus convinced that we were one of the very best in the system that he was to lead. He made a short speech about *A Look to the Future*, which outlined his priorities: access to education; competitive faculty and staff compensation; facility expansion and maintenance; and teacher education. All these objectives fell perfectly in line with the very goals of CSU, Chico.

In August, after undergoing a rigorous vetting process I became a Board member of the Sierra Health Foundation in Sacramento. I was very proud of this appointment and particularly happy to work closely with its director, Len McCandliss, a Chico State graduate and a former director of our own University Foundation. I also became a member of Chico Enloe Hospital Board of Directors. Being on these two Boards afforded Gloria and me an opportunity to enjoy annual retreats at very nice locations, places which we would never have even considered on our own. There were two essential differences between the two Boards. Being with the Enloe Hospital cost us money. We were expected to be generous donors. On the other hand, the Sierra Health Foundation had a policy that encouraged its Board members to be philanthropists, but for every dollar we gave they gave three. Gloria and I took advantage of this generosity to help Enloe Hospital, the Boys and Girls Club, and CSU, Chico.

When we formed The Center for Excellence in Learning and Teaching (CELT) in late 1995, we did not anticipate that it would become such an important asset. To allow it to achieve its potential it needed more institutional support. In 1998 we allocated $250,000 ($150,000 of which comes from the Chancellor's Office for faculty productivity projects) to support faculty development relating to teaching and learning. Under the very able direction of Provost McNall this program was becoming one of the most successful tools to enhance the education of our students. Also, with an eye on enhancing academic programs by building a state-of-the-art technological learning environment, with the help of a $500,000 competitive award from the Chancellor's Office, we created a 24-hour a day Student Computing Laboratory, a focal point for students seeking help with computer problems. The goal that we had set up to provide all faculty with desktop computers all linked to the internet was achieved by the end of 1998.

Our constant improvements on the quality of academic programs went hand in hand with our efforts to remove some of the old buildings and replace them with state-of-the-art new buildings. This was an arduous and lengthy process. Years could go by between the project being approved by the Trustees and money allocated. But with some creative financing and cooperation with other entities such as Associated Students we started to make real progress toward a rejuvenation and beautification of our campus. The academic year 1998-1999 saw a great deal of activity in this area. On January 23, the Dean of the College of Communication and Education, Stephen King and I cut the ceremonial ribbon to officially open a new Yolo Hall. The 70,626 square-foot building included 12 research labs, 14 classrooms, three seminar-rooms, faculty and staff offices, computer labs, and a state-of-the-art SlimEx hydrotherapy pool. In September of the same year, an old building on campus was demolished to make room for a new police station.

The Bell Memorial Union was sold as a sort of facelift and renovation. The end result, however, would look like a totally new building that would take the equivalent of a whole block. It was to have a 52,000 square foot, three-story bookstore and a 15,000 square foot, multi-use room. This multi-use room would hold 1,000 people for concerts and events and up to 400 for dinners, a venue that would prove not only versatile but perfect for many university events. Other features included a basement level recreation area; a game room with pool tables and arcade games, a fully equipped computer lab, increased and larger meeting rooms, and an expanded Garden Cafe. The two individuals who had held the position of vice president for Business and Finance, Gordon Fercho and later, on an interim basis, Bob Sneed, had been reliable, honest, knowledgeable about the ins and outs of government and CSU rules and regulations but they had not been very creative. Dennis Graham, whom I hired to succeed them, lacked some of his predecessors' attributes but gained in imagination and resourcefulness. I had charged him with the responsibility to work with Associated Students and see how we could partner and build something that would be a benefit to both. He did. By using some resources that the university had earmarked for construction and remodeling we were able to add to the $26.5 million contributed by students and come up with a building that would house several of the university's functions. Associated Students (AS) president Elsom said, "how gratifying it was for the AS to work so closely with the administration and facilities planning … it was an opportunity to override the 'us vs them' philosophy that separates students from university personnel."

Improving the quality and increasing the number of buildings on campus, including some of the physical education facilities, became one of my secret goals for the immediate future. Colusa Hall, built in 1921, was in desperate need of remodeling. The soccer stadium, home of our winning soccer team, was a small disgrace. We had attracted men's and women's professional teams to use our facilities. With donations and a loan, we planned to have a brand-new facility no later than 2002. I was determined to also build a recreational center for our students. I knew there would be opposition from the community as most students now used local gyms. If we built our own, they would lose revenue. I was convinced, however, that I could get plenty of allies not only from the students themselves, of course, but from major community leaders who could see the long-term benefits to having a great facility that would make recruitment of students easier. In the ten years I was president we were able to bring to campus more than $100 million in construction. The face of the campus was changing slowly but inexorably.

Since I had just passed the end of my fifth year as President, I decided to publish a lengthy President's Newsletter to provide a summary of what had been accomplished and what the future held for our institution. It had five parts:

1) A *Look Back,*
2) *Externally Imposed Changes and Their Implications,*
3) *The Present Situation,*
4) *Specific Achievements and Examples of Excellence,* and
5) *The Future.*

My main goal was to remind faculty, staff, students, parents, alumni, donors, supporters, and the larger Chico community of everything that working together we had been able to accomplish. It was also important to everyone that we were in a constant struggle against external changes and vagaries that required us to be flexible, nimble, and adaptable. Our Strategic Plan, which grew out of the presidential task forces I established in my first year, had positioned us to respond well to all new trends and exigencies. We needed to follow as closely as possible the fundamental principles that we identified in our Strategic Plan to be faithful to our mission and vision and to meet present and future challenges. The reason for including specific achievements and examples of excellence was to demonstrate that there was no exaggeration nor excessive self-congratulatory chest beating if we proclaimed that we were one of the jewels if not **the** jewel in the crown of the CSU, the university of first choice. Finally, as much as I was the first cheerleader of our institution, I did not want anyone to think that we had made it, that we could sit on our well-deserved laurels. So, I outlined for everyone what I perceived as some of the likely challenges that were in store for us in the future and how we should position ourselves to meet them head on. Before writing it and making it widely available, I feared that I might get some snickering and accusations of sugarcoating reality. My fears were quickly allayed when I received countless words of encouragement and congratulations on a job well done. The first eighteen months of my tenure, when I had suffered setbacks and unsettling criticism were now in the rearview mirror. I looked at the future with confidence. In fact, my Newsletter was so well received that I decided to make it one more arrow in my quiver to reach as many audiences as possible.

On 9 September 1998, Gloria went down to Santa Barbara to witness the birth of our second granddaughter, Monica. I had to stay in Chico but at least Gloria got to be part of a very auspicious moment. We could not have been happier. I know that many men have felt incomplete without a son or grandson. Gloria and I had one daughter, and now we have two granddaughters. All three of them have made our lives fuller and more complete.

Just before the end of the calendar year I attended the 1998 Annual Meeting of the Council of Colleges of Arts and Sciences (CCAS) held in Minneapolis where I was the speaker of the plenary session. My speech was entitled *Distance Education: A Dispassionate Review*. It was published in the proceedings (January-February 1999, pages 8-15).

This and the holiday reception at our home capped a very exciting year, particularly since we counted among our guests two very special people. Jason and Elaine, my nephew and niece-in-law, who had come to Chico State for their Masters' degrees. Jason for a Master of Fine Arts and Elaine for one in Marine Biology. We were so elated, and we loved them so much that we bought a little, somewhat rundown house within walking distance from the university. We charged them a modest rent and they took it upon themselves to fix it up into a very comfortable and welcoming home. Jason and Elaine filled our little free time with joy, and they were our special guests to every one of the receptions and dinners we held at our home. They were and are a delight. Other than having our own daughter with us for two long years we could not imagine having anyone else who managed to make every moment of our time with them incredibly valuable. Jason is a great conversationalist and raconteur. He is also an extremely talented artist. (Although he tried and failed to follow in the footsteps of his grandfather and his uncle, me, his attempt at glassblowing produced nothing of any lasting value. But we did laugh a great deal looking at what he was able to produce). Elaine is a great scientist but also a talented artist in her own right. In addition, she is a person who makes everyone around her love her. They brought a lot of sunshine into our lives. When they left in 2000, Gloria and I felt an unfillable void.

I couldn't possibly put a final point to 1998 without mentioning a letter that was published in *The Chico Examiner* on 11 August. It was written by a man who signed it *Patriotically, Roy Giampaoli.* Supposedly this man had been following me and my career since my days at HSU, where he claimed he had a radio program until "being inappropriately sacked." Now, the reason for his letter was to reveal a secret about me: "Here is some more interesting info on Manny: when Robin Wilson (exCIA employee) retired his CSUC presidency, it was necessary to find a replacement. Esteban was probably recommended by HSU President Alistair McCrone (likely CIA functionary) to take over. ... While Manny Esteban's official title is CSUC President, his loyalty is probably to the CIA!" I admit that I found this letter, which is mostly incomprehensible and filled with crazy ideas and conspiracies, rather amusing. Not too long ago I had been accused of having the face of a Mexican asshole, now I was an American CIA spy or operative. I did not realize how adaptable and versatile I was!

On a personal level, 1999 was going to be a key year. In early February Chancellor Reed sent an open letter to the University and to the community at large indicating that following Trustee policies, I was to be reviewed. He outlined the process to be followed. First there would be a canvassing of opinions from the various constituencies, administrators at every level, the Academic Senate, the Alumni Association, the Associated Students, and the University Advisory Board. A sampling of faculty, staff, community members would be selected at random as well. All would be invited to submit answers to a set of specific criteria and submit, if desired, individual comments. After the written responses had been received and summarized, a team of four (a non-CSU executive, a retired CSU executive, a faculty member from another CSU campus, and a member of the Board of Trustees), would make a site visit to campus during the month of April to conduct a series of individual interviews. Following the campus visit a confidential report would be prepared and discussed by Chancellor Reed and President Esteban and then presented to the Board of Trustees at their May or July meeting. Chancellor Reed wanted to assure all participants that nothing in the report that I would receive would in any way reveal their identity. The process would be confidential from beginning to end.

I am writing this paragraph precisely on Saint Patrick's Day. This brings to mind that, although in 1999 we were far from the days *Playboy Magazine* branded CSU, Chico as the #1 party school, students had not stopped drinking. Saint Patrick's Day was especially dangerous because drinking and partying by our own students and many people from outside the community often got out of control. In anticipation of what might occur, I called a meeting that included business owners (many of whom were bar owners), police officers, students, teachers, administrators from both Chico State and Butte College, and any other interested parties to work together and look for solutions to avoid some of the tragedies that had marred this type of celebration in the past. I knew first-hand the pain parents experience when they receive a call informing them that their daughter/son had died of alcohol poisoning. I had made such calls more than once. I wanted all of us to do everything in our power to avoid a repeat of similar tragedies.

Following this meeting, at a news conference we held March 11, we had a common front. Many of the concerned citizens who had attended the forum gathered to send a clear message: A united community is ready to take a more aggressive stance to combat drug and alcohol abuse and violence, and it won't tolerate what has occurred on previous St. Patrick's Day. Together we came up with a lot of alternatives to drinking and carousing. Students, for instance, endorsed our collective idea of organizing free morning pancakes and other alcohol-free events. We also urged bar owners and store owners who sell alcohol to show restraint, by stopping early-morning openings, drink-specials, and special sales that invite excessive consumption of alcohol. Their help was essential if we were to have a salutary day. I was not certain that students would have heard about our collective decisions and message. I did not want to run the risk that the message had not reached the community we meant to protect. Consequently, I sent e-mail messages to each and every one of our 14,000+ students. I concluded my message to students with the following words: "I'm convinced that you, the students, will be the ones who will lead all of us in curbing the drug and alcohol-related deaths, alcohol-fueled violence and other tragedies we face all too often." On March 19, the *E-R* ran an editorial entitled *Joint Effort Pays Dividends*. In it they praised the collective efforts so many constituencies had made to mitigate what had happened in previous years and gave me a lot of credit for organizing the community meeting and sending the e-mail to all students. It also agreed with a conclusion I had publicly expressed, namely, that "if the students are not on board, if they don't realize they have to make smart choices, if they don't realize that they have to act responsibly, nothing that we legislate will deal with this problem." After retiring, I collaborated with Professor Schafer, who as a faculty member had been focused on these student drinking issues for many years, in co-authoring an extensive report on the history of the alcohol issue at Chico State, efforts over the years to prevent alcohol abuse, and lessons and recommendations. This was published as *Confronting College Student Drinking: A Campus Case Study*, in the California *Journal of Health Promotion*, in 2005 (Vol 3, Issue 1, pages 1-55).

The biggest news to hit the campus and the community at this time came when the results of my six-year evaluation had been concluded and Chancellor Reed made its results public. On July 13, Chancellor Reed sent an open letter to the Chico State community. After explaining the process that was followed, the two step assessment, and providing the names of the four members of the on-campus visit team, he proceeded to detail the findings:

What was learned from the review?
Dr. Esteban is a very successful campus executive. The campus is functioning very well, morale among the faculty and staff is high, community relations are in good condition, and the president is well regarded by faculty, staff, students, and the local community. The visiting team concluded that Dr. Esteban is performing his duties and responsibilities in a highly professional and competent manner. In short, he is doing an outstanding job.

Major accomplishments of the university and Dr. Esteban include:

- *Restoring enrollment;*
- *Building a strong, competent management team;*

- *Improving and sustaining faculty and staff morale;*
- *Opening the decision-making process;*
- *Improving significantly the town-gown relationship, including local government, service organizations, and the newspaper;*
- *Increasing donor funds to the university;*
- *Creating a student-centered environment;*
- *Instituting the Presidents' Scholars program;*
- *Establishing a strategic planning process that involves a wide constituent base;*
- *Establishing Founders Week*

These accomplishments, taken together, healed the campus and created a sense of stability and progress.

Dr. Esteban serves the CSU's system-wide interests through leadership roles on the Financial Aid Advisory Council and the Commission on Technology Infrastructure.

Dr. Esteban's style is one of grace, patience, and politeness. He is a man of integrity, honesty, and is extraordinarily well-liked. He exhibits a great passion for CSU Chico. The president's accessibility contributes towards his successes.

President Esteban, the Board of Trustees and I have established the following goals for the next several years:

1) *The president should keep doing what he does.*
2) *Remind members of the campus of the strategic plan, its goals and achievements.*
3) *Identify a few tangible initiatives related to the goal of academic excellence that the university community will support and that the public will recognize as an attribute of CSU Chico.*

In summary, Manuel Esteban is a highly effective president for California State University, Chico who strives to offer high quality academic programs for students attending CSU Chico. Dr. Esteban is doing a spectacular job for which he is to be commended.

During the discussion Dr. Reed had with me immediately after showing me the results of the evaluation, he asked me if I had plans to move on to a "bigger and better university." The Chancellor felt that my six-year review would make such a move relatively easy. I responded that I was proud to be president of CSU, Chico and did not wish to go elsewhere, that both Gloria and I were privileged to be associated with the university and the city of Chico. My response to the Chancellor was recounted in the pages of the *E-R*. I knew it would be. But my response was not meant as public relations. I meant it with all sincerity and Gloria shared my sentiments completely. We were happy about it. We were surrounded by very good friends. We felt supported and appreciated. Chico had become our home.

Needless to say, I was very happy with the outcome of my six-year review. What pleased me the most is that, after a relatively difficult start, a lot of challenges to meet, the dysfunctional environment I had inherited, the clear opposition and animosity displayed by a few disgruntled faculty, local newspapers who seem to enjoy fostering division internally within the campus and between the campus and the community, and the initial stumbles that I had created for myself, the faith I had in my own abilities, my determination, and willingness to work tirelessly had paid off. I had been vindicated.

The *E-R* recounted some of my earlier gaffes, echoed what the Chancellor had written in his open letter, and concluded: "A person's true character sometimes takes time to surface. Esteban has recovered from the difficult initial months and become, in many respects, a model president." Quite a compliment. I could have exclaimed: *My oh my, How you've changed!*

At my fall convocation, if the audience had expected me to bask in the glory of all the positive aspects of my review, they would have been dead wrong. I had long ago learned that my primary role was to recognize the talents that already existed in the institution, provide avenues for those talents to blossom, find collective goals that all could identify with, convince them that we were on the right track, demonstrate that far more can be achieved through collective effort toward a common goal. What I tried to do in each of my convocations was to highlight the accomplishments and successes of our faculty, staff, and students, to reinforce the benefits of cooperative efforts not only within the institution itself but, better still, with the private sector. I likened our campus to a landscape of valleys and mountains. "This valley," I said, "is created by the unsung and all too often unrecognized daily activities, work, sacrifice and unselfish devotion you all manifest to both our students and to the very community of which we are all part and parcel ... You are the reason that our graduates love this institution and remember it with so much affection." My parting message was that, in my opinion, Chico State was doing so well at that point that our biggest challenge was going to be to top our own successes.

After years of enrollment declines, reductions in faculty and staff positions, freezing new hiring, and budget cut upon budget cut, we began to see the light at the end of the tunnel. Enrollment was up considerably. We were so confident that, with the able help of Bob Hannigan and his staff, we could hope to reach the milestone of 15,000 students, or for the purpose of funding, 14,000 FTE (Full-time Equivalent Students). Of course, we would need more faculty. We were on our way here as well. We had just hired fifty-two new tenure-track faculty. This was the largest contingent of new faculty since 1948. This was bound to raise faculty morale, a necessity to continue on our path forward. There was another good reason for us to walk around with a huge smile on our faces. CSU Chico's budget for 1999-2000 had been increased by $9.5 million. My goal to reach $10 million to enhance our Presidential Scholarship fund had reached $6 million.

The only clouds I could visualize on the horizon were both in the area of technology. The first was what was called a "collaborative management system (CMS)." This was a system wide plan to switch all CSU campuses from their divergent administrative software packages to a single software program. Our participation in the CMS initiative was a massive effort, one that would entail the replacement of our administrative information systems in the areas of human resources, financial management, and student information system with new 'Peoplesoft' software. The work for the transition alone was bound to be nightmarish. Unfortunately, this was not the worst of it. Over the four to five years that the full implementation would take, the cost to CSU, Chico alone would be in the range of $12.5 to $15 million, for which there was no additional state funding planned.

The other huge cloud was what became known as Y2K. There existed nationally among technological geniuses the fear that the moment 1999 turned into 2000 all kinds of serious problems would affect all electronics-based technology. It was feared that it could threaten many aspects of our communications, services, instruction, and research, including systems and equipment with embedded chips, such as heating and cooling, security and alarms, voice communications, instructional lab equipment, food services, and housing, to mention the major ones. I certainly did not know enough about technology to doubt the admonition of our experts. Our own technology guru had even built some shelter in the woods and stocked it with anything and everything for survival. In preparation for this "predictable" disaster we had spent a great deal of money, money that could have been used with better results elsewhere. My only strong reservation was that I had not seen Europeans or Japanese panic the way we were doing in the U.S.A. Why is that I asked myself. After all, Japanese in particular are exceptionally good at technology. But everyone told me, better safe than sorry.

We decided to bid goodbye to the 20th century by taking a trip with Walt and Teresa both to Barcelona and then to London. In Barcelona, we visited Gaudi's Sagrada Familia church, other Gaudi sites, attended a wonderful Messiah concert at the medieval Santa Maria del Mar Church, went to a Barcelona-Español soccer match, and saw all the lights and winter decorations always on display at Christmas in front of the Cathedral. We also ate at some wonderful restaurants and, more endearingly, at Gloria's cousins' home, where Ramona displayed her culinary talents in the most impressive fashion. What Gloria and I liked in particular is how well Walt and Teresa and Benedicto and Ramona got along despite some language barriers. All in all, this trip with our friends bound us even closer than we already were.

After this, Gloria and I spent Christmas and New Year with our daughter and family. For New Year eve everyone in the house went to bed before midnight. Because of all the fuss about Y2K, Jackie and I watched with trepidation as the clock struck midnight. Nothing at all happened. Perhaps it had to be midnight somewhere else for the world of technology to come to an end, we wondered. Still nothing after a few more hours. At the end, exhausted, we went to bed. In the morning the world was still all in one piece. How could so many intelligent and expert people be so wrong? The painful reality was that we had squandered hundreds of thousands of dollars to prepare ourselves for something that never happened. A very painful lesson.

Spring semester 2000 started well. I don't recall exactly what the process had been, but the end result was that I was selected as the only academic from California to be on a 13-member U.S. delegation to a Salzburg Seminar. The home of the seminar was the Schloss Leopoldskron, an eighteenth-century castle, a wonderful setting for an incredible encounter with people who until very recently had been attempting to erase some off the face of this earth. Gloria and I took advantage of this invitation to arrive a few days before the start of the seminar and travel by train to Vienna. It was cold and particularly windy in Vienna where we saw an older gentleman swept off his feet and land spectacularly. Despite the weather we enjoyed our short stay in Vienna.

The project's unspoken focus was to assist educators from Serbia, Montenegro, the Federation of Bosnia and Herzegovina, and Croatia, where issues of globalization were pressing and most difficult to deal with because of economic and political instabilities. The first order of business was to explore the term "globalization" and to distinguish among the various concepts attached to it: an inevitable move toward internationalization; a process threatening the heterogeneity of cultures, language, and knowledge; the development of a world economy as a result of multinational mergers; and the creation of an information technology in which there were no national boundaries. The question was: How can universities play a positive role in the process? How can they assist in both establishing peace among different peoples and preserving the integrity of various ethnic groups, languages, and religions?

Most of the people who attended were intelligent, worldly, educated, and willing if not eager to set aside past wars. Gloria was also invited. We both were incredibly impressed by the humanity of the people from those regions of the world. We spent many evenings talking to them, playing foosball with them, engaging in profound discussions, and, above all, listening to their heart tearing experiences. The formal presentations were something else. They were heart wrenching. I remember in particular the presentation made by Srbijanka Turajlic, from the former Yugoslavia. She delivered a very moving and provocative commentary on what a university can and cannot do to assist the process in South-Eastern Europe of "reconciliation" and, indeed, what Yugoslavian universities actually did during the civil war. She told the audience that if we visited the region "What you would see at a glance is a deeply wounded land with many scars still painfully visible. What you would not be able to see, but can almost palpable sense, is the scars that are left in each and every human soul." The region, she suggested, is in "deep need of an incubator to cultivate the notions of such things as 'dialogue; and 'reconciliation." She wasn't sure that universities could play a very positive role in this respect and for these deep-seated wounds.

The only thing I could do was to play the role I had been assigned. My presentation was entitled: *The University: Model for Multiethnic Relations and Cultural Diversity: Various Perspectives.* My main point was that California was a very multiethnic, multiracial, and multicultural society. The CSU was a reflection of this society. Its mission, I insisted, is not only to educate and train students, but also to prepare them to be good citizens and function comfortably in an increasingly diverse country. This meant, among other things, that students must learn to be tolerant of other people, to better accept and understand other people, and to realize that their lives are enriched by this better understanding. They must also come to realize and accept that the world is becoming one; the economic well-being of California and of the nation is dependent upon a well-educated citizenry, regardless of race and ethnicity. Our universities must teach tolerance, we must teach respect and civility, and we must learn to share each other's experiences. I then provided a long list of what we were doing in the CSU as a whole and-at CSU, Chico in particular to achieve these lofty goals. Given the environment in which we now live in 2021, my speech and providing the U.S. as a role model makes me wonder whether I was excessively optimistic and even naive.

Gloria and I were happy that Chico was such an attractive place that many of our friends wanted to come visit. Over the years, we received visits from Lonna and Alan Baum, who came from Michigan several times, Bill and Gaye Ashby, from Santa Barbara, Fred and Marilyn Dorer, from Bakersfield, Rex and Karen Wilson and Rafa and Celina, from Eureka, Richard West and Christine Helwick from Long Beach, Julio and Nory and also Serge Zaïtzeff, from Calgary. We enjoyed their visits enormously, however brief they often were. They afforded us a respite from our many university obligations.

Days after we returned from Austria and Serge left for Calgary, I flew to Guam. I had already been in Guam before as a WASC team member. I was now there to lead a new team as part of our accreditation assessment of the University of Guam. We met with senators to gauge the support the university received from its government. Since our last visit the government had reduced their allocation. Senators felt that they were very generous with the university. President Jose T. Nededog had a very different view. He had requested $37.8 million and received $24.8. We were there for almost one week, interviewed many faculty (several of whom complained that they had been recruited under false pretenses and been lied to), administrators, and students. We looked at their curriculum, and their facilities. We came to the conclusion that the university was still a long, long way from meeting the most basic requirements for accreditation. We could not recommend reaccreditation. Before we left, we were interviewed on television. As the chair I had to communicate to the university and the island in general what our conclusions had been, and what the university needed to do to merit reaccreditation. Our team was happy to leave directly from there to the airport. We did not leave many happy people behind us.

Soon after being back in Chico, I was off to Los Angeles with our new dean of the College of Business for a presentation to the board of directors of the national SIFE (Students in Free Enterprise) organization. We made a presentation about the future and goals of volunteer service, called "service learning" as a university graduation requirement. Governor Gray Davis had indicated support for the idea. I expressed my sincere wish that students would continue to volunteer in a number of ways. It was good for them to give back to their communities. I was, however, against making it a requirement for graduation. I could not possibly imagine how we could require 15,000 of our own students to volunteer. Besides, how could a community of less than 100,000 inhabitants absorb such an influx of student volunteers.

Our SIFE team always came at the very top of the list nationally. Our civil engineering students won the National Steel Bridge Competition, for the fourth year. Chico. Chico State' Model U.N. team earned top honor as the Outstanding Delegation from among over 200 collegiate delegations from across the U.S. and overseas. Our cross-country athletes were leaving most of their competitors in the dust, finishing in the NCAA top ten. Our baseball team swept the national championship again. JJ Jacovac became our golf star by winning a number of trophies and tournaments, including two NCAA Division II Championships. The women's rugby team captured the national championship. *The Orion* was once again named best student weekly in the nation. Enloe Hospital came to understand that nurses graduating from our program were choosing to by-pass the local hospital for greener pastures, so to speak. They needed to do something quickly. The Enloe Foundation came up with a way to attract and keep them closer to home. They provided $202,500 to fund two additional sets of classes and make room for 20 more nursing students per year, hoping that some of them would end up at Enloe Hospital. Tri Counties Bank gave us the first of three checks for $25,000 to support basketball tournaments. And if that were not enough, we had raised $13.6 million in donations. Not an awesome sum by modern day standards but a tremendous amount at that time and given that we had just recently been given the mandate to raise at least 10% of the amount allocated to our campus from the State coffers. We were on a roll.

That all of our collective efforts were beginning to pay off became patently clear when the *U.S. News and World Report* ranked Chico State as fifth among western public universities. We were beaten only by Cal-Poly

San Luis Obispo, a perennial winner, Western Washington University, Cal-Poly Pomona, and Montana Technical University. University rankings were determined based on various elements in six different areas: academic reputation, retention of students, faculty resources, student selectivity, financial resources, and alumni giving.

My job required me to do a lot of traveling. Ever since the flap about my salary I was incredibly conscious of spending any more than was absolutely necessary. I am somewhat parsimonious by nature but became more so at Chico State. If I could bum a ride with any of my colleagues, I always did. If it was essential that I rent a car, I had instructed Amy, my secretary, that she try to get me the cheapest one. She did. When I got to whatever hotel my presidential colleagues and I were staying at I never used valet parking. Why spend money when I was quite capable of parking the car myself. My car was always the smallest and cheapest looking one. It did not bother me. Whenever Gloria had to travel with me, however, she was somewhat embarrassed that we looked like misers arriving in our dismal automobiles. One time, the car I was given was so bad that Gloria almost cried. You would have sworn that I had rented through a Rent-a-Wreck. The sideview mirrors were held together with duct tape. The motor sounded like the engine was about to fall off. Gloria refused to ride in it. I tried to exchange the car but was told that this was all they had. Take it or leave it. We took it. When we arrived at the hotel, she saw several of my colleagues drive to the front door of the hotel in limousine-like vehicles. I had to quickly park the car and hide it as far away as possible. When we returned from our trip, Gloria went to see Amy and made her promise never again to listen to me and rent such pieces of junk. She said to me that she understood my not wanting to be seen as a spent thrift, but what I did to avoid this perception was undignified and belittled the importance of the presidency. Besides, she added, how did I know that my colleagues did not make fun of me? I told Amy to rent a better grade of car whenever Gloria came with me. On my own, I continued to spend as little as possible. No one would ever accuse me of misusing state resources.

In the Spring, Jack Fox, our Alumni director, approached me with an idea. He wanted to know whether Gloria and I would be willing to go on an extended trip to Spain with a select group of outstanding alumni, do-nors, and community leaders. We would be gone from June 3rd through June 18th. He assured me that Gloria and I would not need to be the of-ficial guides. He would find a qualified Spanish person to carry out this responsibility. But no trip would be possible without our company. Our fellow travelers were interested in seeing Spain, to some extent, through our eyes as well as theirs. We agreed. It was a wonderful trip. Those who signed up for it were sophisticated and savvy travelers. They were also some of the people whose company Gloria and I enjoyed the most. The trip could not have gone any better. Everyone was satisfied and happy. It was perfect until we hit Heathrow Airport or on our way back. Everything was paralyzed. There was an Air Traffic controller strike. There were thousands of people at the airport, and nothing was going out or coming in. Jack Fox and I went up to the ticket counter to rebook the 27 of us. The employee looked at us and said that he could get four of us out in four days, three out the days after that, and perhaps the rest in nine days. We were appalled. Fortunately, Jack was an experienced travel organizer. He called his travel agent in San Francisco. It was a Sunday afternoon, and he was having a barbecue in his backyard. Jack explained how dire the circumstances were and he immediately got to work on it. An hour later he called and said that he had managed to rebook all 27 of us for 10:30 the following morning.

Of course, we were all relieved. Among us were a lot of wealthy people. Money did not help, though. We could not leave any earlier nor could we find any hotel rooms at all. We were forced to spend a very long night at the airport, with thousands of people all around us. The airport personnel didn't seem to think it was important to cater to any of us. At around 10 in the evening everything shut down. Even the heat. Before the closure we had managed to buy three sandwiches and a few bottles of water. We cut the three sandwiches into 27 pieces. A succulent and copious meal it was not! It was getting quite cold. We went around scavenging for newspapers to cover ourselves while we laid on the floor. We decided that one of us had to stay awake and vigilant. This was a great hunting ground for pick-pockets. Amazingly, not a single person complained. Nancy Fox took lots of photos of all of us strewn on the floor looking anything but comfortable. But we were all good-natured about it and it brought the group even closer together. Not something we would have chosen but something to recount. It was a memorable trip and experience.

When everything seemed to be moving along almost if nothing could disrupt our gains and successes, a horrible tragedy struck our campus at its core. In the spring we conducted a survey to determine the extent to which our students were involved in alcohol and drug consumption. We discovered that our student consumption figures were higher than those on most other campuses. With that in mind we accelerated and expanded all the tools at our disposal to educate, help, discourage excessive drinking, and demonstrate the dire consequences of excessive drinking. After pleading with the students to exercise moderation, what I feared most happened. We found ourselves mourning the tragic death of our student, Adrian Heideman, a member of Pi Kappa Phi. Reportedly he drank a bottle of blackberry brandy at the fraternity party. I went to meet with Adrian's parents. I could not leave this unpleasant, difficult, and painful task to anyone else. It was a meeting I will never forget. As I told the parents: "this is something no parent should have to go through. I never want this to happen again." Right there and then I made the decision to suspend the fraternity immediately until investigations into the death were complete. I also wrote a letter to the university community. I wanted to make patently clear that this senseless loss underscored the need for faculty, staff, administrators, and student leaders to improve our efforts. I urged all of us to multiply our efforts "to build a campus climate that encourages and rewards academic engagement, intellectual excellence, and healthy lifestyles … to make clear that irresponsible drinking is neither normal nor cool." In my most direct manner possible and clear language I told an audience of 200 students attending a forum on National Collegiate Alcohol Awareness Week that "I don't want to forget about Adrian. I don't want the university to forget about Adrian. I don't want you to forget about Adrian … You must not surrender to the culture of drinking in which students view drinking to excess as a badge of honor … Imagine, as a parent, hearing our son or daughter suffocated in his or her own vomit." I was angry, very angry. In the ten years I was president I had to call parents to tell them that their child had died in an alcohol-related incident a total of five times. Five horrendous times. This alone kept me awake on many, many nights, particularly around Saint Patrick days.

The academic year 1999-2000 had started brilliantly. Because of Adrian's death it ended tragically. I asked sociology professor Walt Schafer, my running partner, confidant, and very able researcher to devote his efforts to working closely with my Advisory Committee on Alcohol and Drug Abuse and the Campus Alcohol and Drug Education Center (CADEC), the vice presidents, and the deans to assess what we were doing to reduce alcohol abuse and to make recommendations on how we could improve these efforts. We could not wait passively for yet another tragic death. In August of 2001 the University received a $276,590 federal grant for a two-year program to reduce alcohol abuse among freshmen, directed by Professor Schafer.

Who could possibly have guessed or even contemplated that 2001 would shake America to the core? However, the catastrophe would not happen until September, so we began the year, once again, full of hope and celebration.

My dream that one day not too far into the future CSU, Chico would have a Wildcat Activity Center was beginning to materialize. On March 7 and 8, Chico State students were to vote in a referendum to determine whether they would levy a fee increase on themselves to permit the Associated Students to build a state-of-the-art recreation center and intramural facility to correct what a consulting group described as "woefully inadequate," recreation facilities on campus. Both Jeff Iverson, the then Associated President and I had lofty goals for this facility. It would be 125,000 square feet and would have two stories. The Aquatic Center would add an additional 45,000 square feet and contain a large Olympic-size pool for lap swimming, a leisure pool, a warm-water spa, and a sauna. This project fit perfectly with the campus's number one priority of the *Strategic Plan for the Future of California State University, Chico*. Other than the fierce opposition from the local gym clubs in the city, the biggest stumbling block was the price, about $65 million. We hoped that, if the referendum passed, we would open the center in the academic year 2003-2004 and the Aquatic Center in 2005.

Schofield, the winner of the wheelchair race and the biggest owner of Chico's gyms, was adamantly opposed to the Center. He had support from other gym club owners. They devoted a lot of money to derail the project. But what surprised both Iverson and me was the bizarre alliance that he had been able to cobble together. The Republican and the Democratic Clubs, the Progressive Student Union, and the Chico Cannabis Coalition all joined forces with the club owners to defeat the proposed hike increase, even though the student newspaper, my administration, and the Associated Students all recommended a positive vote. The *E-R*, seldom on the side of students, recognized that "Chico State's recreation facilities are abysmal, and even the addition of a new physical education building, which is in the works, won't be nearly enough." I was informed by the Chancellor's Office of legal counsel that I had the authority to raise fees, but I declared that I was opposed to acting unilaterally, that "It would make a mockery of the referendum if I was to simply impose the fees without taking into account the will of the students". Ultimately, the project was scaled back somewhat and eventually students voted in favor. The Center was open as I was leaving the presidency. Nonetheless, I was proud that at least it was conceived and approved during my tenure. It turned out to be a beautiful facility.

March turned out to be a bad month despite some nice successes. On the 16th I received a phone call from Gloria. She was in Calgary visiting her mother and staying, as usual, at Julio and Nory's home. She told me that my mother had refused to take any more medication and had long ago stopped eating. Her health was declining quickly. Gloria did not think she had much longer to live. When she called me, it was too late for me to fly to Calgary. I had to wait until the following day. The only flight I could get on such short notice did not arrive in Calgary until early evening. Julio came to the airport to pick me up. Our mother was not doing well but was still alive. By the time Julio and I got to the nursing home, she had expired. I missed seeing her alive by minutes, Gloria said. I could not believe that I had, once again, as it happened with my father, missed being able to say goodbye to her. She was 82. She had been paralyzed for over ten years. She obviously did not want to suffer any more. I felt empty, forlorn. I had to get lost in my work so that I would not dwell on my sadness.

As summer was approaching, Jack Fox, who by now had married our friend Nancy McDougal and had retired as alumni director, convinced his successor, Sue Anderson, to organize yet another trip. Two trips were organized primarily for alumni participation, one to Peru, led by Roger Lederer, Dean of the College of Natural Sciences, and another to China and Tibet. Alumni were eager to have Gloria and me join one or both trips. We chose the latter one.

Between May 26th and June 14th, we visited Beijing, where we stood in the middle of Tiananmen Square, climbed the Great Wall and visited the Forbidden City, the Temple of Heaven, and the Summer Palace. From there we travelled to Xi'an, where we visited the seven-storied Big Wild Goose Pagoda and the Jade Buddha Temple. Outside Xi'an we came face to face with 6,000 life size terracotta warriors. On our last day in Shanghai, we bid farewell to some of the members of our party, who returned home. Ten of us began the second leg of our trip with a three-day trek down the Yangtze River. On one part of the river trip, men running along the banks pulled us to a tributary in small boats. Whereas the Yangtze is extremely wide and exceptionally polluted (in fact, we saw human bodies floating as well as the bodies of some animals), the tributary was pristine, with water so clear that we could see every colorful rock and pebble lining the bottom of the river. At the end of our river cruise, we travelled through an incredible dam construction to Chengdu, the gateway to Tibet and from there to Lhasa, its capital. Once we became acclimatized to being at an altitude of 12,000 feet, we visited the huge 17th century Potala Palace, where the 14th Dalai Lama would have lived had he not been in exile. Altogether an incredible trip.

The Fall semester began in Chico with a great event: the Grand Opening of the brand new and beautiful Bell Memorial Union. With this building and several of the other ones that we have renovated either partially or completely, the campus was undergoing a process of beautification. The paths that linked the various buildings or separated them were also modified and enhanced. I just enjoyed walking from building to building and observed how happy students seemed to be with the improved surroundings.

I was about to complete my eighth year as president. Gloria had been urging me to consider retirement. As enjoyable as most of our life was, it did not belong to us. We were forever involved directly or indirectly in university events. We managed to go out for breakfast at our favorite place, Morning Thunder, only now and then and almost always on a Sunday. The rest of the week was totally devoted to official functions. I did not want to retire yet. I had achieved a lot of what I had hoped to get done, but there was still plenty to do. Yet, I could see how Gloria thought that it was time for us to be able to spend more time together and do things unrelated to the university. I finally gave in to her. I was scheduled to be down in Long Beach for the Board of Trustees meeting Monday, September 10 and 11. I asked to talk to Chancellor Reed on the 11th. I did not tell him what I wanted to discuss with him. My plan was to inform him that the academic year 2001-2002 would be my last. If he wanted, he could start the search for my successor.

When I got up on the 11th to get ready, I did something unusual, I turned the TV on. What I saw surprised me. I wanted to watch the news on CNN and instead they were showing a movie, I thought. It took a couple of minutes to realize what I was seeing. An airplane had flown right into one of the World Trade Center towers. I immediately called Gloria to tell her to turn the TV on. We were both horrified. Needless to say, the Trustees meeting was cancelled and so was my appointment with Dr. Reed. All the presidents were in a scramble to try to get home. Everything in California had shut down. Those who lived within driving distance of Long Beach left immediately. Those, like us, who needed to fly home, were stuck. The whole country was left in a state of paralysis. No one knew what else could happen. Some old enough to remember compared what happened to the Pearl Harbor attack. President McCrone and I were fortunate that President Gerth from Sacramento had his rented car with him. Dr Gerth offered us a ride to Sacramento. I had left my car at the airport in Sacramento. So, we drove from Long Beach to Sacramento's airport. I got in my car and drove with McCrone to Chico. He spent the night at our home, rented a car and drove to Arcata the following day. We were all in shock. We just could not wrap our arms around the idea that the U.S. had been attacked.

For several days, vigils were organized at the free speech area on campus. There were all kinds of speeches made by a number of professors, students, and community leaders. On one of those vigils, students invited political science professor George Wright to address the crowd. He was a harsh critic of U.S. foreign policy, and like other people in attendance he was emotional in his remarks. He lashed out at President Bush, saying he was continuing policies that militarized the Middle East and sought to capture foreign oil reserves. Some people shouted at him as he spoke. Others hugged him afterwards. His remarks were reported in the *E-R*, then echoed in an essay he wrote for the *CN&R* (*Going down the wrong path*, Essay, September 20). His comments were posted on various Web pages and eventually picked up by national media, such as the *Wall Street Journal* and *Fox News*. Professor Wright received more than 100 pieces of hate email, including death threats. He feared for his life and stayed away from campus for a while. I was called by a number of people who urged me to fire him immediately, or else.

I felt it was my duty to write a guest comment which appeared on *CN&R* October 18. Here are some excerpts of what I wrote in my *In Defense of Free Speech*.

We all have strong feelings right now, especially anger. That is the reason Professor Wright spoke out as he did, in a way that in hindsight he realizes was probably excessive. And that is the reason he prompted such a fiery response. The horrific terrorist attacks left us with no living perpetrators and only a shadowy mastermind: we have a tremendous urge to find the enemy somewhere, anywhere, and strike at him.

But we as a people must not vent out our anger to the extent that we threaten those of us who take a contrary view. In this time of crisis, we cannot toss out our Constitution and exclude citizens who choose to disagree with the majority. As we do so, we grow to resemble the terrorists who would tear us apart.

Most people may view Professor Wright's comments as inappropriate, insensitive or just plain wrong. But we must, as Americans, bear to hear them. They are protected by the First Amendment. ... It is easy to defend freedom of speech when that expression coincides with our own or that of the vast majority. It is far more virtuous, significant, important and necessary to defend freedom of expression when it puts forth views opposite to our own.

Stanley Kurtz, a fellow at the Hudson Institute and a contributing editor to *National Review Online*, wrote an extremely long article entitled *Free Speech and an Orthodoxy of Dissent* which appeared in *The Chronicle of Higher Education*, October 26. In it he devoted a good portion to criticizing Professor Wright, probably because he perceived him as liberal. He praised me somewhat for having defended Wright's protected rights but faulting his timing and his judgement. I wasn't happy that we had become national news but was comforted by the fact that our local newspapers showed restraint and dealt with the controversy with equanimity. Others were not as sanguine. As I said, I received many calls for Wright's termination. Many of those who called me threatened that they would no longer make donations to the university unless I fired Professor Wright. Out of curiosity, I checked our records and saw that none of those people have ever given a penny to the university. In time tempers cooled and life began to have its own regular rhythm. One relevant result of this horrendous event was that I never got to discuss my plan for retirement with Chancellor Reed. When he called to reschedule our meeting, I told him that it could wait, that there was no urgency. Gloria was not happy, but I took the whole thing as a sign that I was to stay on the job one more year.

On September 16, former CSU, Chico's president Glenn Kendall turned 100 years old. I had enjoyed his company and southern charm on many occasions. I felt a strong affection for him. It was therefore a tremendous honor for me to host and preside over the ceremony held to celebrate such a momentous occasion, held at the Albert E. Warren's Reception Center. That it was so well-attended was a testimony to a man who had meant so much for Chico State.

As 2001 was coming to an end, budgetary clouds came to darken our sunny skies. Governor Gray Davis ordered a statewide hiring freeze. When I met with the Academic Senate in October, I informed all present that I was determined to challenge this order. An across-the-board hiring freeze never makes sense for higher education. We could not possibly halt immediately all the searches that were underway for new faculty. If we had no choice but to reduce our budget, we would proceed with care and follow our own dictates outlined in our strategic plan. Chancellor Reed informed each campus president that we should anticipate a 1% (about $1.1 million for us) cut but prepare for as much as 5% ($5.5 million). We were back to the feast or famine years I encountered when I arrived at CSU, Bakersfield back in 1987. By January, however, all predictions and draconian scenarios regarding budget vanished suddenly. There would probably be no increases but, at least, no cuts either. In fact, at least for Chico, we were scheduled to receive $1.1 million to fully fund year-round instruction, and some additional resources to increase our enrollment by 95 FTES.

The winter semester of 2002 was anticlimactic. Everything seemed to be running smoothly. I continued to host faculty and staff in small groups over coffee, went to Academic Senate meetings, had my weekly Cabinet meetings, went to Sacramento for legislative days now and then, attended the monthly meetings in the CSU headquarters in Long Beach, had AASCU and WASC meetings at different locations regularly, went monthly to the Sierra Health Foundation meetings in Sacramento, and to Enloe Hospital Board meetings in Chico, presided over the University Advisory Board reunions, was present at University Foundation and Alumni Board, went to weekly Rotary lunch meetings, and oversaw the many activities that had made Founders Week such an anticipated and successful series of events.

I also went this spring to the Provost Spring Retreat at the remote Eagle Lake, a desolate research property that was owned by the University, as I had done since Scott McNall began to gather all the deans and invited me to attend. McNall loved it and possibly a couple of deans did as well. Others suffered through it, since the living conditions were rustic, to be kind. I was fortunate in that Scott reserved for me the best of the cabins, not that it was anything luxurious at all, *au contraire*. But it was a fun time, it created an *esprit de corps* as well as a time when a lot of very important decisions were made in academic affairs. Everyone had a task and/or a report to prepare and all participants listened carefully and critiqued it appropriately. I participated sparingly. Only at the end of the two-day retreat did

I offer my opinion on what had been discussed and agreed upon. I always came away from these retreats impressed by the seriousness with which all participants assumed their particular roles and contributed constructively.

I finally had my meeting with Chancellor Reed. I informed him of my decision to retire from the presidency. When I took the job, I said that I would do it for 8 to 10 years. I did not want to be like some of my presidential colleagues who never seemed to know when it was the right time to go. Though I could have worked for at least a couple more years, since I felt that there were several projects that I wanted to lead to term, I could no longer be deaf to Gloria's entreaties. She wanted to enjoy a life with me, without having to share me constantly as my job required. Chancellor Reed tried to convince me to stay. I politely refused. I was giving him a whole year to find a replacement.

On August 22, during my annual Convocation I announced that I would step down at the end of the 2002-2003 academic year. The convocation, as was reported in the local press, was an emotional event for the standing-room-only audience. Harlen Adams Theater grew hushed. No one had expected that I would keep my word to stay at the helm for no more than ten years. As I concluded my remarks, I was almost moved to tears by the spontaneous standing ovation. Faculty and staff rushed the stage to wish me and Gloria well and to thank both of us for our contributions to the university. I told everyone that I still had a full year of work ahead of me and did not plan to slow down.

When I learned that the presidents of CSU, Sacramento and Cal Poly, Pomona had also announced they were leaving, I wondered whether the Trustees would be able to conduct three concurrent searches. We learned quickly that CSU, Chico would be the last of the three. This meant in all likelihood that there would be an interim president for a while, something the faculty were very unhappy about. When Chancellor Reed came to campus for a 24-hour visit to meet with students, faculty, administrators, deans and the press, he declared that he wouldn't do anything to speed up the search for a replacement for me. He indicated that Chico State "has stable, outstanding senior leadership under Esteban, the other two campuses are not in nearly such good shape." He also said that in consulting with local constituencies, he heard that "the best candidate would be a 'clone' of President Esteban." Nice compliment. But perhaps the nicest one came from Jim Postma, the chair of the Academic Senate who said to a reporter: "Although Esteban will be a hard act to follow, he's actually made the job of replacing him easier. He's made Chico State a very desirable place to be the president of, so I think we'll get some pretty good candidates." The logical person to be selected as the acting president was Scott McNall. And this is what happened. I felt comfortable with the decision. I knew Scott would do a very good job.

The press in general gave me high marks for what I had accomplished. To my surprise, they seemed to know more than I would have assumed. They indicated that I had served in several national and regional organizations, including the American Council on Education, the American Association of State Colleges and Universities, and the California Joint Policy Council on Agriculture and Education. They also highlighted some of my other responsibilities, such as my membership in the Sierra Health Foundation in Sacramento, the Enloe Medical Center in Chico, the Chico Rotary Club, and as a director of the Chico Chamber of Commerce. They also credited me, among many things, for having

1) had the university re-accredited by WASC,
2) developed the University Strategic Plan,
3) created a Center for the Excellence in Learning and Teaching,
4) worked with the Nettletons to provide an enviable home to Chico State Wildcats and Chico Heat,
5) created a University Research Foundation,
6) expanded the membership of the University Advisory Board to include many important community and philanthropic leaders,
7) established the President's Scholars Program, and
8) collaborated with the City of Chico on the Warner Street Project to widen Warner Street, build a parking structure, and a bridge over Big Chico Creek.

Those were not necessarily the achievements that filled me with the greatest pride. I would have liked to see them bring up my effort to bring Nobel

Prize winners. We had had no fewer than seven of them. In my opinion, this played a very important role in changing the culture of the campus and demonstrating that we were the intellectual and cultural hub of the region. But it was nice to see a press that at the beginning of my tenure had been exceptionally critical and full of acrimony converted into such a strong supporter. In fact, on January 23, 2003, the *E-R* editorial made the case that I should lead the university in the interim, while a successor was identified. They urged the Chancellor to call me immediately to ask me to postpone my retirement. The editorial continued: "Esteban is a unique leader. He's about as close as you'll come to being universally liked and respected on a college campus. And he has the knowledge, based on his 10 years as Chico State's president, to guide the campus through a difficult time. It's an expertise no interim president can possibly have."

In the meantime, there was reason for further pride and celebration. On October 22, Governor Gray Davis came to campus and informed those of us who had worked on a building that would house a Natural History Museum that Prop 40 had passed and we would be granted $3 million to start planning and construction of the museum. We already had the drawings. It was going to be another beautiful addition to our campus.

Before the end of 2002, on 12 October to be precise, we traveled to Saint Louis, Missouri, for a very important family event. David, our nephew, married a wonderful young lady, Lynn. It was a joyous wedding, and we were happy to be reunited with a lot of our family members who came from Canada and from several parts of the U.S.

Gloria and I sent out our last invitation to a holiday open house. It was incredibly well attended. Everyone seemed eager to wish us well as we entered a new stage in our lives. For us, it was a bittersweet time. On the one hand, we were looking forward to spending more time with each other far from the limelight. On the other hand, we were quite sad. Despite a difficult beginning and a few hiccups here and there, the last eight years had been almost idyllic. It would have been very difficult to have had a written script that would have had a better finale to it than the one we were actually living. We had been living an unimaginable dream. We had made lasting friendships that endure to this day, almost twenty years after my retirement.

The last semester of my presidency began well. In March I wrote my last Newsletter. I was already beginning to feel the pull of nostalgia. I began to reminisce. Before I gave a summary of the state of the university, as a way of saying goodbye, I looked back in time to August 1993. This is what I said:

When I assumed the presidency at CSU, Chico in August 1993, I saw clearly how much the people, events, and traditions had shaped this campus into the wonderful institution it had become. The foundation laid by the founding fathers and mothers, the beautiful setting, and the courage and foresight of community and campus people down through the years have all contributed to the success and enduring greatness of CSU, Chico.

As I approached the inauguration, I wanted to keep sight of the university's remarkable history and, at the same time, celebrate present contributions and achievements. In April 1994, the first Founders Week was held, and since then it has been an annual opportunity to cherish our rich past and honor our present.

Don Heinz, chair of the first Founders Week committee, wrote this eloquent description of the celebration: "CSU, Chico is constructed of land, culture, people, traditions, memories, hopes. During our annual Founders Week, we celebrate what we have been and what we will strive to become. We welcome you all – friends, neighbors, colleagues, forerunners – as we build the community we are and hope to be. Join us this week in our diversity and unity – all who celebrate university life together in intellectual discussions, games, music, and dance."

This year is the tenth annual celebration of our rich historical legacy, and we applaud all those who continue to bring accolades and acclaim to themselves and to the university.

We were about to enter another period of famine, but I was determined to ensure we all faced the future with hope and dedication. We had survived previous budgetary famines and would survive this one again. I knew that I was going to be asked to make the rounds and be asked to summarize my ten years. I was not going to dwell on the bad moments, although there were quite a few, particularly at the beginning. I wanted to use the few remaining months to give evidence that everyone involved in any way with the university ought to be proud and continue on the track we had chosen. The future was theirs to mold. No outside force could derail their progress if they persevered. We had not gotten where we were by accident. Inertia was not an option. Collectively and sticking to our wonderful master plan, whatever clouds were on the horizon could not dampen the spirit that had shaped CSU, Chico. I wanted to leave a clear message. The president, whoever he/she is, can help, can be a force for good, but the actual work to move an institution from good to excellent is done by all, in a collective effort.

April 20-28 was the last Founders Week that I was going to be involved in. It was a wonderful week filled with the typical events that had made this the highlight of the year. Gloria and I enjoyed it probably more than in previous years because it was going to be the last one where we would play an active role.

Who would have thought that Arno Rethans, former Dean of the College of Business and at the time the Vice President for Academic Affairs, a serious, somewhat mordant, always incredibly efficient and effective man, would also be a poet? On April 12, he wrote an

Ode to Manuel and Gloria

In 1993, Humboldt State sent us its very best
And in Chico he would build his new nest
Along came Gloria, his honey
Some said maliciously both of them in search of mo' money

From the very first inning
The town Manuel was winning
Everyone he met, ended up grinning
And that was just the beginning

Soon after his arrival, came out of the can
The evolving document known as the Strategic Plan
And for the next ten years it would guide
The campus community back to a sense of pride

In 1998 he faced the inquisition
When some disgruntled professor wanted his deposition
To account for alleged crimes of commission
Against all of which a wise judge ultimately slapped a prohibition
Whenever Manuel felt under the gun
With Walt Schafer he would go run
Along nature's trail they would travel
Until their problems would flow into the gravel

At Eagle Lake the game of "Piquitos" he would teach
To unsuspecting deans, he would beseech
And inevitable "I win, I win" he would screech
While at breakfast the next morning his winning he would preach

Now that Manuel and Gloria are to retire
We truly wish them all that they desire
As you go, know that you are people whom we admire
And to whose many accomplishments we aspire.

Over the years I have discarded plenty of cards and notes wishing us farewell, but kept this one because it is too loving and too swell. There I rhymed!

The Orion was the first newspaper to want a retrospective from me. The staff writer wanted to give me a lot of credit for what I had accomplished for athletics. My response was "As much as I would like to take credit, I have had nothing to do with it. It'd be presumptuous of me to assume anything like that." It was true that I had played perhaps an important role in some progress, most notably Chico's move to the California Collegiate Athletic Association (CCAA), a necessary move that we made in 1998. It placed us in the most competitive Division II conference in the country, something that required us to raise substantial funds for athletic scholarships. This permitted us to recruit better student athletes which, in turn, resulted in securing many national titles in a good number of sports. Gloria and I did all we could to help raise funds for athletics and attended as many games as was humanly possible. Our support and commitment were never questioned. This was recognized by our new Athletic Director, Anita Barker when she summarized it this way: "He was a friend to the whole sports department. He was a fan. He went to games and supported our teams. We're going to miss him greatly." This was enough credit for me. In another article, *The Orion* reminded me that I had often said that I was a cheerleader for the university. I accepted this description of me but made it clear that "For the past ten years, I don't consider any progress made to the university due to me. The university was good before I came. And if it's better, it's due to the efforts of the individuals at the university. It's a collective effort that comes from a love of the institution."

Provost McNall was quoted as having said about me that "he never asked or expected me to be somebody I was not. Few people have that kind of freedom or working relationship." This is what I would have said of my relationship with President McCrone and it was nice to hear the same praise from McNall about me. McNall was quoted as remembering something about the many road trips that we had taken together. He was always ready to take detours to explore. I always believed that the shortest distance between two points was a straight line and that the fastest way to get there was without stopping. "No matter how I hinted, the man has the same capacity as Fidel Castro," he said about me. I guess I should have realized that not everyone has the same bladder capacity.

There were two constituencies whose support I most valued and for whom I devoted most of my work and dedication: students and faculty. To be praised by them filled me with pride. To see that the Associated Students president, Jimmy Reed, like several other AS presidents, considered me "an inspiration" and that, whether students agreed or disagreed with my decisions, they knew that I was always driven by a deep desire to do what was best for them; or to read that Professor Jim Postma, chair of the Academic Senate and a member of the campus search committee that brought me to campus in 1993, indicated that the "he has never regretted the committee's choice," filled my soul with gratefulness and satisfaction.

After thanking me profusely in writing for having always been accessible to the press, the journalists and editors of *The Orion* were amazed that

"From attacking each other with lawsuits to partnering in a campaign for improving the Halloween celebration, the city of City and Chico State University have come a long way. The Chico City Council wants to thank University President Manuel Esteban for playing a crucial role in leading that journey. ... City Manager Tom Lando, will present Esteban with the resolution giving him most of the credit for the successful link between the university and the city." It was another source of satisfaction for me to see that the City of Chico credited me for a better working relationship. But it is yet another example that no one single individual can make change happen. He/she needs willing partners and Chico was more than willing to partner with the university to create an atmosphere of cooperation.

Even the *E-R* wrote an incredible lengthy article about my ten years at the helm of Chico State, including a number of photos: of me walking on the bridge that united the athletic field, where I always tried to exercise with my dear friend Walt Schafer, of the administrative building that housed my office, of me in my office with a coffee cup that my staff gave me as a present when I completed my first year in office (it said "I survived my first year!"), and one that showed Walt Schafer and me running in the University Stadium, another where I am embracing the former Associated Students President Amber Johnsen, and a last one showing Gloria and me at one of the many receptions offered in our honor where we both beam of happiness.

One of the nicest tributes appeared in the *CN&R* May 22, 2003. I appreciated the fact that they gave Dave Waddell, faculty advisor to *The Orion*, the honor of being the guest commentator on a day where it was obvious that the editor of the *CN&R* would have wanted to be the recorder of that moment. It was a classy move. Waddell had a lot of very complimentary observations about my tenure. I particularly enjoyed reading the following: "Another thing Esteban did regularly was participate in freewheeling, off-the-record discussions with *The Orion* staff. He could be both very opinionated and very, very funny. During one particularly divisive campus issue, Esteban expressed astonishment at the profane language some students put into angry emails to him. *Orion* staffers, I think, were both surprised and delighted when he told them what those words were."

I found the editorial in the *CN&R, Adios, Manuel,* rather ironic. "We're going to miss Manuel Esteban. The community had best hope Chico State University finds a new president half as good as the Latin leader who saw the school through the last decade. ... His door was open to faculty, staff and students. ... Esteban's accessibility extended to the community and the media – and a warm relationship with the press is an exception among school leaders. ... Esteban's missteps can be counted on one hand. *The News and Review*, like almost everyone else in town, likes Esteban: his personal style, his leadership abilities and that cool accent." What? Had the *CN&R* really forgotten how they treated me and portrayed me on their front page as a doll in my underwear with royal vestments ready to dress me as a king? By golly, the editor even suggested that the new rec center should not be called Wildcat Activity center but The Manuel Esteban Recreation Center. My, how things had changed!

At my last Graduation Ceremony, I was proud to do something that, to my knowledge, had never been done at CSU, Chico. The University granted two honorary Ph.Ds. One to Steve Nettleton and one to Judy Sitton, an incredibly valuable member of the University Advisory Board, a member of the national SIFE advisory board, and an overall supporter of almost any academic, charitable, humane agency. This was in 2003. Steve, unfortunately, passed away last year. Judy continues to play a preeminent role in Chico. They both deserved to be publicly honored for their tireless work to promote Chico.

The May 15 elegant retirement reception that was organized in Gloria's and my honor seemed like a series of eulogies – with the happy difference being that I was still alive to enjoy it. Gloria and I sat surrounded by numerous plaques and commendations. The College of Engineering, Computer Science and Technology certified that I had been officially designated an Honorary Faculty Member of the College. With this official designation came a beautiful office that the College had found for me to move into given that I would no longer be able to occupy the one that had been my home away from home for the last ten years. We even had an American folded flag that had flown over the Capitol. It was awarded to me by Congressman Wally Herger. He was a nice person but someone with whom I shared not a single idea or belief. Perhaps one of the most unusual honors Gloria and I received was from Carolyn S. Shoemaker and Eugene M. Shoemaker. They named an asteroid (16641) they had discovered in 1993 in Gloria's and my name. Hereafter this asteroid was to be named: (16641) Esteban=1993 QH10. Carolyn Shoemaker, one of our most illustrious alumni, wrote to us a beautiful and moving letter. She finished with these words: "Enjoy looking at the sky and knowing that you are there for thousands of years to come!" Talk about a unique honor!

To be lauded by colleagues as a "born leader," "open and forthright," "genuine," and "dedicated and skillful" was of course nice to hear. I was particularly glad that Gloria got to hear it as well. I did not get the same adulation and admiration at home. Perhaps she would now show me the respect and veneration that I deserved!

The Members of the University Board organized a retirement dinner honoring Gloria and me. There were 230 guests. It was one of the classiest events Gloria and I have probably ever attended. From the very classy, invitation cards, to the decoration of the tables, to the number of tuxedo clad men and evening-dressed ladies, to the short speeches made by a selected group of individuals, to the fact that Jackie, Rafael, Julio, Nory, and our nephew Jason were present, everything, turned that evening into a magic night. Nancy Fox's splendid album chronicling our ten years contains pages upon pages of the photos that were taken of the many guests who came to express their love for us and to wish us well on the next leg of our journey. We were moved beyond words.

I had made it very clear that we did not want people to go to the trouble of getting us gifts. Instead, I let it be known that if anyone felt like doing something for us, I would appreciate contributions to the President's Scholars Program. I could not believe it when Carol Berg informed me that the Program would be richer to the tune of $125,000. I wish I could have hugged and kissed everyone who had so generously donated to one of my favorite projects.

How could we not take a cue from all those generous donors? Before we left, Gloria and I funded a scholarship for aspiring young tenors. We named it after my father, a wonderful tenor who never had a single lesson.

He would have been honored to know that someone would benefit in his name. We also created an endowment in the form of a $100,000 life insurance policy that upon Gloria's and my passing will provide the College of Agriculture with $50,000 for scholarships. The other half of the policy will add to my father's Aspiring Tenor Scholarship Endowment. Because tuition and fees keep going up, and the $125,000 originally created to support the President's Scholars Program will soon begin to be depleted, Gloria and I have decided to make an annual donation to this program to ensure its perpetuity. CSU, Chico gave us a lot. We want to give back as much as we can.

There was a very special thing that I believe Carol Berg organized, a book that contains hundreds of notes, short in some cases, and much longer in others, from staff members from throughout the university. Several of them moved me to tears then and again as I have read it in preparation for this memoir.

Chancellor Reed also organized a beautiful farewell dinner party for three Trustees whose terms had come to an end and the three CSU Presidents who had chosen to retire. It was a grand event. What surprised me the most was the beautiful booklet that was presented to Gloria and me. Its cover contained a photo of the two of us in the middle of the cover and and on the side, a vertical band of additional photos that seemed to capture many of the major events that encompassed my ten-year presidency. Inside, it contained a series of letters from each of the 22 other CSU campuses plus letters as well from Dr. Reed, Richard West, and Christine Helwick. A nice gesture and a good souvenir.

Recently (4/25/2021) I received a brief note from former Dean of Humanities and Fine Arts, Don Heinz. I had mentioned to him that I was writing my autobiography. He told me that there were two little events that he wanted me to know about. The first had to do with the very first time I addressed the whole university community. According to him, Dale Steiner, who at the time was the chair of the History Department, leaned over to him and said: "Just imagine—he's speaking in his fourth language, after Catalan, Spanish, French, and now English." Don Heinz said that he has never forgotten this comment. Don also confessed that at one point, early in my administration, he intimated to a colleague that he thought that "Manuel had a strong need to be liked" implying the impossibility of making hard decisions. Much later, Don wrote, "I realized something else was going on – you were determined to reach out to the town and be a generous and conspicuous presence. You would be president at the university and simultaneously a kind of academic missionary to the citizens of Chico. This was the opposite of Robin Wilson, who was widely thought not to give a damn about the city." Coming from Don Heinz, a person I have always held in high esteem, these are comforting words because they capture part of my strategy as I sized up the situation I encountered as soon as I arrived in Chico.

Over the ten years at CSU, Chico I had come to admire a few people who combined everything I value in a professor: an excellent record of publication, a commitment to students, respect for the institution, an unusual degree of collegiality, and an objectivity not commonly found in academic stars. One of these individuals was Robert Cottrell, a professor of history who over his 36 years at CSU, Chico has excelled in each of the traits I mention above. He has been honored as Outstanding Professor, Outstanding Teacher, Outstanding Service and has more than once been chosen to provide presentations for the Presidential Lecture Series. He has offered more than 30 different courses at CSU, Chico and additional ones in London, Puebla, Mexico, and Moscow. A true scholar and gentleman. Because I hold him in such high esteem as a professor and a person, I could not refrain from marveling at what he recently wrote about me. If the reader forgives my lack of modesty, I will quote what he said:

I recall Manuel Esteban's stewardship of California State University, Chico, with great fondness and a measure of regret. His ten-year reign coincided with my most pleasurable stint at the institution. That, in my estimation, is no coincidence, for his presidency was unquestionably the finest during my thirty-five years of service at Chico State. As he did for so many others, Manuel made me feel included, having an open-door policy that I shamelessly took advantage of on several occasions.

What else did Manuel offer? I recall best his warmth, genuine friendliness, collegiality, many kindnesses, graciousness, intelligence, professionalism, class, and concerned nature. From the outset, he strove diligently and successfully to repair town-gown relationships. He restored the flagging spirits of those employed at Chico State. He and his lovely wife made frequent appearances at public events hosted by the university. He displayed a commitment to ensuring that Chico State embodied the best that it was capable of: quality instruction at a multi-purpose public university in Northern California. He exemplified the scholar-professor turned administrator, while never losing his reverence for scholarship, insistence on teaching excellence, and dedication to faculty, staff, and students. Always impeccably attired, Manuel invariably displayed civility and decency even during sometimes indecent times, as when he had to contend with inanities directed his way by certain of my colleagues.

As for the measure of regret I referred to, that pertains to the relative brevity of his presidency. Because I recall that period with such affection, I had forgotten the actual amount of time that Manuel graced the halls of Kendall Hall and Chico State. This institution and I personally, undoubtedly like so many others, rue the fact that Manuel chose to depart when he did. But he did so having accomplished so much, going out on a high like few others have been able to do. He resuscitated and restored Chico State's good name, both in Chico and within the larger academic world. He demonstrated that a top-level administrator could remain close to those working at his home institution, while acquiring an excellent, even exceptional reputation for both that school and himself.

I'm proud to be considered a friend of Manuel Esteban, one of the most honorable, decent public servants I've had the pleasure to encounter and had the privilege of getting to know. He is the embodiment of what I consider an ideal university president of a university like Chico State to be: a well-trained steward exuding both the requisite confidence and humility. Manuel managed that feat in virtually flawless fashion. All the while, he always appeared to operate as a good man striving to make Chico State the most representative, concerned, and committed institution it could be.

When I decided back in 1984 to try my hand at administration, I promised myself that I would never want to be like many of the administrators I had met. My goal was to remain as much as possible in the shadows but do everything in my power and to the degree my abilities allowed me to facilitate and improve the environment so that faculty, staff and, above all students could reach their potential. I wanted to leave any institution in which I was fortunate to work in a far better place than I encountered. I did not consider these modest goals, but I did view them as imperative. I don't know whether what Professor Cottrell wrote spontaneously about my tenure at Chico State is shared by many, but whether it is or not, it fills me with pride to know that someone was able to judge what I did as I had wanted it to be judged. Because of comments like these, I had to consider my administrative career as a success. And Gloria had been at my side throughout providing support and encouragement.

California State University Chico

Dr. Manuel A. Esteban, President
Gloria Esteban, First Lady

August 1, 1993 – July 31, 2003

I could not possibly leave the academic world without clarifying in my own mind the opinions I held based on a career spanning thirty years. The academic world is not monolithic. There exist extreme differences between and among the various types of higher education institutions. Private and public colleges and universities function in two separate and unequal universes. Private ones have more freedom, are most nimble, and are able to make decisions quickly. Generally, they respond only to their boards and, in some cases, to major donors. They are usually unencumbered by burdensome bureaucracies. Public ones are different, but also quite dissimilar among themselves. Two-year community colleges have a very different mission than four-year colleges. Community colleges usually provide a mixture of programs. Some provide academic programs that prepare students for transfer to four-year colleges and beyond. But they also train people for specific and practical jobs. Four-year colleges, whether private or public, have a very discreet mission, to prepare students for a bachelor's degree in the sciences, in the arts and humanities, or, in some cases, in specialized technical fields. Teaching is the primary and primordial *raison d'être* of their faculty.

Comprehensive universities are also quite distinct in some very important ways. Those that offer PhD and other terminal degrees often pay only lip service to teaching. The cruel reality for top universities in this category is that success in grant-writing, publication, and national and international recognition always trumps excellence in teaching. Few professors, if any, ever obtain tenure and promotion solely on their teaching, regardless of their brilliance in this area. In fact, there are many professors who rarely if ever teach undergraduate students. This is left to graduate teaching assistants, lecturers, adjunct faculty, or those whose prowess in research is not sterling. It stands to reason that in some fields graduate students help their professors advance in their career. Professors who teach primarily graduate students have the advantage that what they teach and the research they carry out are intimately linked. So, teaching and research become one and the same, one feeds into the other and vice versa. This is not the case when professors, either at PhD-granting institutions or those whose terminal granting degree is the Master, teach primarily undergraduate students.

What they teach and the research and ultimate publication they are expected to produce are worlds apart. Take for instance a professor of foreign languages, something I know something about. If he/she teaches upper-level language classes or even some upper-level literature courses, chances are that what they are required to teach has absolutely nothing to do with the work required to conduct high level research that leads to publication. These professors are at a great disadvantage compared to those who mostly teach graduate students, particularly students in PhD programs.

Now, let me turn to the type of institution I am most familiar with, which is, as a perfect example, the one that by state regulation is limited to offerings that cannot go beyond the master's degree. There are some cases, and Chico State was one of them, where we were able to work jointly with one of the University of California campuses to offer some of the courses that would eventually lead to the PhD. or a doctorate in education. But the granting institution was always the UC, not the CSU. What is the relevance of this situation for campuses such as those within the CSU? In a real-world sense, they are neither fish nor fowl. In theory, excellence in teaching is supposedly the *sine qua non* of such institutions. In reality, however, a professor would be committing professional suicide if he/she actually fell into the trap of believing that superior teaching would automatically result in tenure. Most of the system in place rewards primarily grant-writing, securing external funding, and publication. Yet few professors enjoy what professors in research institutions do, a direct correlation between the general nature of the courses they teach, and the specific and highly specialized work required for publication.

Most people don't realize that this carries implications that are never visible to the public in general. The greater the success in grant-writing and attracting external contracts, the more money enters into the institution's coffers. And this is not just money like any other. These are resources that escape the bureaucratic state rules that govern any dollar that comes from the state. This is where budget cuts hurt more deeply into state institutions that stop at the Master level. This is also, in my opinion, why faculty at universities such as the CSUs lead a far more schizophrenic existence than those at PhD granting universities. What is expected of faculty is far clearer in the latter, although of course not necessarily always easier. Further, since professors in institutions such as the CSUs are supposedly not required to devote as much time and energy to research and publication, they are expected to teach more hours and courses, making it even more difficult to carry out the work that ultimately leads to tenure and promotion. I must add that there are also distinct differences among institutions whose mission is basically the same. As I evaluated presidents of several CSU campuses, I became aware of these differences. Each campus has a particular "personality" so to speak. A great deal depends on the age of the institution. The older they are, the more likely they are to have developed a particular DNA, a sense of destiny, a panoramic view that allows them to focus on the future without losing sight of the past. There is little doubt that CSU, Bakersfield, is very different from HSU, and both are set apart from Chico State, and so on. This, too, is important to recognize as one is asked to lead one of these universities. Although everyone expects new things from a new person at the helm, no one expects that person to lose sight of the past and what has contributed in making each institution what it has become.

With Professor Schafer. Last run as President of CSU, Chico. 2003

Whether in private or public institutions, most faculty perceive themselves as independent contractors. Other than the threat of not giving them tenure and/or promotion, no one really has any leverage over professors. This, more than anything else, makes the job of top administrators quite different from that of running a company of any type.

CHAPTER IX

Post Presidency

▲ ▲ ▲

Gloria and I had planned to spend the summer of 2003 in Invermere and then take a two-month long trip with Julio and Nory to Spain, Italy, and France. But just before we left for Canada, I received an interesting message from a certain professor, Clay Steinman, a person I barely remembered. He had been at Macalester College in Minneapolis since 1993, the year I went to Chico State. He had learned about my retirement and wanted me to know that he had nominated me to be the next president at his college. He thought that I would be a perfect fit for a liberal arts college with a reputation for multiculturalism, civic engagement, and academic reputation. I told him that I had received a letter from Macalester College informing me that I had been nominated. I had wondered who had put my name forward. I thanked him for his faith in me but let him know that I had retired to spend more time with Gloria. She had waited long enough and patiently enough for me to fulfill my dream. It was time now for her to have some say in what we were to do for the rest of our lives. Though flattered, I had to decline. We immediately left for Canada.

A couple of weeks before we were to start our trip to Europe, Richard West and his wife, Kathy, came to visit us. They wanted to see where we would be spending our summers. We had a great time with them. On their second night there, while we were having dinner, we received a phone call from the nursing home in Calgary. We were urged to go immediately. Gloria's mother was suddenly very ill. We apologized profusely to our guests and took off. We got to Calgary around midnight. Gloria's mother was having a very difficult time breathing. In fact, her whole body was in convulsions with each breath she took. She may have had a few moments when she recognized Gloria. The nurse told us that even though her condition looked terrible because of her convulsions, she was not in any pain. We found this hard to believe. But there was nothing we could do. We could only watch with impotence. After a few hours, she stopped suffering. She had passed away. She was ninety-three. She had had a very rich and fulfilling life. Nonetheless, Gloria was inconsolable. We spent a few days in Calgary taking care of many administrative and bureaucratic details. We also made the arrangements for the cremation. When all of this was done, we went back to Invermere. We had lost our four parents. In a way, having to go on our trip to Europe represented a palliative for Gloria.

We returned to Chico quite refreshed. For the first few years after I retired, I continued to be active. I was recruited by the Office of the Chancellor to be part of the teams that evaluated CSU presidents. I was involved in four of them. I did not find the task particularly pleasant, especially in cases where the president was in serious difficulties. In 2008, after I was done with the evaluation of the President of the Maritime Academy, which had become part of the CSU, I asked Chancellor Reed not to count on me any further. For a few years I remained active in WASC visits and continued to serve in AASCU. This activity, too, became less attractive the more removed I became from the daily tasks of administration. It took me a few years before I decided to resign from the Rotary Club. With all our frequent travels and time spent in Canada I found it increasingly difficult to meet the attendance requirements. For as long as Gloria and I still held some sway, we were involved in fundraisers for a number of causes, not always associated with the University. And for several years Gloria and I were constant guests at the dinners for our Distinguished Alumni, at most Founders Week celebrations, and at sports and music and arts events.

Value: Priceless

By Rick Satava
World Renown Glass Blower

and

Manuel Esteban
Former CSU Chico President
And Accomplished Glass Blower

I was quite conscious that I should not step into any of the roles our new president, Paul Zingg, was expected to play. In fact, I seldom did anything semi-official without checking first with him. We had a good relationship. During his first two years he asked me to help him maintain the relationships I had built with our regional community colleges, and any important regional organization with which we had enjoyed a good cooperative effort. In particular, he engaged me to work with the Redding McConnell Foundation. This Foundation had for many years limited its generous giving to only two counties. It was considering expanding its reach to other counties. Over the years I had developed an excellent relationship with the Foundation's president, Lee Salter, a member of my University Advisory Board. I was directed to work with Lee Salter's daughter, who was in charge of many of the new Foundation programs. I also met with President Zingg, whenever he wanted to discuss any issue, he felt he could benefit from my contacts and experience. On April 18 of 2005 I was very honored to be asked by Paul Zingg to participate actively in his inauguration. I should add, by the way, that whereas my own inauguration had been controversial at the time, this one went off without a hitch and without any kind of adverse notice from the press. Times had certainly changed.

The beautiful office Dean Derucher set up for me in the College of Engineering, was my home away from home for a while. It was there that Walt and I worked closely together on the monograph on student drinking mentioned previously. After we finished this time-consuming report, I did not think that I would be doing any more research. My need for an office, particularly once I had my own in our beautiful new home, had vanished. I donated a good percentage of my thousands of books to the university library and vacated the premises after having thanked Dean Derucher and the College Faculty for their generosity in welcoming me in their midst.

So, what was in store for us after basically withdrawing from most activities related to the University? Before I retired, I had gone to a seminar on the transition from the presidency to retirement. The main advice was, particularly for those who lived in small towns, to move away. We were going to find out who our true friends were. We needed to accept that we would go from being "the toast of the town" to being "toast." as we were warned. It is true that some of the people whom we had seen often at our home, because we had a lot of dinners and receptions, stopped calling.

They were busy cultivating the new president. But, at the same time, we were gratified that some of the people we liked the most continued to be our best friends. In fact, we even gained new friends who up to this point had been reluctant to invite us to their homes because they did not want to be perceived as hangers-on.

We did not become toast, but we were certainly no longer the toast of the town. If we continued to have a high profile it was because we were still involved in a number of associations, boards, and fund-raising activities. I personally never felt bereft or deprived of any powers or notoriety. I had always admitted to myself that much of the fuss surrounding me was directed at the president of the university, not at me. So, it was normal then that I did not feel affronted by the sudden loss of attention. I certainly did not miss for a minute all the attention I had received from the press. Our life was more normal. We could go to Morning Thunder Café for breakfast and not be besieged.

CHAPTER X

Years of Leisure and Travels, 2003–2019

▲ ▲ ▲

THE TIME HAD COME FOR us to make serious plans for the future. We decided to spend the summer months in Invermere. We wanted and needed to be close to Julio and Nory and keep in touch with family and friends from Calgary and Medicine Hat. Invermere is a lovely destination in the summer, and we encouraged friends and relatives from Europe, the US, and Canada to come spend time with us, which they did to our great delight. We also made the commitment to spend four to six weeks each year in Barcelona, sprinkled with visits to cities and towns throughout Catalonia and other parts of Spain. Whenever appropriate, we would also spend time in France. We hoped that we would also leave time to discover other countries.

And discover other countries we did. Over the years we have been very fortunate to find amazing fellow travelers willing to go far afield to visit far away countries on four different continents. We thank Julio and Nory, Staff and Carol, Jack and Nancy, Bill and Gaye, and Brian and Ana for having been such gracious travel companions. I doubt that our experiences would have been as rewarding had it not been for their enthusiasm, strong desire for exploration, adventuresome nature, tolerance, and downright friendliness. Our travels have taken us to no fewer than 30 different countries, enriching our lives beyond expression.

In 2011 Gloria and I made a very important decision. After having lived in Chico for 18 years, living now in the house of our dreams, and surrounded by countless friends and acquaintances, we chose to move to Santa Barbara. Ever since we got married, Gloria and I had moved a lot. Because of my studies and different jobs, although I always consulted her and would not have made a decision contrary to her wishes, she was always in tow. This time, she was the one who insisted that it was her turn to choose where we lived and she wanted to live in Santa Barbara, something she had always dreamed of doing ever since she fell in love with the city and the region back in 1970, when I attended UCSB. We did not think we would have a difficult time selling our wonderful house in Chico. But we did. The real estate market had gone bust. Gloria, however, was undeterred. We spent a lot of time looking for something we liked and could afford in Santa Barbara. The two seemed incompatible. Much of what we liked was beyond our means, and what we could afford was of no interest to us. We could not possibly leave our wonderful home in Chico to move into a shack, since this was what seemed available for what we thought we could afford or were willing to pay. Ultimately, we did find a very nice townhouse with a nice partial view of the ocean. We bought it before we sold our home in Chico. Bill and Gaye were very excited that we would live so close together. They had been one of the main reasons for our move.

When we informed our friends in Chico of our decision to leave, they could not believe it. Gloria and I were very moved to see how many people, primarily the ones we had been close to for so many years, were sorry to see us go. We were feted many times over at the homes of many of them. Instead of just one single painful event, similar to removing quickly and violently a band aid that is firmly stuck on hairy skin, we had many goodbyes, like stripping the band aid little by little, and thus causing pain over a longer period of time. As difficult as these farewell parties were, Gloria and I were excited about yet again another interesting period of our lives.

We loved being back in Santa Barbara immediately. Jackie loved the place and could see herself retiring in it when Gloria and I were not around anymore. I joined Bill and a group of regulars three times per week to play golf. Through them we met another couple Ray and Sally Rapozo, a wonderful and very entertaining couple who have become close friends of ours.

In April of 2017 Paul and Katy Crapo came to spend a few days with us in Santa Barbara. In May it was our friends from Calgary, Brian Gill and Ana Val, who paid us a visit. They knew that we were about to make yet another major decision regarding housing and wanted to make sure they got to visit us in beautiful Santa Barbara. As always, we had a wonderful time with them. Both Ana and Brian are very funny. Their sense of humor, however, is very different. Brian has a British, dry, caustic sense of humor. Ana, on the other hand, is more direct and openly funny and always happy.

As usual, we went to Invermere to spend the summer. While we were in Invermere, I received a message from the curator of the new Medicine Hat Art Museum. When Altaglass, where my father, Gloria's father and I had worked, closed down, its owners donated all the tools and equipment as well as the remaining inventory to the museum. In June of 2011 there was to be a grand opening to highlight Altaglass. They had actually reconstructed with great detail the setup at the studio. The walls were festooned with human-size photos of our parents working. The many glass displays showed some of the most creative and typical pieces made by our parents but also by other artists that came after their retirement. To my surprise, since I had not worked there since 1968, there were some of my more iconic pieces. What the curator asked me was to make a public presentation about what Altaglass had meant for our families, to me in particular, for the city, and for tourism, since Altaglass had been one of the top tourist attractions in Medicine Hat. I was honored to accept the invitation. Almost every single member of our family that resided in Medicine Hat was present. So were Bert and Erica and other friends from our years in the city. Julio and Nory were there as well, of course, and our daughter flew in from California to be part of this ceremony that paid tribute to her grandfathers. For me it felt like going back in time, and the fact that I was surrounded by life size photos of my father and Cisco at work filled me with nostalgia. I was overwhelmed by a mixture of emotions. I will always treasure the chance that the curator gave me to be an integral part of such a historic moment, one that celebrated the work that my dad and Cisco had done and the role they had played in attracting attention to Medicine Hat to an art form that had not received sufficient recognition to that point.

While we were there we also participated in the celebration of my uncle and aunt's 60th wedding anniversary. We were surprised to see my first cousin from Mallorca, Cati. We had not seen her since she and Jackie were both 18. It was a very nice family reunion. The only sad part of this period was the fact that our very dear friend, Serge, had recently passed away.

We got back home in the USA in early September. But not to Santa Barbara. We had just moved to Tucson. Many wondered about our decision to move. Why in the world would you leave Santa Barbara, the town Gloria had been dreaming about for thirty years? Well, everything has a reason and a story behind it. One day, our friends Chris and Ruth, who by now lived in Ann Arbor again, after Chris had retired from his presidency, invited us to join them on their own visit to see Dick and Susan Nisbett, who happened to live in a 55+ community near Tucson. We did in January of 2017. It was a very nice visit. It was wonderful to be reunited with Dick and Susan after many, many years during which we had not had a lot of contact.

The community they had chosen to live in is called Academy Village. It was founded by the former president of The University of Arizona. His concept was to create a community where retired faculty and administrators as well as artists and some professionals could create an active intellectual, cultural, artistic, and health-oriented community filled with activities that would continue to force mental and physical acuity. While there, we attended some concerts, went to social events, and went for a few hikes. We liked the community a great deal and were impressed by its members. When we got back to Santa Barbara, I suggested to Gloria that we might consider living in such a place. If we did, we couldn't possibly keep both the house in Santa Barbara and the one in Invermere. Since the summers are so hot in Tucson, we needed the one in Invermere for the weather and to be close to Julio and Nory. We would need to sell the one in Santa Barbara. Gloria's first reaction was to wonder about my sanity. I could not blame her. We had only been living there for seven short years. I knew that it would take a while to pry Gloria away from her beloved Santa Barbara.

After a while, I suggested that perhaps we could rent a place in Academy Village to see what it would be like to live there. I said that perhaps three weeks would give us a chance to get a better feel for what kind of life we could expect to have. We rented a huge house and invited Jackie, Julio and Nory to come spend some time with us. They did. We all loved the general atmosphere, the friendliness of the people, the overall facilities and activities provided, and the intellectual and cultural life that we could sense and see. When we got back to Santa Barbara, Gloria and I had some serious thinking to do. There was no real hurry, so we went on a long trip with Julio and Nory.

When we got back, I asked Gloria whether she was more amenable to move. I also mentioned that housing was a great deal cheaper in Tucson than in Santa Barbara. This would allow us to have spare change to take lots more trips and be less concerned about finances. Gloria was not ready. We went back to Academy Village for one more week. We spent time with Dick and Susan and asked about what they thought of the community. They had spent their winters in Tucson for the last 13 years. Everything they had to say was very positive. They did not push us to make a decision but mentioned that the people diagonally across from them were considering moving and selling their home. We went to see it. We loved it. When they told us how little they wanted for it, including most of their furniture, we could not believe it. After a couple of sleepless nights, we decided to make one more move. We sold our house in Santa Barbara, moved everything into the new home in early June, and without unpacking a single box we left for Invermere.

On the 3rd of September we left Canada and moved into a new house, a new city, and a new state. How had I managed to convince Gloria to move? She was in shock. I took it a lot better. After so many years of moving from country to country, from province to province, from state to state, and from city to city, this was for me just one more move. We have now been in Tucson for the last four years. I love it here. And we have had many, many visitors, particularly in the winter.

A very happy event took place in October of 2019. Adriana and Rajan got married in Seattle. Family and friends from Canada, many different parts of the U.S. and Spain came to the wedding as well. It was three days of constant happiness. We have hundreds of photos that chronicle in great detail the three days of festivities, before, during and after the wedding. Gloria and I put an end to 2019 by going to Port Coquitlam, outside of Vancouver, to spend Christmas and New Year with Julio and Nory. Jacqueline, Adriana, and Monica stayed at a hotel in the heart of Vancouver and came a couple of times to be with all of us and our nephew Jason, his wife, Elaine, and their two kids, Miró and Mobi. We were grateful to be together once again.

What can I say about 2020? As Queen Elizabeth said of a particularly bad year, for millions of us 2020 has been an *annus horribilis*. Other than a few visits from our daughter, and dinners with two couples who formed part of our bubble, this has been a horrendous year for us and for the world. We are five months into 2021 and the situation seems to be improving but who is to tell what could still happen with all the variants to the virus. When things are back to normal, what will normalcy look like? Are we going to be able to go back to our travels and visits to Canada, Spain, and France? The only thing I can say about these last 18 months or so, is that boredom got me to write my autobiography, something I had been meaning to do since I retired in 2003.

CHAPTER XI

Lessons Learned

▲ ▲ ▲

I STARTED GOING OVER MY life with the hope that, somehow, I would discover how I have become the person I am. I also wanted to find out what sort of influence my parents had on my development as a person. I don't know that I am any more informed today than I was when I started to ponder this fundamental issue. There is little doubt that my mother infused me with a strong sense of family and friendship. For her, one should never take for granted the bonding that brings members of a family together. The love she displayed for her mother, sisters, brother, aunt, and cousins was admirable and worthy of imitation. She also passed on to me the softer touch, a strong sense of empathy, and the ability to get into other people's shoes to understand their perspectives and their motives. My father, as I have recounted, had clearly cut all possible ties with his blood relatives, preferring instead an adopted family. Yet he was in constant need of love and affirmation. His love for my mother, my brother, and me was abundant and constantly in evidence. From him I learned primarily a sense of personal respect, the value of perseverance, discipline, duty, and hard work and the courage to take on life's challenges. It is probably a truism to say that I am my parents' product to a large extent. The adult I have become was already in gestation when I was a child, even when I was an irresponsible and somewhat lost adolescent in Barcelona. That being said, however, I look at the person who left Barcelona at fifteen and a half and I don't recognize myself in that person. I wasn't interested in learning. I wasn't disciplined in the least. I did not have a work ethic. I cannot see much empathy in the person I was then. Of course, one can argue that I was young, still a child in many ways. But I had already been working for 18 months and I did not show much promise. I had to leave most of the several jobs I held in such a short period of time just ahead of being fired.

Would I be who I am today as a person had my parents stayed in Barcelona instead of moving to France? I fervently believe that I would not. I was quite aware as I started life in Souvigny and Moulins that I was in a process of personal change. I became far more aware of who I was as an individual, how people reacted to my words and actions, how much better I felt and was treated when I did things well rather than how I had behaved to that point. Both good and bad experiences have an impact on your psyche. The 18-year-old adolescent who left France for Canada was already a changed person. Would I be today the same person who left France had I not experienced the travails, challenges, disappointments, successes, and adventures I encountered in Calgary and Medicine Hat? I doubt it. I was probably not changing dramatically, but I sincerely believe that as time went by and I lived life, as a son, brother, husband, father, friend, student, and professional, the person in me was being fine-tuned. I was becoming, hopefully, a better version of myself.

It is this better version of myself, I think, and the richness of my seemingly constantly changing lifestyles, that allowed me to often successfully choose the right path and choices that presented themselves to me or that I created for myself. I believe that faith in oneself, perseverance, and an unwillingness to concede defeat are essential qualities without which bumps on the road of life can easily become insurmountable obstacles.

Nothing of consequence is achieved by going at it alone. Everyone needs allies, supporters, cheerleaders. I have been fortunate to count on some of them, primarily my brother and, above all, Gloria. I was also coming to accept the reality that I could not just wait for luck to come to me. I had to create my own luck. Passivity or inertia was not an option. I had to learn to identify opportunities as open doors and be valiant enough to go through them. This is why, when I learned that I could stagger the exams that could lead me to the high school equivalency and thus access to college, I lunged forward. Sure, I was lucky to have my brother who helped me through it. But ultimately, I had to do the studying. I had to deprive myself of a peaceful and pleasurable domestic existence to make up for incredible lacunae in formal knowledge that often put me at a serious disadvantage compared to other college students who had gotten there the traditional way. These circumstances created a new me, little by little. I was, of course, deep down the same person, but I was covered by layer upon layer of experiences, actions and reactions that were slowly preparing me for a very different type of future. If I had not insisted that my brother help me study for the high school comprehensive provincial examinations, would I now be in a position to recount my successes? Absolutely not. If I had not studied hard to overcome the deep gaps that existed in my formal education, would I have been able to complete my studies first at the University of Calgary and later at UCSB? Clearly not. Would I have ended up with a professorship and an associate deanship at the University of Michigan, Dearborn if I had not defied the odds stacked up against me? Not likely.

Needless to say, I did not get to the presidency of Chico State without having gone through trials and tribulations, all of which enriched my specific knowledge and taught me to learn as I went along. My years at UM-Dearborn taught me how we, as professors, thought, understood our duty, and reacted to expectations. They also taught me to be distrustful of many administrators as, in my opinion, they did not have the interest of faculty and students as their priorities. As an administrator at that same university, I began to sharpen my skills as a negotiator, communicator, persuader, and leader behind the scenes. CSU, Bakersfield presented a totally different set of challenges and opportunities. I realized quickly that the first few weeks in a leadership position are golden. This is the time when most changes can be conceived and implemented. Each institution has a particular culture, a history, and certain traditions that must be learned and, unless they are detrimental, must be respected. HSU presented a totally different scenario, a very different culture, a far richer sense of mission and destiny, and challenges and opportunities. My abilities were tested further. My responsibilities went far beyond whatever I had experienced. I wondered often whether I had the mettle to succeed. But I was confident that, given the opportunity, I would not only prevail but leave a small legacy behind.

No administrator can lead by mandate or administrative fiat. The only real power a president possesses is the art of persuasion. Faculty and anyone else associated in any direct or indirect way with the university have to be convinced that what is being proposed, the changes that are being contemplated, will ultimately make their lives easier and the act of educating more effective. I believed that if given the chance I could do just that. I came to the conclusion, which I hoped would be the right one, that my personality, my personal attributes, my sense of justice, my willingness to consult widely and bring as many constituencies as possible into decision making, my ability to listen and learn, my dedication, my honesty, transparency, humility, and my self-deprecating humor, would win out in the end if I just buried myself in work and behaved as if I nothing could distract me from my belief that I could contribute decisively to improving the reputation and quality of Chico State.

Throughout my life I have made it my obligation to always keep on learning from others and from my own experiences, successes and, above all, mistakes. What lessons have I learned? First of all, no one is so supremely better than others to assume that one can do it alone, and this is particularly true in academic environments where almost everyone around is exceptionally well educated and in possession of a great deal of knowledge and experience. The wheel was invented centuries ago. No one should be presumptuous enough to believe that they can disregard the past that others have toiled to fashion, in order to create a totally new one. Let's remember the old dictum that "those who forget the errors of the past are doomed to repeat them." Take time to listen, learn, consult, and build alliances. Even if you are convinced that yours is the right action to take, you are never certain that those you are expected to lead will follow you. You must communicate clearly, you must convince, you must achieve buy-in. Only then can you hope to move forward effectively. Decisions that can affect complete institutions and many constituencies are to be taken slowly and judiciously. As the Italians say, *Chi va piano va lontano, chi va forte va a la morte.* Dramatic changes are always difficult and often painful. The change of old habits and institutional norms cannot be completely achieved without disruption and even pain. But every effort must be exhausted to ensure that both disruption and pain are mitigated. The imposition of new norms must never be seen as permanent. Almost everything in life is in constant evolution. Institutions are living organisms. They too must be allowed to evolve. Once a leader has been successful in implementing institutional changes, that leader must be willing to relinquish control of these changes and allow for the natural process of evolution.

I can unashamedly say that I love Chico State and thank it for having given me a chance to accomplish something that was unimaginable. How could an uneducated kid from Barcelona progress in life to have such an incredible journey. To quote Frank Sinatra, "I did it my way" but with a lot of help from many along the long journey. Thank you to all those who made such an extraordinary journey possible.

Made in the USA
Las Vegas, NV
02 December 2021

35847807R00187